Legal Writing, All Business

Legal Writing, All Business

J. Scott Colesanti

PROFESSOR OF LEGAL WRITING

HOFSTRA UNIVERSITY MAURICE A. DEANE SCHOOL OF LAW

CAROLINA ACADEMIC PRESS

Durham, North Carolina

Library of Congress Cataloging-in-Publication Data

Names: Colesanti, J. Scott, author.
Title: Legal writing, all business / J. Scott Colesanti.
Description: Durham, North Carolina : Carolina Academic Press, [2016] |
    Includes bibliographical references and index.
Identifiers: LCCN 2016026679 | ISBN 9781522105282 (alk. paper)
Subjects: LCSH: Legal composition. | Law--United States--Language.
Classification: LCC KF250 .C55 2016 | DDC 808.06/634--dc23
LC record available at https://lccn.loc.gov/2016026679

e-book ISBN: 978-1-5221-0529-9

CAROLINA ACADEMIC PRESS, LLC
700 Kent Street
Durham, North Carolina 27701
Telephone (919) 489-7486
Fax (919) 493-5668
www.cap-press.com

Printed in the United States of America

For James and Giovanni,
whose words inspire me every day,
and who have been perfect since first draft.

Contents

Preface

When I started teaching "Legal Writing" 9 years ago, I naturally reviewed the range of available texts. My review had quite an impact, literally: One of the larger treatises fell off an overmatched coffee table, nearly shattering my toes.

It was then I became wary of "comprehensive" books on the subject. Weighty texts addressed everything from research to client contacts to oral argument. The craft of Legal Writing was described as requiring mastery of a series of acronyms and structures mercilessly enforced. The exercises were often drawn unpredictably from a broad array of subjects. Attached appendices included detached, professional-caliber Memos, Briefs, and Motions that added to the bulk.

Subsequent years in the 1L classroom taught me that a course is only as comprehensive as its instructor. More importantly, speaking at length about *writing* is a hopeless cause. For the motivated student, it is akin to listening to someone talk about eating a chocolate sundae. For the unmotivated, it is hearing of the sundae's melting. Overall, I found some very talented students were not giving the Legal Writing course a chance. And few students selected a Legal Writing text as their favorite law book to read.

Thus, when given the opportunity, I fashioned a shorter coursebook with a much more direct message: All Legal Writing centers on a user-friendly presentation of a Rule of Law, which is then applied to a new set of facts via a Rule Application. With this modest aim in mind, any student of any background can succeed at Legal Writing, and learning the process can have numerous takeaways.

Accordingly, herein are offered short Chapters designed to minimize lecture and maximize practice. The Chapters fall into two categories. Part One (Chapters I–VI) provides instruction on the central aim of identifying the Rule, and applying it. In service of the "learn as you go" approach, each Chapter commences with a short list of objectives, continues through a lesson, lists examples ("Weak" and "Better"), and intermittently requires completion of an Exercise.

Part Two (Chapters VII–XIII) was designed to get the student started in his/her preparation of the documents that Legal Writing courses and summer internships value. Here, I attempted to update examples to reflect modern tasks of—and opportunities for—1L and 2L law students. There are Chapters on office memos, e-memos, law journal Notes, and industry comment letters, among others.

Overall, the approximately 30 Exercises offer themed practice and repetition. They uniformly involve business law topics and settings, covering a range stretching from the generic and historic (e.g., vacatur of arbitration and tax liens) to the specific and timely (Bitcoin statutes, online fantasy sports, and "vapor shop" regulations). These Exercises, the majority of which involve actual statutes, and nearly all of which employ real case law, reveal business law standards, statutes, doctrines and trends, while consistently stressing the significance of primary authority.

The teaching methods are varied. The lessons repeat the stressed two-part formula, by way of conventional introduction of standards, narrative anecdotes explaining the author's painful lessons "on the job," the incorporation of newsworthy trends and examples, and insights into writing maxims memorized by rote. The Exercises may call for starting points, ending points, or both—specifically, a student may be requested to provide an outline or a list of "bullets" before being asked to actually verbalize a response. The five Appendices at book's end offer lists designed to further a Chapter's explanation or to prepare a student's attempts at a particular document.

The book's title refers to a compact, no-nonsense approach to the subject, as well as the subject matter through which the approach is learned. It is hoped that the text possesses appeal both through its trumpeting of that subject matter and the sheer volume of opportunity for practice it affords. At all times, the book remains focused on the need to identify a Rule and apply it via Rule Application in each task and document. Overall, the book offers several levels of takeaways, both skill-building and substantive.

In 15 years of teaching law students, I have designed courses ranging from Legal Analysis to Corporate Governance. The Legal Writing course steadfastly poses the toughest challenge, as its registrants hail from widely varying curricula and come of age at a time when people are increasingly communicating via fragments and pictures. Moreover, it seems that students take constructive criticism of their writing quite personally: A first year student accepts an initial weakness in a "doctrinal" subject, but no student wants to hear that he/she cannot yet write effectively. Small wonder that most 1L students inform me that they would rather spend time with a Torts text or Contracts study aid. To be sure, the popularity of Legal Writing coursebooks can grow. In purpose, design, and method, this work should prove—if not captivating—at least as popular as other subjects. And it is of a size that will endanger no one's toes.

J. Scott Colesanti, LL.M.
June, 2016

About the Author

J. Scott Colesanti, LL.M., Professor of Legal Writing, has taught at the law school level for over 15 years. In 2006, while serving as an adjunct, he was selected "Professor of the Year" by the Hofstra Law Review. He has developed and taught 10 courses and has had over a dozen articles published by law reviews. His writings are included in treatises on securities law and as expert commentaries to seminal cases.

Professor Colesanti is a member of the Bars of New York, Missouri and Washington, D.C. In 1987, he was the first law clerk to a Chief Hearing Officer of the New York Stock Exchange; he subsequently served as Investigative/Trial Counsel for the New York Stock Exchange Division of Enforcement for 10 years. Afterwards he served within the NYSE Office of the General Counsel, and as a securities industry arbitrator for over a decade. He has handled appeals before the Securities and Exchange Commission, the Social Security Administration, the EEOC, and the New York State Division of Human Rights. Overall, he has authored articles, commentary, case decisions, speeches, motions, editorials, comment letters, complaints, charging instruments, and settlements.

Professor Colesanti regularly lectures on the Financial Crisis, and he also coaches high school mock trial teams. He previously instructed at the Saint Louis University School of Law, and on several occasions has taught abroad as part of the Hofstra Study Abroad program. He served on the editorial board of the *Journal of Securities Law, Regulation and Compliance,* and is a former contributing co-editor of the *Business Law Professor Blog.*

PART ONE

Chapter I

Choosing Collars (Getting Started)

Chapter Objectives:
- Viewing Undesirable Legal Writing
- Favoring Efficiency Over Attempted Eloquence
- Appreciating the Need for Organization Prior to Actual Writing
- Developing a Rational Frequency to Citation
- Drafting a Preliminary Rule of Law

Substantive Takeaways:
- Sources of Federal Securities Regulation
- Automobile Registration Protocol in Missouri
- California Law on Claims Against "Employers" of Dogs

I. Background

An old joke starts with one farmer describing to another his problems with a wandering goat. The farmer explains that he had to resort to placing a shock-causing collar on the animal. "Does he stay home now?" the second farmer asks. "No," responds the first farmer, "But he's quit smoking."

While the goat probably should never have been indulging in tobacco, the larger point is that some choices can cure the wrong ill. In the paragraph above, I could have written "itinerant" instead of "wandering," thus displaying my rapt attention during one week of 11th grade English. But you would have had to slow to recall the word's meaning (as I did when confirming my memory), or re-read the sentence to glean its definition from nearby text—either way, I would have hindered the flow of the passage.

As in the writing of jokes, news segments, articles, and dinner speeches, *Legal Writing* demands that the text never slow the reading. Indeed, the craft is quite counter-intuitive in that long sentences do not indicate intellect, and long passages do not reflect hard work. The 50-page thesis that earned an "A" in college would be cut to ribbons by the Legal Reader. The transition to effective Legal Writing, therefore, requires the immediate choice of new set of restrictions, or collars.

That selection is your first challenge, and you must choose wisely. Apart from long passages and ornate language, other ineffective "collars" abound among 1L students. At one end of the spectrum, there is the tendency to substitute "common sense" for productive legal research. At the other end, there is the habit of citing repetitively to countless cases, statutes, and secondary materials as a means of generating apparent credibility. All of these choices can be easily fixed.

To begin your journey as an effective Legal Writer, this Chapter offers three steps: Choosing the most direct language, choosing uncommon sense, and choosing rationally when citing to authority.

II. Choosing Direct Language

You shall see soon enough that your paramount goal as a first year Legal Writer is surprisingly consistent: Identify the relevant law, and apply that law to facts. Your dual results are presented within a "Legal Formula." That is often the totality of the first year associate's entire law firm experience.

However, to attain these modest goals, you have to ensure that someone trusts your ability to fulfill countless duties. These duties include telling complex stories of ongoing disputes, identifying issues of every variety, finding common ground between differing authorities, and citing correctly to cases and statutes.

Such varied tasks afford a multitude of opportunities for the Legal Reader to disengage, starting with the first sentence that he/she reads. Accordingly, whether it be explaining a new rule governing e-discovery, or summarizing the facts of a trade secrets case, start with the aim of keeping the Legal Reader's eyes glued to the page. Your nouns should be described with a sole adjective, your adverbs should be monosyllabic, your sentences should be short, and your paragraphs should be focused on a sole premise (indicated through a topic sentence). Whatever the document containing your Legal Writing, it should be read in one sitting. For whenever a Reader puts down your paper to rub his eyes, daydream, smoke a cigar, or feed the cat, you have not written well.

Writing well in this profession can be counter-intuitive. There are many poor choices to be made when producing Legal Writing, but use of legalese (or repetition) is not foremost among them. To the contrary, I have found that I most readily ascertain a student's meaning when he or she employs terms such as "a fortiori" or "inter alia." Rather, the chief detriment to the Legal Writer's progress is distracting the Legal Reader. It is axiomatic that if your Office Memo meanders, the Reader will simply read the underlying authorities herself. Likewise, if your Trial Motion raises more questions than it answers, the judge will decide to rely on a lengthy oral argument (which raises more work for you, and others). If your Complaint does not plainly state a case for relief, it shall be dismissed.

Thus, directly rewarding the Legal Reader's most likely questions takes precedence over catering to your own stylish impulses. Lawyers are busy people, as evidenced by their charging by 5-minute increments. They have no time for wordsmiths flexing their muscles, or topical experts sputtering out jargon, or young associates hesitating with a prediction.

As initial guidance on direct Writing, adopt these 3 standards:

- Keep sentences under 20 words.
- Fit at least 2½ paragraphs on each page.
- Eliminate all phrases requiring the Reader to use a reference guide.

You will, of course, modify these standards as your style emerges. Additionally, Chapter VI of this book provides practical sets of permissible and impermissible language, and dwells on the high degree of attention that must be paid to the micro-structure of sentences and paragraphs. Before addressing the specific language that should be used, let us view some language that should not.

A. Avoiding Flowery Prose

Consider the following examples of a Rule section that one might see within a Brief for the defendant seeking to avoid criminal prosecution of an insider trading violation:

WEAK:

> Securities regulation is a truly eclectic mix. Spawned by New Deal legislation, eight federal statutes concatenate to establish what one Professor has labeled "an amorphous but dangerous mosaic." The 50,000 Securities and Exchange Commission agency missives issued since 1934 often engage in internecine warfare, or simply lapse into disuse. Amid this cacophony, State Attorneys General have, as of late, attempted to cabin Ponzi schemes and corporate

misstatements with S.E.C. interpretations dating back to the 1950s (and expert witnesses nearly as antiquated). Meanwhile, private attorneys—equally split between class action specialty firms and sole practitioner arbitration experts—display the persistence of Sisyphus in attempting to apply the ever-changing mix of law and regulation. Regardless, judges are left to ponder whether a case before them either exemplifies a good faith attempt at corporate communication, or a machination that "out-Herods Herod" in extravagance.

Many college professors would be proud of such a passage. It used a half dozen S.A.T. words to recall 80 years of American economic history (and somehow involved Greek mythology in the process). But random statistics and showy quotes, while sounding informed, fail to rank authorities, and such details thus exemplify the wrong approach.

A basic re-ordering and emphasis on the nature of the authorities leads to a more direct summary. Now armed with a lean structure, the Legal Writer can offer an improved product—dependent upon a much simpler vocabulary:

BETTER:

Under its authority to regulate interstate commerce, Congress federalized the regulation of securities sales via laws of 1933 and 1934. In the next decade, six more federal statutes targeted stock market abuses. All of those laws are enforced by the Securities and Exchange Commission, an agency that brings civil actions. Court cases between 1946 and 1980 greatly expanded the antifraud provisions within the 8 statutes; that era showed that these provisions and laws can be equally utilized by civil and criminal authorities.

The use of criminal enforcement has gone in and out of favor, as scandals ebb and flow. In our Circuit, there has of late been a clear tendency to defer to civil authorities. In those cases, the testimony of legal authors and other experts can often be dispositive.[1]

By linking simple truths, the Rule both reaches the target tone (i.e., flexibility) and emphasizes a top-down rule of law (i.e., discretionary prosecution). Moreover, the Rule arrives at a conclusion, thus making the history lesson

---

1. To maintain emphasis on the initial lessons of the book, footnotes will be added gradually to the examples in subsequent passages.

more palatable. Finally, the Rule contains an obvious "punch line" or reward—close to home, courts nowadays are listening to the experts, rather than the prosecutors.

Thus, the goal should be a straightforward revelation of assertions, free of references that trigger marginally relevant thoughts, and always housed within short sentences and paragraphs. Such a focus naturally reveals the productivity of your research; accordingly, wandering prose is interpreted as masking imprecise identification of the most relevant principles.

B. Avoiding Verbosity

Most of the time, the difference between effective and ineffective Legal Writing is the work required of the Legal Reader. That work is directly related to how many words must be read. Simply stated, the length of a passage does not indicate its strength, wisdom, or dominance. Note the examples below:

WEAK:

> The plaintiff, who sued corporations in the past, brought a class action lawsuit, choosing federal court instead of state court, and naming the CEO, the CFO, and three corporate directors, for their misstatements to the public via newspapers and press conferences in connection with: a 1999 initial public offering of stock, a 2001 public offering, a 2005 private offering, and a 2007 public offering.

BETTER:

> The experienced plaintiff brought a federal class action against corporate managers for their alleged misstatements concerning public and private offerings between 1999 and 2007.

Both passages attempt to fill the duty of a topic sentence. The first example above masquerades as diligence. The passage provides details that are readily combined (e.g., the stock offerings) and unnecessary elaborations (e.g., federal vs. state actions). Further, it relinquishes text when it switches to the colon format ("in connection with: ...). The second example conveys the same information in less time and in a consistent manner; to the extent the details on the varied offerings are germane, subsequent sentences shall surely distinguish their differences.

Overall, both the use of flowery language and too many words are emblematic of the first year Legal Writer's desire to please. By itself, that desire is healthy, but it is much better served by the next bit of guidance.

III. Choosing Uncommon Sense

A. The Futility of Personal Beliefs

I recall my early days of working as a lawyer, riding the railroad to and from Manhattan each rush hour. People outracing the closing doors often gathered themselves and asked anyone nearby, "This train go to New York?" or "How many stops until the transfer?" Unresponsive answers offered, "It better, or else I'm lost," or "For all the money they charge, I never know where we are." Then a conductor would pass and offer simply, "Express train, 3 stops until Manhattan." Instantly, we were all reminded of the universal appreciation for (and poetic beauty of) the most expertise answer to the question.

The lesson? As a Legal Writer, do not be another bystander. Resist the common, knee-jerk reaction. Exercise *uncommon* sense. Reject the role of pointed critic or passionate journalist, both of whom seek foremost to highlight inconsistencies. Legal Writers are asked to translate the applicable legal principles, sum up the current problem, and predict/urge[2] an outcome. Indeed, *all* of Legal Writing may be summarized as the hunt for a perfect Rule (i.e., the relevant set of guiding principles) and subsequent Rule Application (i.e., the result when such principles are applied to the instant case).

Therefore, an equally important consideration for the emerging Legal Writer is to avoid the temptation to join the crowd of those adding personal opinions and unsupportable beliefs. Referencing an unnamed community of reason is pointless; nonetheless, first-year law students write "logically" and "it is human nature" far too often. As I like to tell my students, you *have* no opinion, unless someone more experienced had it first. Familiarity with that uncomfortable truth will expedite your growth.

The resistance of instinctive beliefs can yield immediate rewards. Consider these two topic sentences, centering on the Uniform Commercial Code's "reasonable notice" provision (§ 2-309) for the termination of a contract for the

---

2. Many Legal Writing texts and courses bifurcate instruction between "predictive" writing (e.g., the office memo) and persuasive writing (e.g., the appellate brief). But such nomenclature can be likened to distinguishing an apparition from a ghost—if either fulfills its duty, the viewer cares little for its name.

Thus, this book posits that a more meaningful distinction focuses on degree of description and expected scrutiny by its audience. Concurrently, the communicative lessons relayed herein speak to both prediction and persuasion, with differences in audience covered by the exemplar documents within the latter Chapters in the book.

delivery of goods. The plaintiff has urged a 2-day notice period; you (as defendant's counsel) are arguing for a more lenient standard:

WEAK:

> Logically, not all 50 States will interpret the U.C.C. provision so strictly.

BETTER:

> Eleven of the 13 States that have considered the issue have rejected such a strict interpretation of U.C.C. § 2-309.

The second example far outshines the first. It urges the Reader to adopt a position embraced by the majority of relevant jurisdictions; the fact that such position mirrors what best serves her client seems a happy coincidence for the Writer. Why would a Writer even consider a statement as bland as the first? Because, as bystander language, it feels harmless to assert. Conversely, the second statement confidently indicates that the writer has researched the relevant case law—she has not only done work for the reader, she has also furthered the discussion by distinguishing majority and minority viewpoints.

And "viewpoint," as undesirable as that term sounds, is not a setback to Legal Writing. Having recognized that personal beliefs are not allowed in Legal Writing, understand a crucial qualification: *Unsupported* personal beliefs are not permitted. You are most certainly free to feel a kinship with your words, as long as those words are supported by a citation. At this point in your career, you are not going to create new law. But you quite often are going to be asked to deliver a set of principles by which determinations in a field are best made. That set of principles is called the *Rule*, and it dominates all other Legal Writing constructions.

B. The Singular Importance of a Rule of Law

Many students rush to locate a solitary statute or case that defines the Rule. The Rule can be concise but most often incorporates various authorities, as illustrated by the example below. The example sheds light on the process by which an entity determines if it is subject to money laundering restrictions imposed by federal law.

EXAMPLE:

> In the United States, the Bank Secrecy Act, 31 U.S.C. § 5311 et seq. (2012) requires registration by all entities serving as a "Money Services Business" ("MSB"). Under the federal statute, both banks and non-banks can be classified as MSBs. The registration re-

quirement, created by effectuating regulations, applies to those entities exchanging cash for other forms of legal tender (e.g., the purchase of money orders totaling $10,000 or more in a single business day). *See* 31 C.F.R. § 1010.100. There are exceptions for certain government entities, such as the U.S. Postal Service.

The above example includes authorities from the top-down, supports those authorities with citations, makes statements with authority, and, overall, educates the reader. To be sure, there are terms that will require elaboration, and this book shall soon explore expanding the Rule. Understand that learning to include the most relevant information in the most digestible fashion is a skill that you will perfect your entire career. In the short term, recognize that the Rule determines the scope and content of every other section of the document you are endeavoring to create. That mutually beneficial relationship shall become evident as you attempt different types of documents later in this book. For now, the two steps below will assist you in your initial attempts at creating a sturdy Rule.

1. Gather and Join Authorities (i.e., the Words of Others)

Lawyers earn their pay and their praise on a case-by-case basis, generating credibility in each document they create. And that credibility can be lost in a sentence. Remember always that the best lawyers in the country aspire to the role of Supreme Court Justice, a job that, while guaranteeing lifetime tenure, nonetheless demands reference to a statute, case, or principle (with citation) each time a paragraph is penned. In other words, even the most heralded of judges is not entitled to unsupported, purely personal opinions.

That daunting challenge laid bare, you should always strive to locate the most relevant words of others. For example, imagine the television news reporting that a Beverly Hills celebrity is suing a public company and its CEO over a dog bite on corporate property. The celebrity, who was nipped during a social meeting at corporate headquarters, never went to the hospital. The CEO's dog weighs 2 pounds and is named "Madame Snowflakes." The lawsuit (against the CEO and the corporation) asks for $5 million dollars.

The "bystanders" may make comments about the petulance of the citizens of Hollywood, the targeting of CEOs during the Recession, or overly accommodating courts. Nonetheless, as a law student, your mind should race to the following:

Has anyone ever received such a payout for that tort in California?

Is there a state statute on point?

What's the test for recovery?

Has any lawyer ever been sanctioned for filing a similar case?

The last question may be the most challenging, but it is actually derivative of the first three. The apt Legal Writer thus seeks to address the questions of whether the law presently speaks to such conflicts, and what principled guidance it offers. Avoiding remote authorities (e.g., the Supreme Court) and distracting personal judgment (e.g., "Trivial lawsuits such as this ..."), the efficient Legal Writer thus offers something akin to the following:

> While many jurisdictions evaluate the dog's known, aggressive tendencies, California has a strict liability statute governing this issue. Since 1988, Section 3342 of the Civil Code imposes liability upon any dog owner for any and all injuries sustained by a victim. Damages normally approximate injuries (i.e., medical costs) but may be reduced by the victim's degree of negligence.

> Defenses exist for owners of police dogs and against trespassers, parties provoking the dog, and those performing a paid service involving the dog. Commentators generally favor the modern approach, as it is seen as both protecting communities and preventing litigation between families and friends. While additional grounds for suit exist in the context of an employer-employee relationship, there is no known case finding the corporate employer liable.

The 2-paragraph Rule thus succinctly offers a standard while tracing its progression. It answers the questions of whether there is an applicable statute (Yes), whether payout is possible (Yes), who can be found liable (the CEO), and even serves the question of whether someone is going to be sanctioned by the court for starting this ostensibly frivolous lawsuit (We cannot presently tell.). The Rule also adheres to guidance on paragraph and sentence length. Most importantly, the Reader feels he now possesses something of value—the author and he are not just mere bystanders. The Writer avoided the self-indulgent traps of both flowery language and personal belief. The Writer also succeeded in imparting the relevant legal guidance in organized fashion; the weapon of choice for such endeavors is *the outline.*

2. Create an Outline (i.e., Your Own Words)

An outline ensures that you have authority for every assertion you might make. It serves as both menu and calorie counter. It precedes all effective Legal Writing. Outlines come in countless forms but all serve the same purpose: Ensuring that the Legal Writer is ready to write.

Above all else, Outlines rank authorities. An elementary listing of the authorities in order of their importance (i.e., the famed "Hierarchy of Authority") looks something like this:

I.   U.S. Constitution

II. Federal statutes/Agency pronouncements/State statutes

III. Case law

IV. Commentary/Secondary authority

Obviously, not all of the above authorities will be revealed by each of your research projects. But realizing, for example, that a regulation has the force of a statute (and thus trumps case law) helps to explain both, while ultimately leading to your best statement of the relevant standard.

In the Exercise below, create the most basic of outlines—the list of "bullet points." In preparing a responsive, sole page, do not become distracted by dates, repetitive items, or direct quotes. And strive to avoid the dual pitfalls of ornamental language and personal belief.

Exercise One: Outlining Authorities

This year, the Environmental Protection Agency has taken a bold stance on factory emissions. In recent months, a temporary worker at your company compiled the following random notes on the topic within a word document titled "EPA 2015."

> In February 2015, the Environmental Protection Agency proposed regulations that newly interpreted the federal Clean Air Act of 1990 ... Three pro-business groups have filed lawsuits over the measures ... The rules would require all industrial plants to reduce the amount of mercury and other emissions. New York, New Mexico, Utah and Oklahoma support the EPA's plan ... Numerous States oppose the regulations, compliance with which would cost "untold millions" according to one Senator ... Section 111 of the 1990 Act empowers the EPA to regulate air pollution from any "stationary source" ... The move was designed to lessen climate change. Michigan, California, Florida and Pennsylvania oppose the EPA's 2015 plan. Section 112 of the Act ("National Air Standards for Hazardous Pollutants") empowers the EPA to regulate over 100 emissions, regardless of source ... A noted Harvard professor has written a Washington Post editorial calling the EPA plan "an extraordinarily unconstitutional piece of administrative rulemaking" ... Lawsuits against the EPA normally center on final regu-

lations. The regulations would require a 30% decrease in covered emissions ... The two Act sections have never been cross-referenced, or reconciled ... The EPA proposal does not address section 112 or tungsten gas.

Your public company employer operates plants that may emit a modest amount of tungsten gas, which indisputably originates from a stationary source. The press has been calling to learn your company's official position on the controversy. Accordingly, the CEO of your company plans to seek a vote from the Board at the quarterly meeting next week. In a well-organized background memo taking the form of a sole page of "bullets," briefly explain the dispute and the relevant authorities to the CEO. Be sure to reveal the authorities in the order of their importance. Write short sentences.

Even the most organized delivery of information can still frustrate the reader if the overall message is that of a layman. Simply put, the next task ensures that you have dug deep enough, and that you have added value of a legal nature to the problem at hand. In the following exercise, organize the varied thoughts into a "lawyerly" Rule.

Exercise Two: Writing A 5-Sentence Rule

Imagine that the supervisor at your law firm is moving to Missouri, where he just purchased a townhouse. Her last assignment for you is to briefly advise of the Rule in that State governing the registration of a newly purchased automobile. Your internet access is down, but an insurance agent friend in St. Louis has been kind enough to send you the following text:

Car registration? That's a bit tricky here. You have to have your auto insurance paid up. Oh, and also a certificate from the State that you've paid your property taxes for the year. You can visit any licensing office of the Department Motor Vehicles, but some counties require separate emission inspections (on top of the 2 required vehicle inspections). Oh yeah, a motor vehicle law section says you have to complete all this within 30 days of the purchase, or else there are fines. Your boss wouldn't like that. Of course, you'll need a Missouri title certificate. And that certificate has to clearly state the latest odometer reading. I remember when I moved here and went through the process. Completely forgot about the State sales tax (I think it's about 7.5%, and more for "luxury" vehicles). I got through all the paperwork and then was asked if I wanted the 1-year or 2-year registration. I still don't know the advantage of one or the other. Best bet: Tell your boss to count on several trips to the DMV.[3]

Your supervisor, naturally, does not wish to make several trips. Create for her a plain Rule including all of the requirements disclosed above. Where possible, distinguish the origin of certain requirements; throughout, be detailed but brief (and leave out the personal commentary).

Note that, once having identified the key principles, both a set of instructions for the Legal Reader and a resultant tone emerges. Principles are thorny prizes; some might say they are like distant relatives—once they finally arrive, they never want to leave. It is up to the Legal Writer to combine, trim down, and rank the list of instructions in the cause of providing a thorough revelation of the Rule. As previously discussed, that Rule and its relevant Application comprise the Formula. These two key components shall be further explained in subsequent Chapters. For now, let us stop to consider how often we wish to interrupt the text of a Rule to provide supporting authority.

IV. Choosing When to Cite, Rationally

Once having located the highest authorities and concisely communicated their relevance, your goal becomes most mundane. Local court rules—most often revealed via dedicated web sites—dictate such matters as font, spacing, page limits and indentation. The *Bluebook* is the most oft-utilized reference manual for citation. Whatever your manual of reference, its punctual and consistent use is urged by the profession, and even by the manual itself.

Far more intellectually challenging is the question of *when* to cite. Stated otherwise, proper usage of a citation manual is rather low on the ideal list of writing skills (i.e., it can be learned through mere repetition). The more distinguishing skill is thus employing correct cites to maintain credibility without engaging in mind-numbing repetition.

And thus the third principle of this Chapter: Use authority when required, use it properly, but only use it as often as is necessary.

In my 9 years of teaching Legal Writing, I find a short list of questions to repeat each semester:

---

3. Adapted from David O'Brien, *Registering Your Car in Missouri* (Dec. 2014), *available at* http://stlouis.about.com/od/livingworking/a/MO_registration.htm.

Must I cite after every sentence?

When can I <u>not</u> cite?

Doesn't the reader already know where to find the source case?

The answer to the above questions is quite basic—we cite when necessary to maintain credibility. Different audiences may require it to different degrees. For example, many law reviews adhere to strictest possible standard of including a footnote after each sentence.[4] But such religious observance of the *Bluebook* may serve foremost to winnow down the voluminous submissions an editorial board encounters.

The more universal practice lies in establishing trust. Trust is established by citation when providing clarity and ease of reference. For example, locate the point at which the trust was lost in the passage below, likely to be read in an introductory class on business law:

> The standard for determining the presence of an investment "security" comes from case law. The *Howey* decision is often cited as the authority for the relevant investment contract test. *SEC v. W.J. Howey Co.*, 328 U.S. 293 (1946). In that case, what was essentially a real estate deal was characterized by the Court as an investment. The Court granted the SEC injunction, upholding the Second Circuit determination that a Florida land deal, accompanied by service or leasing agreements, could come within the securities laws. *Howey*, 328 U.S. 293. The resulting 3-part test has been cited countless times by subsequent federal and state courts. *See, e.g., U.S. v. Leonard*, 529 F.3d 83 (2d Cir. 2008).

Here, there are numerous cites, but not much clarity. First, the opening sentence, while admirably clear, asks for indulgence by the reader (i.e., at some later point, the Reader shall learn from where the definition emanates). Second, the Reader is left to wonder whether the Court expressly re-characterized the land deal, or the author is imparting a bit of his own analysis. Third, the reader knows not where to find the part of the case decision relating the holding—all that has been provided is "293," the first page of the case.

Overall, the above Writer appears to not be trying to skirt obligations, but the effect is the same. The Reader loses trust when the passage ceases honest revelation of the distinction between the words of the Writer and the words of others.

---

4. The wall to the office of my law school journal consistently displayed 2 pages of a student Note entirely taken up by a footnote. I still do not know if such homage was offered in admiration or in jest.

Now read this passage:

> Conversely, whether or not a financial arrangement qualifies as a "note" (i.e., undeniably resembles commercial paper) is governed by the test set forth in *Reves v. Ernst & Young*, 494 U.S. 56 (1990). The *Reves* case, although dated, remains instructive. In the case, a farmer's cooperative went bankrupt after issuing millions of dollars of "demand" notes. *Reves*, 494 U.S. at 57. The Court relied heavily upon the nature of the sophisticated instrument. The test favored the unsophisticated purchasers. *Id.* at 61–63.

Here, the Writer has revealed a standard and distinguished the parts of the underlying decision addressing facts, holding, and outcome—and the Reader is much appreciative. And not every sentence required a cite.

Recognize that citation is not just to show authorities agree with you—that minimal goal is achieved via a healthy bibliography. Additionally, citation is not purely cosmetic, for a skilled advocate can use a robust Table of Authorities to persuade (e.g., via articles that through their titles reveal skepticism of a Rule). Likewise, a parade of "id."s actually alienates the reader, who believes you have become a bit lazy. Citation is a skill that requires constant balancing of the profession's requirements with the needs of the Reader.

To be sure, effective citation also requires a mastery of *Bluebook* formalities on spacing, capitalization and punctuation. Those strict requirements are readily available in the form of court rules or the *Bluebook* (two Exercises on which are included in "Appendix A"). But knowing when to cite is the skill that demands a bit more adaptation and practice. Indeed, accomplished Legal Writers eventually develop a rhythm for when an assertion needs support (much in the same way a teacher senses she is losing her audience). For starters, complete the Exercise below.

Exercise Three: Frequency of Citation

Indicate where you would include cites in the following passage. Strive to so indicate on a frequent basis, but avoid simply including a cite after each sentence. Vary your cites to the situation/strength of authority.

> The private cause of action for trademark infringement is briefly and clearly stated. Section 43(a) of the Lanham Act both outlaws "false designation of origin" and creates a cause of action for plaintiffs, defined broadly as "any person who believes that he or she is or is likely to be damaged by such [false] act." Damages are assumed, and jurisdiction resides in varied federal courts.

Likewise, since the Act's adoption in 1946, federal courts have been eager to enjoin defendants utilizing marks without permission. Since 1961, the Second Circuit's disjunctive *Polaroid* test has been used to arrive at a determination of whether there exists a "likelihood of confusion." Chief among these factors are the plaintiff's intent to occupy the field, the strength of the mark, and the defendant's bad faith.

However, on occasion, a corporate plaintiff will face a solid defense in the very factors revealed by *Polaroid*. Specifically, in a decision involving the famous Muppets of television and theatre fame, a Second Circuit judge found the defendant's naming of a character as "Spa'am" (which sounds like "Spam," a meat product sold by the plaintiff) to be simply a creative, comedic variation that would not confuse the grade schoolers who bought the merchandise of Muppets. The court thoroughly applied the eight *Polaroid* factors and, if influenced by First Amendment concerns, did not so indicate in the written decision.

V. Conclusion: In Choosing Collars

Too many names are bestowed upon the "secrets" of Legal Writing instruction. There are a broad array of wonderfully colorful terms such as IRAC, CREAC, "the Paradigm," macro structure and micro structure. As you shall learn, Legal Writing essentially seeks to identify the most relevant principles and then apply them to the present case.

To commence your Legal Writing approach, acknowledge that, if you want to impress a law professor, a supervisor, a firm partner or a judge, you need to convey in short order a comprehensible mixture of legal background and the present issue. Successfully concocting this mixture may require you to absorb some startling new ideas, such as the deliberate inclusion of legalese, the adherence to mechanical word limits, or the elimination of descriptive detail.

Relish the amount of choice you nonetheless maintain. As an attorney, you will be consistently reminded of the many things that are beyond your control. Witnesses forget, statutes and regulations change, and judges sometimes rule unpredictably. But effective communication of all of these realities is within the grasp of any diligent attorney or law student who has a plan. Keeping the overarching, 3-step guidance offered in this Chapter atop your list expedites the development of that plan.

Specifically, this Chapter asks you to commence your career as a Legal Writer by concentrating on the following 3 potential pitfalls:

- Avoid distraction. Its chief tool is language that gives pause, so do not make words your goal.[5]
- Further, do not settle for the role of bystander. Dig deeper than commentators. And eschew personal judgment for opinions that can be supported. In Legal Writing, there can be viewpoints, but they must be supported by authorities.
- Finally, adhere to the formalities (foremost being citation). But do so in moderation.

To be sure, there are deeper lessons to be learned, but mastery of these objectives will surely set you on the right path. For some, Legal Writing is to be resented for its segmented structure and unforgiving technicalities. For successful students, it is a challenge met by adapting collegiate skills to a new environment. Regardless of your initial opinion of the subject, Legal Writing shall present countless fact patterns, potentially unknowable standards, and ever-changing Rules. The one constant shall be your reliability in relating those unknowns. In short, we may never totally fence in the wayward goat, but we can all at least choose the right collar.

---

5. Remember always the wise advice of Kipling's timeless poem, *If* ("If you can think and not make thoughts your aim.").

Chapter II

The Magna Carta and the Dominance of Rule of Law

Chapter Objectives:
- Recognizing the Universal Structure of All Rules
- Implementing a Short Checklist for Rule Efficiency
- Focusing on the Mantra: "to Assert and Support"
- Drafting a Thorough and Informative Rule

Substantive Takeaways:
- Model "Bitcoin" State Licensing Statutes
- "*Chevron* Deference" for Agency Decisions
- Delegations of Duty in Health Provider Licensing

I. Introduction: Appreciating the Dominance of the Rule

The year 2015 marked the 800th anniversary of the Magna Carta, the iconic agreement credited with birthing the "Rule of Law" that characterizes democracies. Procured at sword-point, hopelessly cryptic, and even contemporaneously negated by the Pope, the document did prove to be lasting by contributing the phrase "lawful judgment by peers" (or something similar), and thus deserves its dominant role in jurisprudential history.

Likewise, the Legal Writing *Rule of Law* dominates the Formula. For if the Rule is drafted properly, it makes the ensuing section (i.e., the Rule Application[1]) an almost routine task. Conversely, if the Rule is drafted incompletely

---

1. The Rule Application part of the Formula is dealt with in detail in Chapter III.

or haphazardly, the entire Formula confounds the Legal Reader. At its best, the Rule serves as a thorough and thoroughly comprehensible presentation of relevant principles. At its worst, it reads like the manual to an appliance you resent. The difference often lies in the Legal Writer's appreciation for its singular importance.

Follow the 3 steps below to at once deepen your drafting skills and concisely introduce the Legal Reader to the information he requires from a Rule:

A. Account for the Full Range of Authorities, Even the "Outlier"

This step includes identifying the jurisdiction, a must in the days of Internet and global commerce. A lack of immediate clarification proves a setback to both comprehension and credibility. Compare the two examples below:

WEAK:

> The Secretary of State can sometimes enjoy both investigative and prosecutorial authority. These powers are largely due to Oklahoma case law.

BETTER:

> In Oklahoma, the Secretary of State enjoys both investigative and prosecutorial authority.

The latter example both clarifies the jurisdiction for the present matter and sounds more confident. The first example equivocates enough to remind of the bystander language rejected in Chapter I; concurrently, the "weak" example prompts editing before the Rule is anywhere near completion.

To avoid such a false start, simply get in the habit of commencing every Rule you write with the phrase "In the State of X," or "In the United States." The relevant jurisdiction is always going to be the court that would hear a contested matter on the subject of your Writing. If these two conventions prove uncomfortable, begin by noting the most important statute (thus indirectly informing the Reader of the relevant jurisdiction).

EXAMPLE:

> Pursuant to Congress' Video Privacy Protection Act of 1988, video rental establishments must keep confidential a customer's rental history.

Perhaps more importantly, another guide for drafting a Rule asks that you abandon the collegiate practice of hiding unpleasant news late in the document, or in a footnote. Legal Writers confront ugliness head on, if for no other reason than Legal Readers are diligent researchers who are ultimately going to unearth any truth that has been buried. Additionally, it is often the identification of the rare case (a.k.a., "the outlier") that serves best to define the mainstream law on a topic.

Evaluate these two passages, both dealing with the requirement that plaintiffs under the federal Age Discrimination in Employment Act of 1967 be at least 40 years of age:

WEAK:

> No case focused on herein found someone under age 40 to be a plaintiff.

BETTER:

> Nearly all of the cases uphold the statutory age requirement. While one case did allow a 38-year-old male to bring suit for discrimination, the facts in that case simultaneously disclosed outrageous efforts by the employer to alter the plaintiff's birth records.

The first example appears to deliver information "in short order." But, as the second example clarifies, there is an outlier that will eventually emerge, and the complete lack of reference thereto will detract from the Legal Writer's credibility. Thus, the second example proves the better approach because it at once reveals the rare case and relegates it to the unpersuasive role of outlier.

B. Order the Authorities, and Offer a Conjunctive/Disjunctive Test

After naming the jurisdiction and accounting for the range of relevant principles, the Hierarchy of Authority is, again,[2] the primal consideration. Although there are many variations of that ranking of sources, it can be generally summarized as follows:

CONSTITUTION → STATUTE/REGULATION → CASE → COMMENTARY

Bypassing this prioritization—even in an uncontroversial matter—leads to Reader frustration. For example, imagine your law firm's managing partner had his cell phone searched during a routine traffic stop. The managing partner is outraged at what he feels was an invasion of privacy. A junior associate

---

2. The Hierarchy was introduced in Chapter I.

has been assigned the research on the legality of this search. Consider the partner's reaction upon receipt of the research in this manner:

> The law on the legality of cell phone searches by police officers is in a great state of flux. One state, Arizona, has evaluated the danger to the officer posed by the overall situation. Another state, California, has favored the use of a warrant. Of course, the Supreme Court decision of 2014 seemed to end the kitchen table debate, but some commentators question whether dinner is truly over.

In the interest of forging a communion with the reader, the Writer has initially lowered expectations (and then barely met them). Remember always that, when craving guidance on a topic, Readers care little about the Legal Writer's own priorities (or sense of irony). The following passage, surely more orderly and less metaphoric, is undoubtedly more informative:

> In 2014, the Supreme Court ruled in <u>Riley v. California</u>, 134 S. Ct. 2473 (2014), that police searches of a private cell phone incidental to an arrest require a warrant. Since that ruling, one State court has followed the ruling without question, while another has interpreted the ruling as allowing for an "officer safety" exception. No agency or other state authority has weighed in. Commentators generally extol the high Court ruling for providing a bright line test.

The difference is due to the second passage religiously adhering to the Hierarchy of Authority. Indeed, the Hierarchy is much more than a mantra; the list actually serves to deepen research and evaluate efficacy.

Thus, locating a principle's source takes precedence over fully understanding it. To relay that plain but elegant lesson, each semester I commence my first lecture with a simple quiz: Which local, professional sports team has the best ballpark? The students rush to offer irrelevant, highly subjective reasons. "The Yankees have the most championships and a Hall of Heroes." "Cardinals games are broadcast throughout the Midwest." "My parents met at a Mets game at Shea Stadium." When the fun subsides, I ask the volunteering students to attach third party support to their subjective views, and silence ensues.

I then note that a debate based upon such highly personal rationales would be ceaseless (and emotionally charged). Viewers would ultimately sympathize with neither side. Conversely, a debate commencing with universal standards would more likely reach an agreeable resolution. I thus ask, "Is this a Constitutional, statutory, or case law debate?" There is more silence. I then explain that in fairly recent times, appellate judges in Minnesota were tasked with deciding whether the public should fund a new ballpark. Those skilled jurists listed a number of relevant factors that could be used to evaluate the contributions a ballpark makes to its host community. The factors included whether the stadium was open for use for many occasions, created public debt, and/or whether a team leaving a State for lack of stadium would create a sense of loss in the community.[3] By overlaying the Hierarchy, the most relevant guidance emerges: Persuasive authority, in the form of State appellate court decisions, rare (but pointed) in nature.

By following the incontrovertible order of authorities, the incontrovertible universal elements of each Rule begin to appear. Students are naturally adept at placing the strongest authorities atop the list; students are not as readily inclined to place the remaining authorities in a numeric order. But such a detailed ordering is of great utility to the Legal Reader, both among authorities and among their resultant principles.

And such structure is timeless. I once had an MBA student challenge the Hierarchy of Authority as "a textbook creation." I answered his challenge by asking him to select any Constitutional provision he liked for analysis. He chose the Fifth Amendment, which governs the rights of the accused in government investigations. I pointed out to him that, with very little modification, the text of that famed protection can be stated as the following Rule:

> The Constitution's Fifth Amendment guarantees that the criminally accused shall be afforded protection from 1) being tried without a grand jury indictment, 2) being tried more than once for the same offense, 3) testifying against himself, 4) being denied "life, liberty, or property" without due process, and 5) his loss of private property (for public use) without compensation. An exception from the grand jury requirement exists for members of the armed forces during wartime.

While the original text possesses a poetry and preeminence that this book could never replicate, the above *conjunctive* test may be the better choice for a memo to a litigator facing a deadline for a criminal appeal. Note also the corollary progression that results from the varied provisions, both in the original text and the Legal Writer's summary thereof. The drafters of the Constitution first revealed the very event that defines the accused (i.e., indictment); the above summary concludes with the unknown (i.e., why only one exception exists). Thus, the guidance for ordering the disclosure of varied rights might look something like this:

EXACT → SPECIFIC → GENERALIZED → UNKNOWN

---

3. *See, e.g., Lifteau v. Metropolitan Sports Facilities Commission,* 270 N.W.2d 749 (Sup. Ct. Minn. 1978); *Metropolitan Facilities Commission v. Minnesota Twins Partnership,* 638 N.W.2d 214 (Ct. App. Minn. 2002).

In short, proceed from highest authority to lowest authority, and from the most clear principle to the vaguest.

Separately, wherever the authority to be summarized includes one or more optional elements (e.g., the various means of running afoul of the tax code), a *disjunctive* test is utilized, signaled to the Reader through the use of "or" instead of "and."

EXAMPLE:

> Pursuant to Congress' Video Privacy Protection Act of 1988, video rental establishments must keep confidential a customer's rental history, unless disclosure of such information is 1) pursuant to a court order, 2) coincidental to the establishment's business, or 3) with the notice to and consent of the customer.

The disjunctive test utilized above actually conveys 3 defenses for a defendant (i.e., the defendant need only prove one of the three numbered items to avoid liability for disclosure).

Such tests[4] and progressions are rhythmic and predictable. Further, a seasoned Legal Reader will expect them. And the Legal Reader's expectations are a key consideration, as the next point advises.

C. Answer the Unspoken Question Posed

Many Rules lose the forest for the trees. The Legal Reader is often most concerned with a sole, threshold question: Has this case ever been heard before? To that end, effective Rules often answer the unspoken question with a simple declarative statement, such as "No case could be located directly on point," or "This appears to be a case of first impression." Both choices are often shied from for the reason referenced throughout this book (i.e., the unfortunate hesitancy of 1L research). But such express language readily distinguishes superior Rules from average ones, a goal many 1L students seem to share.

As an example: Online purchases of digital currencies such as "Bitcoin" have skyrocketed in recent years. Correspondingly, the entities enabling such purchases have so grown as to prompt some State regulators to require a "Bitlicense" to engage in such commerce. Imagine that your supervisor has an appointment in 2 hours with an out-of-State client who needs to know whether his fledgling entity needs to be concerned with licensing in this State.

---

4. Equally effective are tests including discretionary factors, explained in Chapter V.

WEAK:

> In our State, the finance department guidelines require entities "buying, selling, or storing" Bitcoins to register for a license. There is an initial fee of $1,000. Also, an initial application must be received within 45 days of commencing business. There is a provision speaking to "foreign entities," but there are also provisions speaking to "other States." An applicant must grant access to State regulators for examinations at any time, but such an applicant may refuse examination and hire outside auditors instead. In such case, the accountants would have to prepare and retain records each year.
>
> Going forward, the registrant would have to annually pay $1,000 (to cover "the State's cost of compliance and examination"). In the enabling statute, there are exceptions from registration for 1) subsidiaries of chartered banks and savings institutions, 2) Canadian enterprises, 3) companies earning less than $10,000 a year, and 4) subsidiaries of registered insurance companies.

BETTER:

> In our State, entities "buying, selling, or storing" Bitcoins must 1) complete an application within 45 days of commencing business, 2) pay an initial and annual fee of $1,000, and 3) agree to examination upon request by State regulators, or hire an external auditor to annually compile records. Exceptions are made for, inter alia, entities that will derive less than $10,000 in gross revenue from their first year of business. It is not clear from the statute whether entities headquartered outside of the State are covered. However, on related topics, State regulators have been reluctant to expand jurisdiction.

Indeed, the second example above took time and thought to arrive at a shorter passage (reminiscent of historic admonitions that more direct speeches take longer to prepare[5]). The passage utilizes both conjunctive and disjunctive language, and it answers the ultimate question (i.e., Of what effect is the client entity's newness?). The passage uses the same term repeatedly ("entity") to avoid confusion;

---

5. Among others, President Woodrow Wilson is credited with having clarified the inverse relationship between preparation and length of presentation. *See* http://quoteinvestigator.com/2012/04/28/shorter-letter/ ("[A] ten-minute speech ... takes me all of two weeks to prepare ...; if it is a half-hour speech it takes me a week; if I can talk as long as I want to it requires no preparation at all. I am ready now.").

additionally, it embraces a bit of necessary legalese ("inter alia," which may be the most economical Legal Writing term ever constructed). Finally, the Rule answers the unspoken question (i.e., Does the client need to fear the statute?), albeit in a manner that contravenes traditional guidance on the placement of topic sentences.

To be sure, there are additional considerations in drafting a Rule, and there are more fundamentals (such as legislative trends), enhancements that this book shall address soon enough. But the above three steps will assist in Legal Writer in delivering what the Legal Reader wants, namely, a set of guiding principles that could fit on an index card carried in a breast pocket.

In the Exercise below, state a Rule that lists the barest of essentials, in the proper order, while mindful that the "client" has a practical outcome already in sight. Remember to account for the scope of authorities, employ a conjunctive/disjunctive test, and answer the Reader's unspoken question.

Exercise One: Writing a Draft Rule

Poor Professor McElvoy. His Teaching Assistant moved to Guam, leaving in disarray the research he had begun on the famed *Chevron* case. That landmark Supreme Court decision guides lower courts on the deference that should be displayed for agency pronouncements. Business lawyers re-visit the federal standard each time their clients weigh litigation over an onerous agency regulation.

From the scattered notes of the departed Assistant below, create a preliminary multi-part test that best communicates the breadth and spirit of the *Chevron* decision. Note that many study aids tend to sum up the test a bit too briefly, and Professor McElvoy is known for the depth of his lessons.

> Chevron v. Natural Resources Defense Council, Inc., 467 U.S. 837, is the standard since 1984 ... The rule only relates to final declarations having the effect of law ... The justices ultimately found the "bubble theory" to be within the scope of the EPA's discretion ... Agency pronouncements will only be struck down if "unreasonable" ... The petitioner has to show that the underlying law is ambiguous (thus nullifying the discretion exercised by the agency) ... Enabling statutes create agencies; effectuating statutes delineate the scope of their authority in an area ... The court indicated its reluctance to intervene in "interstitial rulemaking" ... The relevant agency must have "expertise" ... The Clean Air act had previously been interpreted ...

II. The Pitfalls

Of course, Rules are sometimes easier said than done. And what is offered effortlessly by one court as a universal standard can be undone by a parallel court the very next month. To ensure your best effort at providing both the most vital information to your Reader and the most consistent structure to your Formula, avoid the traps detailed below.

A. Dignifying the Author Over the Principle

Remember that the "Rule of Law" establishes the dominance of principles; thus, even the hallowed creators of authorities take a backseat to the idea itself. It is thus inferior to explain the governing law in an area by first crediting a judge or author, particularly when such identifying information fits neatly into a citation. Compare the two examples below:

WEAK:

> As Professor Colesanti explains, Section 2-206 of the Uniform Commercial Code acknowledges any form of assent as establishing a "meeting of the minds." [cite]

BETTER:

> Section 2-206 of the U.C.C. acknowledges any form of assent as establishing a "meeting of the minds" required by the law of contracts. U.C.C. § 2-206(1)(a) (2012). *See also* Colesanti, *When Minds Collide*, 124 U.S.A. Intell. Prop. J ...

On very rare occasion, the author of an authority may be placed on a par with her principle (e.g., "Justice Ginsburg's ruling that 'feigning fidelity' may satisfy the fraud required in an S.E.C. Rule 10b-5 action"). However, overall, it is best to explain Rules with notions, and give credit for these notions in cites.

B. Forgetting the Finer Points of the Hierarchy

The Hierarchy of Authority, which helps Writer and Reader alike to compartmentalize new information, contains sub-classifications that are often forgotten. Foremost among these additions are the following:

- Higher courts come before lower courts
- Newer cases take precedence over older ones
- Cases with facts more directly on point outshine others.

Forgetting these dictates not only results in a Rule that is difficult to follow but also in a Formula that ultimately collapses on itself (as will be discussed in subsequent Chapters).

C. Forgetting to Paraphrase

Terms of art (e.g., "knew or should reasonably known was false") deserve to be quoted. Nearly everything else can be paraphrased. Further, quoting too often appears slothful, a perception that should be avoided at all costs. Witness the relative strength of the two passages below.

WEAK:

> The court ruled that "although the argument had been made in the past, situations had now changed enough to warrant reconsideration of whether the trademarked name now offended the public consciousness." The ruling did not provide further specifics.

BETTER:

> The court ruled, without specifics, that situations had changed since petitioner last challenged the trademarked name as violating section 2a.

Legal Writing seeks to add value. The first passage, at the very least, slows reading; at worst, it seeks to relay to the Reader the duty of comprehending the court's words. The second passage, although perhaps not ideal, nonetheless conveys that the Writer has embraced the duty of analysis for the Reader.

D. Engaging in Narration

Legal Writing is a series of countless discretions, assertions, and decisions. Do not call attention to their selection by including pointless introductory language that equates to "I included this assertion for a reason." Witness the comparative strength of the two examples below.

WEAK:

> A principle that deserves our attention is "the *Polaroid* Test," which, since 1961, has offered 9 factors for consideration of a claim of likelihood of confusion.

BETTER:

> Since 1961, "the *Polaroid* Test" has offered 9 factors for consideration of a claim of likelihood of confusion.

In Legal Writing, simply assert and support. Do not also remind the Reader that you are doing so. Truly, a wise Reader will know that any assertion not "worth mentioning" should not be part of the Writing to begin with.

E. Writing a Rule that You Cannot Apply

Often, there are numerous approaches to a legal problem within a jurisdiction (e.g., the statutory vs. the common law approach). In turn, there are countless ways to state a Rule on a vexing subject—as I like to tell a class of forty students, "I anticipate reading forty different Rules in your memos, and all of them being correct."

The challenge thus becomes to identify a Rule that is eminently supportable and most helpful to your client (yet another reason why this book avoids distinctions between "objective" and "subjective" Legal Writing; it's all ultimately subjective). Again, the Hierarchy steers the decision-making and language, as evidenced by the two examples below:

WEAK:

> Throughout the country, there are a number of ways of to evaluate alleged violations of the right of publicity. The statutory approach often confines analysis to a short list of protected attributes, such as "name, picture, portrait or voice." Alternatively, the common law approach may add to this discrete list by also factoring damage resulting from total context, or to an expanded list of victims such as family members. In fairly recent times, state statutes have embodied a collective statutory/common law approach, which both lists expanded lists of factors (e.g., including "likeness in any manner") and separately allows courts to look at existing common law for surviving causes of action.

BETTER:

> In recent times, courts and legislatures have acknowledged both statutory and common law right of publicity claims. *See, e.g., Midler v. Ford Motor Co.*, 849 F.2d 460 (9th Cir, 1988) (upholding the dual approach embodied in California Civil Code § 3344(g)).

The first example reads like the opening pages of a college thesis, and—by providing for 3 subsequent means of analysis—probably foretells of a page limitation problem. The second example confidently asserts that the California approach is being utilized. Subsequent cites and sub-sections shall explain why. In the latter case, the Writer is not "hiding" a problem. Rather, the Writer is clarifying the Rule that drove her analysis; the Writer shall, in short order, explain why she did not subscribe to a separate approach. Such fine tuning is a far more effective way of communicating results than undertaking multiple analyses at once. If the Writer still feels that initially leaving a contrary approach out of a Rule is a bit dishonest, that is why the Bluebook has given us such handy signals as *But see* and *Contra*. Remember: The Rule of Law is dominant. As such, there can be only one.

III. Conclusion

As the pitfalls make clear, drafting an effective Rule can encompass a good deal more discretion than just gathering principles. Elevate one set of principles, and then account for the relevant authorities. Dignify notions, but not their authors. Only reveal that which shall be applied. Truly, there are multiple challenges to generating credibility, both in your research and in its presentation.

In the Chapter's final Exercise, you are asked to utilize all of the guidance of the first two Chapters in creating a Rule. The Exercise focuses on the growing tension between businesses struggling during the recent Recession and active City Councils attempting to regulate them. You shall later examine the full context for such a Rule. For now, focus on crafting a Rule that you can later apply to the offered facts.

Exercise Two: Writing a Final Rule

Authorities

(i) NYS Constitution Article I, sections 1 & 8 (establishing the authority of the State executive).

(ii) McKinney v. Comm'r, 15 Misc. 3d 743 (March 8, 2007) (explaining that the legislature may not delegate absent intelligible guidance).

(iii) Boreali v. Axelrod, 71 N.Y.2d 1 (1987) (reminding that agencies which act beyond the scope of their delegated authority violate the ultra vires doctrine).

(iv) Carter v. Carter Coal Co., 298 U.S. 238 (1936) (holding that Congress may not delegate its legislative duties to private parties).

(v) Chevron v. Natural Res. Defense Council, 467 U.S. 837 (1984) (establishing a 4-part test for determining when deference to administrative agencies is due).

Background

The national Center for Study of Communicable Diseases announced in February 2015 that, for 2014, 57% of all flu vaccination shots were deemed ineffective.

Outraged, the Governor of the State of Luxury issued a press release declaring, "The period of convenience store health rip-offs is over." Shortly thereafter, the Governor signed legislation creating Luxury's "Center for Disease Action" ("CDA"). The relevant provisions of the State's "Disease Action Law" appear in their entirety below:

DAL 111—There shall be established a Center for Disease Action. The Center's mission shall be to restore order and decency to the private marketplace for health aids and products. The Center shall promulgate such rules as necessary for the education of consumers as well as the fair and orderly administration of private health remedies, vaccinations, and health aids. The Governor shall have the right to amend or reject such regulations.

DAL 112—The Center shall be headed by a Commissioner who is a physician and who shall be unaffiliated with any private vendor offering health remedies, vaccinations and health aids. The Commissioner shall be advised by a Health Panel that is comprised by health practitioners, or small business owners.

Instructions

Your firm has been hired by a group of private vaccination providers to challenge the legality of the CDA. Note that the Luxury State Constitution mirrors that of New York in all relevant aspects (including equating *legislative* delegation with *executive* delegation). Utilizing relevant case law and doctrines, write a Rule that will later provide the basis for two arguments against the operation of the CDA. Remember to identify a jurisdiction, account for all authorities, employ a conjunctive/disjunctive test, and answer the Reader's pivotal question. For specific guidance on formatting, see "Appendix D."

Chapter III

Locating Facts and Writing a Rule Application

Chapter Objectives:

- Defining a Legal "Fact"
- Reiterating the Formula (Rule and Rule Application)
- Introducing the Skill of Applying a Rule of Law
- Reiterating the Need for Repetitive Editing

Substantive Takeaways:

- Internet Privacy Law
- State Elder Abuse Statutes
- Federal Reserve Regulation T and Credit for Securities Transactions

---

I. Background

The Legal Writing Formula which this book offers (i.e., a Rule, followed by a Rule Application) assumes that the Writer can confidently assert a set of facts to which the Rule is applied. It could be argued that such an obligation is hopelessly idealistic: Judges and juries determine the Facts; the rest of us locate "likely facts." Nonetheless, Legal Writing demands that we best present the facts as we know them, and then apply the law to them.

In Chapter II, you were shown how to draft a basic Rule. The present Chapter has two primary goals: 1) to define "facts," and 2) to explain how to draft an effective Rule Application. Both the Rule and Rule Application will be amplified in the next two Chapters.

II. The Fleeting Notion of a Legal "Fact"

Curiously, in Legal Writing, a *fact* is often defined by what it is not. *Pleaded facts* are but aspirations, to be blessed or dashed by the judge or jury. *Dates and numbers* are often approximated, thus making them qualified facts, at best. *Inferences* are unstated (i.e., ultimately, they are facts finalized by the Legal Reader). *Characterizations* are dismissed as attempts at persuasion. Even *stipulated facts* are subject to disrepute — my first supervisor frequently reminded me that, for purposed of expediency, two parties to contested matters may stipulate that "the sea is shallow and the sky is green." Further, *Conclusions* find parties liable or guilty based upon a combination of all of the above.

Indeed, the more one studies a legal Fact, the less actual meaning it contains. Consider the following examples, each relating to events one might witness at a workman's compensation hearing and resulting order:

(i) The claimant was physically exhausted, having tried in vain to follow numerous instructions that he was to keep working, "Come hell or high water."

(ii) The foreman loudly scolded the claimant, repeatedly.

(iii) The written decision did not mention witnesses who could corroborate the claimant's prejudicial and self-serving version of events.

(iv) The decision is on appeal, and the review is expected to be heard in late fall.

Of these four examples, perhaps (iv) comes closest to embodying a Fact (i.e., an appeal will be heard sometime before the holidays). The first example ("(i)") contains the distraction of a trite phrase; at its core, the sentence merely conveys that a witness testified to a version of the ultimate truth. The second example ("(ii)") contains two adverbs of varying interpretation (i.e., "loudly" and "repeatedly"), as well as a verb that means different things to different Readers (i.e., "scolded"). The third example ("(iii)") appears to commence with a Fact (i.e., the existence of a written decision), but, in reality, the statement cannot confirm 1) that there were no other witnesses, nor 2) that there were no other helpful witnesses; all that is confirmed is that there may/may not have been other witnesses, and these witnesses may/may not have helped the claimant (in the same manner in which he attempted to help himself).

The fourth example ("(iv)") provides a somewhat narrow time for an appeal, but even that modest goal — upon inspection — reveals only one bit of incontrovertible information: There is an appeal.

It being so simple for lawyers (and layman alike) to dispute Facts, it becomes imperative that they be offered economically. Still, Legal Writing requires storytelling beyond what a police report or pie graph can offer. Further, practitioners often make a strong argument for the Facts section being the most valuable component in a Motion or Brief, for it motivates the judge to apply the law in the way favorable to the most deserving party in the present circumstances.

Facts being simultaneously scarce and in high demand, principles for their location are necessary. Below are five bits of guidance that help us to identify a legal "Fact."

A. Embellishments Are Not Facts

A good rule of thumb speaks directly to multi-word descriptions: Avoid them. A distinct item is not *very unique;* by definition, unique means "singular in nature."

Likewise, even single-word descriptions can place the Facts in shadows. Examine the passages below:

WEAK:

> The greedy plaintiff repeatedly filed suits against public companies three times, in 2012, 2013, and again in 2014.

BETTER:

> The plaintiff sued public companies in 2012, 2013, and 2014.

In the first Example, the additions of "greedy" and "repeatedly" are more than just redundant. The highly subjective language reveals the transparent attempt by the Writer to urge a conclusion by the least cumbersome means (i.e., if the plaintiff can only evidence greed, the cause of action must fail). The second Example includes all the verbiage that is necessary to show that the plaintiff has tried his luck three times.

B. Conclusions and Inferences Are Not Facts

Like embellishments, *conclusions* and *inferences* are not Facts. In drafting Facts, there is a good bit of guidance to be drawn from the most effective trial attorneys. Such professionals often advise that their overriding goal is to lead a jury to the brink of a conclusion, but stop short of making that decision for the jury members. Likewise, in drafting a Fact, let the Reader come to the final judgment of its worth.

WEAK:

> The heartless customer service department answered the needy 75-year-old's written complaints only once, in a mere two-sentence letter.

BETTER:

> The plaintiff, who does not own a computer, handwrote 5 letters to the company. She received one response, a form letter advising only that "No further action shall be taken."

In the second passage, the desired result is still obtained (i.e., someone in customer service has some explaining to do). But the Reader is spared the uncomfortable determination that the company is liable, the ultimate purpose of the contested legal matter (and a virtually impossible decision before learning all of the Facts, or the applicable law). In a sense, we all learned this trait of delaying subjectivity in grammar school ("Show, don't tell"). In a larger sense, repetitive characterizations and commentary serve to discredit the Legal Writer in a way that cannot later be repaired.

Accordingly, in proofreading your Writing for conclusions, ask yourself whether a single statement resolves the entire dispute (e.g., "The company was negligent."). If so, eliminate the statement, and pen the 3 or 4 Facts that would lead the Reader to that same determination.

C. Pleadings and Assertions Are Not Facts

This principle may be the easiest to absorb. If an alleged "Fact" appears in a lawsuit's Complaint, Answer, or other pre-trial pleading, it simply exists as a wish, to be granted or denied later on. But as is the case with most principles, there is one caveat: Once granted by the judge, the allegation is elevated to Fact (and normally takes on the title of a "finding").

D. Parties Can Stipulate that Non-Facts Are Facts

Closely related to the judge's ability to create a Fact is the power of the parties to grant wishes. Namely, two parties can resolve the dispute over an allegation without the court's intervention. Such agreements are called "stipulated facts," and they have the full force of a Fact.

This possibility should cause some alarm. If the legal process seeks foremost to find the truth, a mini-truth within the process can actually be determined by agreement between the parties (e.g., "The parties hereby stipulate that under 5 letters were sent to the customer service department."). But such is a compromise inherent to the legal system, perhaps characterized as an expedient solution in the service of a higher good (and definitely a necessity in light of the system's ever-growing caseload).

E. The Absence of a Fact Is a Fact

My first pro bono case involved an applicant for disability benefits. The aged male applicant had suffered kidney disease, carpel tunnel syndrome, and damage to his spine. The man had twice been denied benefits, the latter occasion stemming from a brief government physical declaring him fully healthy. Indeed, the case file included a variety of adverse determinations better suited to earn him a job as a lifeguard than assist with his impairment.

My mentor, a securities lawyer, patiently worked with me. Where I saw a dearth of evidence, he saw opportunity to prove the government's inattention to actual events. Where I saw a blank page, he saw a detailed argument. Regarding the controversial (and damning) physical examination, I felt overwhelmed. I did not see how I could opine that a doctor's report was insufficient—I had no medical training, in general, and no experience with disability appeals, in particular.

My mentor asked simply, "Have you ever been through a physical?" He then smiled as he reminded me that my argument would be solely centered on everything *that was not done* during my client's hasty, 5-minute exam. My summation concluding the benefits hearing thus sounded something like this:

> "Finally, on January 3rd, Mr. H was examined by the government's doctor. His temperature and pulse were taken, and he was asked to walk across the room. That was it."

> "Noteworthy is that his reflexes were not tested, and he was not given a hernia test. No X-rays were taken, and blood was not drawn. He did not breathe in deeply or cough, he did not catch a ball, and he was not even asked to bend at the waist. Remember that scoliosis exam we all received in grammar school? He didn't receive that either ..."

"That's enough," bellowed the administrative law judge. The written judgment for my client arrived by mail 3 weeks later. That injured man thereafter received some monthly benefits, and I received a thrilling lesson that the *non-facts* can dwarf the facts.

There exist many such war stories about the importance of stressing Facts of every definition. Before going any further, complete the Exercise below. It is loosely based on a criminal trial in recent years of an American corporate executive, in absentia, who had been charged for failing to protect the privacy rights of an Italian national:

Exercise One: Recognizing Facts

TO: Junior Associate

FROM: Senior Partner

RE: NetBox defendants

Sally Dupuis, a Vice President of NetBox (a "viral chat board"), was convicted last year of criminal negligence in not responding to public complaints about a popular, online video of a young boy being bullied. The video was removed 27 days after the first complaint was lodged. The Italian court rejected the defense that NetBox had implemented policies calling for removal of objectionable videos from its web site "upon reasonable investigation and time period." Under Italian law, authorities now must decide whether an appeal shall be granted.

We have been asked to request an appeal for Dupuis. Our firm's publicists recently put together the timeline appearing below. Before I write the Case Memo for our managing board, I need a lawyer to separate the Facts (i.e., actual events) from the non-Facts (i.e., evidence, characterizations/conclusions, and factual inferences). Please review the items listed below. Then indicate next to each whether—in your estimation—the item represents a fact ("F") or something else ("SE"). Note that some items represent both; in such cases, separate the Fact from the non-Fact.

- "Between 2004 and 2007, Sally Dupuis was an honor student at a nationally ranked business school."
- "In high school, Dupuis had authored a short story that seemed to applaud a school bully."
- "Prior to this incident, Dupuis had never had any run-in with the law."
- "Antonio Gimmono, a native of Naples, was pictured in a 38-second video for over 3 weeks on NetBox. He is 9 years old and autistic."
- "The day the video first appeared, NetBox received a complaint calling the video 'appalling.' "
- "Dupuis knew of the complaint but did not remove the video from circulation."
- "Experts estimated that over 200,000 Internet users accessed the video over the next two weeks."
- "NetBox written procedures were drafted in 2002."
- "These procedures have been revised, but only in superficial manner."

- "The Castillian police formally charged NetBox and Dupuis on November 7, 2014."
- "Dupuis did not answer the charges lodged by the Italian prosecutors, publicly calling them 'superfluous.'"
- "The Dupuis family, who all reside in Kansas, awoke one morning to find news trucks surrounding and dwarfing their house."

III. Linking Facts

The preceding Exercise should make you feel a bit uneasy, for there are often no easy answers to questions on Fact classification. Regardless, Legal Writing requires that the underlying story be told. "Fact" sections permeate Office Memoranda, Trial Motions, and Appellate Briefs. Such sections do not allow for created or embellished Facts; the only variables are the amount of space devoted to a Fact and the order in which the Facts are presented.

Thus, once deciding on a set of Facts, the question becomes how to link them while retaining their objective nature. Fact sections lend themselves to a very short list of modes of organization. The first (and by far most common) mode is chronological. Witness the efficiency of the following passage, furthering the workers compensation hypothetical from above:

> The facts in this case are undisputed. Mr. Taylor was employed by the U.S. Army from 1993 through 1997. After a few months of home rest, he entered the civilian workforce in early 1998. He was next employed as a foreman at an outdoor construction site for six months when he began to experience a condition called tinnitus (i.e., ringing in his ears). His employer did not respond to e-mail requests for a meeting about the high level of noise at the worksite.

> By February 1999, Mr. Taylor was unable to function any longer. In fact, he stopped driving altogether. In June 1999, he filed a claim under the Federal Employment Compensation Act. Approximately six months later, his former construction employer filed a motion to dismiss, arguing, among other things, that Mr. Taylor's injuries were not compensable because they had actually been incurred while he was a soldier.

Chronological order is a natural fit for the above story, which centers on a degenerative medical condition. The organization affords a seamless sequence of events, punctuated by transitional words such as "after" and "next." The convention thus serves as the default mode for many attorneys.

A second means of Fact organization, "issue order," allows for greater flexibility in preparation. Pursuant to that protocol, the above story may be reorganized in more persuasive fashion as follows:

> Outdoor construction sites are dangerous places. Thousands of accidents occur there each year. Mr. Taylor had survived active military duty, but he could not escape the threats posed by three-ton cranes whirring day and night.

> Mr. Taylor had been on the job at one such worksite only six months when he felt the persistent buzzing in his ears caused by tinnitus. He complained to his superiors to no avail. He cut down on his hours. He ultimately just stayed home, but it was too late. He now no longer drives and spends his days preparing for his lawsuit against his former bosses.

> And, to be sure, those owner-bosses were aware of the situation. They did not return his e-mail requests for re-assignment. Yet, they did call him when he stopped showing up for work. When he filed suit, they blamed his physical infirmity on his prior service to his country.

The second example draws attention, in sequence, to two issues: The alleged lack of workplace safety, and the alleged refusal to cure a known wrongdoing. Note that Fact sections may add non-controversial truths (e.g., "Guns can kill"). Above all, the organization reclaims a good deal of the story from the control of a calendar (while highlighting some "non-Facts" in the process).

Both chronological order and issue order are preferred ways of organizing Fact sections. Both should be capable of being preceded by the blanket statement, "Let me tell you a story," a temporary marker and Writing tool I urge upon my students. Whichever mode best fits your Writing style, be sure to cite effectively. That nagging request is explained below.

IV. Citing Facts

Factual citations begin and end with parentheses. This formatting distinguishes them from legal cites, which contain factual information at their conclusion (again in parentheses). This citation rule is not difficult but it is unforgiving—credibility is nowhere more vital than when telling "the story" of the dispute.

Fortunately, the need for, and frequency of, citation closely resembles the characteristics of legal citation. For example, the first passage above concerning Mr. Taylor might be cited as such:

> The facts in this case are undisputed. Mr. Taylor was employed by the U.S. Army from 1993 through 1997. (Transcript before Magistrate

(June 1, 2001) ("Tr."), at. 1). After a few months of home rest, he entered the civilian workforce in early 1998. He was next employed as a foreman at an outdoor construction site for six months when he began to experience a condition called tinnitus (i.e., ringing in his ears). His employer did not respond to e-mail requests for a meeting on the high level of noise at the worksite. (Tr. at 11–14.)

By February 1999, Mr. Taylor was unable to function any longer; in fact, he stopped driving altogether. (Tr. at 31.) In June 1999, he filed a claim under the Federal Employment Compensation Act. (Complaint of June 17, 1999.) Approximately six months later, his former construction employer filed a motion to dismiss, arguing, among other things, that Mr. Taylor's injuries were not compensable because they had actually been incurred while he was a soldier. (Answer of December 31, 1999.)

Note that the full reference to a Fact source appears but once, and that a short cite ("Tr.") appears on each relevant occasion thereafter. Note also that a cite after each statement is probably unnecessary and likely interruptive. Conversely, all exact dates should be entered, even where arguably duplicative of the text (e.g., "June 1999" and "June 17, 1999").

V. Ready for Application

Once facts have been identified, linked, and cited, they need to have the Rule applied to them. Students often believe Application to entail a simple "plugging in" of facts. Further, a common mishap evidences the 1L student's rush to fit the Application within the page limitation for the assignment. Such folly is akin to speeding up before your car runs out of gas.

Successful Rule Application involves a 5-step process that at once resolves issues raised in the Writing and rewards the Reader's expectation of patterned analysis. The section need not be long, but it must be extremely disciplined. The 5-step process is detailed below.

A. State Your Prediction/Conclusion

In Office Memos, the customary language is "likely/unlikely." In a Brief or Motion, use "should/should not."

Aside from using the trigger words, provide the conclusion to your analysis in a sole sentence. The only true pitfall here is a lack of specificity:

WEAK:

> In the instant case, because the plaintiff cannot meet the third element, his case is likely to fail.

BETTER:

> In the instant case, because the plaintiff cannot meet the required element of notice, his case is likely to fail.

B. Summarize the Rule

The best Applications remind the Reader of the applicable standard. Witness the efficacy of the second passage below, which concerns the growing use of corporate-owned medical facilities:

WEAK:

> In the present case, the plaintiff is unlikely to prevail. The plaintiff was allegedly injured irreparably by intestinal surgery on October 8, 2011. He did not bring suit until 2015 …

BETTER:

> In the present case, because the plaintiff cannot meet the required element of notice, his case is likely to fail. A lawsuit upon a privately-owned facility requires three steps: 1) the occurrence of a tort for which case law has permitted recovery, 2) proper notice to the managing board of the facility, and 3) observance of the applicable statute of limitations. Regarding the third element, the plaintiff, who underwent surgery in 2011, did not file his claim until 2015 …

Such repetition of the relevant test is always appreciated by the Legal Reader.

C. State All the Relevant Facts

Students often shave time and space off their submissions by assuming that Facts introduced earlier are still before the Reader. The better approach is to remind the Reader of the key Facts immediately before the law is applied to them. Witness the heightened credibility of the Notice analysis appearing above if a single such cross-reference cite is added:

EXAMPLE:

> … Regarding the third element, the plaintiff, who underwent surgery in 2011, did not file his claim until 2015. *See supra* pp. 3–4.

Thus, more reference to the Facts is better than less. Apart from failing to exercise diligence, the pitfall here is introducing key Facts late in the analysis.

Such a practice undermines credibility (and reveals an unwillingness of the Writer to engage in repeat edits of his work). Thus, if a Fact has not previously been introduced in the Facts section, go back and add it.

D. Apply the Legal Standard

This step, the most informative to the Reader, is likewise the most fulfilling to the Writer. After observing all prerequisites and formalities, the Writing finally provides an answer to the key questions posed by the dispute. Do not let the climactic moment pass too quickly. Apply all of the elements you introduced in the Rule, even if they (temporarily) produce conflicting results.

EXAMPLE:

> In the present case, because the plaintiff cannot meet the required element of notice, his case is likely to fail. A lawsuit upon a privately-owned facility requires three steps: 1) the occurrence of a tort for which case law has permitted recovery, 2) proper notice to the managing board, and 3) observance of the applicable statute of limitations.
>
> Concerning the first element, the permissibility of the tort action, negligence, is indeed a claim allowed by interpretations of the State's Torts Claim Act. *See supra* p.2. The plaintiff has thus established that element.
>
> Likewise, regarding the second element (i.e., notice), the Hospital Board acknowledged receiving the letter of December 5, 2011 advising of a potential lawsuit over one of its surgeries on the Plaintiff. *Supra* p.3.
>
> However, regarding the third element (observance of the statute of limitations), the plaintiff underwent surgery in 2011 but did not file his claim until 2015. *Supra* p.3. He meets no exceptions and can claim no peculiar circumstances. *See Supra* p.2. Having failed to satisfy this component of the 3-part conjunctive test, he cannot succeed.

Such a religious observance of the totality of the Rule reveals the diligence of the Legal Writer—in both understanding the law, and in proofreading her document for coherence.

E. Repeat the Conclusion

This step may seem a bit like overkill, but the repetition actually sounds a trumpet blast that the analysis is over. As issues become more numerous, analysis gets more robust, and documents grow longer, the inclusion of a terse, recognizable marker is greatly appreciated by Writer and Reader alike.

EXAMPLE:

> Accordingly, because one of the required elements is not met, the Plaintiff's claim for negligence by the Hospital must fail.

We shall see that when the Formula parts are varied and strengthened, a reiteration of even such a basic conclusion can counter the potential ill-effects of other Writing tools (e.g., the counter-analysis, which should rarely be the last thing that your Writer sees).

In the next Chapter, the Rule shall be expanded to include elaboration (e.g., case summaries, key definitions), and the Rule Application expanded through various means. But first, let us review the two distinct parts of the Formula— Rule and Rule Application. The Exercise below concerns the growing problem of the financial abuse of the elderly. In the Exercise, utilize the following standards: Anything that provides generalized guidance is a Rule; anything that expressly helps to resolve the present dispute is Rule Application.

Exercise Two: Recognizing Formula Parts

Please read the following Facts and statutory provisions and then label the ensuing 10 statements.

<u>FACTS</u>

While conducting a routine audit of county records, a State official noted the appearance of the same lawyer's name ("Thaddeus Phelpps") on a wide variety of residential mortgage records. The cashier at the County Clerk's office recognized the name as that of a lawyer who often pays all filing fees for the recordation of home deed transfers. Upon referral to the District Attorney's Office, the matter became an official investigation into potential elder abuse.

<u>LAW</u>

The applicable State penal law provides the following:

101—ELDER ABUSE: THIRD DEGREE

(A) A person shall be guilty of elder abuse in the third degree when, without the use of physical force, the person deprives a Senior of cash or property valued over $1,000.

(B) For purposes of this provision, "Senior" is defined as anyone over the age of 70.

105 — ELDER ABUSE : DEFENSES

(A) No one shall be found to have satisfied the intent element of an elder abuse charge brought under this section if found to have acted in ultimate beneficial regard for the Senior characterized as the victim of the alleged offense.

Now identify each of the following hypothetical statements as RULE (i.e., the governing principles) or RULE APPLICATION (the consideration of Facts in view of the Rule).

1. Accordingly, because he did not act in ultimate regard for his landlord, the tenant, Phelpps, will be found guilty of elder abuse.

2. The State statute acknowledges the need to protect individuals placed in precarious positions when in contact with elders.

3. In *State v. Romey*, the court limited the "beneficial regard" exception dramatically.

4. The elder's bank account evidenced over 170 withdrawals in 2009 alone, further casting doubt on the alleged defense.

5. Clearly, the tenant violated the statute.

6. In *State v. Jonas*, a good Samaritan tenant effected transactions valued at over $50,000 in alleged care for his landlord.

7. Courts have been hesitant to convict those defendants put "between a rock and a hard place."

8. In that case, the defendant also participated in multiple deed transfers.

9. Phelpps was contacted by the district attorney immediately.

10. There is no precedent for a lawyer financially abusing a client.

VI. Conclusion

You now have a healthy introduction to the working parts of a legal analysis: the Facts, and the Formula (Rule and Rule Application). Before learning to take these components to an advanced level, try your hand at penning an Application in the Exercise below. The Exercise concerns a famed Federal Reserve Board Regulation implemented after the Great Depression of the 1930s.

Exercise Three: Regulation T and Credit for Investors

Based on the ensuing fact pattern, write a full Application of the relevant Rule. Your Application should answer the following question: Will Nevlin Hardy succeed in his lawsuit against his stock brokerage alleging a wrongfully canceled stock trade?

FACTS:

> Nevlin Hardy is a first-time securities investor. On Thursday, March 3, 2016, he entered a buy order for 1,000 shares of XYZ, Inc. (a public company) at a total cost of $24,000. Pursuant to the advice of his registered stockbroker (himself new to the business), Hardy rendered a check to the stock brokerage for $10,000. The check bore the notation in its memo line, "PURCHASE ON MARGIN." The brokerage house lent him the $14,000 balance of the purchase price.

> On Friday, March 11th, Mr. Hardy reviewed online the extension of credit to a securities purchaser. He saw that a brokerage may lend an investor 50% of the purchase price. Fearing that he had violated a federal regulation, he called the Federal Reserve to request an exception. The Federal Reserve clerk was most rude to Hardy and his request. The same day, the brokerage's Regulation T department cancelled Mr. Hardy's purchase as requiring too much credit; the shares of XYZ, Inc. doubled in price the following week. Mr. Hardy now seeks the advice of our law firm on his possible suit against the brokerage for the lost profits.

RULE:

> The Securities Exchange Act states that the maximum amount of credit that may be afforded an investor on the initial purchase of stock is 55% of the purchase price. The effectuating provision, Regulation T of the Federal Reserve, has since 1975 set this upper limit at 50% of the purchase price of the securities.

> An exception exists for the purchase of government securities. Also, investors can exceed the 50% cap through a formal request effectuated by a registered broker-dealer. That request must be made in writing within seven (7) calendar days of the purchase of the securities. No case located found a brokerage firm liable for a Regulation T violation incurred at the advice from one of its stockbrokers.

Chapter IV

Deepening Analysis:
Statute and Case Summaries

Chapter Objectives:

- Developing a Multi-Read Approach to Scrutinizing Statutes
- Learning to Look Outside the Statute for its Meaning
- Preparing Case Summaries that Travel Through Conflict, Positions, and Ramifications
- Enhancing Analysis Through a Deeper Plumbing of Source Material

Substantive Takeaways:

- State Statutes Outlawing Insurance Fraud
- Federal EB-5 Program for Naturalizing Job Creators
- Statute of Limitations for Breach of Contract Claims
- Dwindling NCAA Concept of "Amateurism"

I. Background

The previous Chapters of this book provided a plan to create a Legal Writing Formula (i.e., Rule-Rule Application). This Chapter examines the skills by which a Legal Writer can provide a deeper analysis within those two segments. Specifically, the diligent plumbing of primary authorities ensures that the Legal Reader will trust the standard being offered.

In some cases, this Chapter's guidance simply enhances prior lessons. As its major point, the Chapter suggests two means of heightening analysis: Adding meaningful statutory analysis (where a statute comprises the majority of the Rule), or adding thorough case summaries (where a Rule is largely dependent upon precedents).[1] Whichever means is utilized, the Legal Writer should appreciate that a lawyer's analytical capabilities are dynamic, starting in the 1L year and growing throughout his or her career.

II. Analyzing Statutes

The reading of a statute is superficially pleasing. With the immutable print before you, the tendency arises to feel comfortably educated after having read the text once. But such blind faith in the often dated words of a generalized measure can be detrimental to a thorough understanding of a measure's full import (or lack thereof). Statutes vary greatly in presentation; moreover, some create new duties, while many simply modify existing obligations. Indeed, many a young associate has studied a law for hours without adequately exploring whether it is the first legislation in its field. Additionally, few conversations with a senior attorney are more disheartening than the one that concludes with the unanswered question of "why" a statute was passed.

In sum, reading a statute and nodding your head in agreement is never enough. There are two ways of fully vetting a statute: looking intrinsically, and looking extrinsically.

A. Intrinsic Evaluation (i.e., From the Statutory Language)

First, you must read the entire statute. This means word by word, preferably aloud. Most lawyers read the full statute twice. If the writing appears thick, take notes. Understand that if you have difficulty deciphering a law, the obstacles are sure to double when you attempt to summarize it. Therefore, plow on. Read and read, and take notes.

Next, focus on the definitional section (if any). Many students pride themselves on purchasing a Black's Law Dictionary early in their career. While that resource can be found in the library of every successful attorney, it is largely irrelevant where the legislature has expressly defined a term for purposes of a particular law. Stated simply, if a statute declares that "adequate notice shall be two days," then "adequate notice" is thereafter defined as *two days*; there is lit-

---

1. Some Legal Writing guides refer to this expansion of the Rule as "Rule Proof." But that term inevitably collides with the more common term, "Proof of Law." Thus this book simply sums up the various means of further explaining the Rule as "Elaboration."

tle to be gained by referencing either a dictionary or other learned source for an alternative interpretation.

Additionally, recognize that statutes often work in tandem. For example, provisions within a State's penal code will often focus on the offense and expressly refer the Reader to a separate provision for an underlying definition (e.g., "with intent"). In such cases, each relevant statute must also be read (and re-read) in full.

After you have defined the key terms, you need to understand the people, entities, and disputes covered by a statute. Is the measure only aimed at entities, or also "natural persons" (a common legislative term connoting 2-legged beings)? Does the law, by providing only for civil fines, prove to be beyond the reach of the prosecutor? Many a young litigator has been embarrassed by preparing a defense to a statute that by its own terms is inapplicable to the firm's client.

Once you comprehend the full scope of the statute, look for exceptions. Did a discrete group ostensibly covered by the statute effectively lobby for (or simply get rewarded with) an exception? For example, New York eateries were outraged by a 2015 city council ban on the use of Styrofoam packaging in "to go" orders until reading the "hardship waiver" section of the ordinance (which permitted exceptions for businesses with less than $500,000 in annual revenue).[2] Simply put, the exceptions to any statute serve as the tail wagging the dog, rendering the more substantive sections promptly irrelevant.

Of equal significance is the effective date of a statute. Controversial pieces of legislation often include a considerable "grace period" to allow the affected to change their practices. Some statutes immediately take effect but "grandfather in" (i.e., exclude) certain parties. And some legislatures are fond of "sunset provisions" that disappear on a certain date after the statute's enactment. To be sure, not understanding that provisions may be subject to time limits is also a source of embarrassment to a law student or lawyer.

Finally, ascertain the statute's general mission. Laws are generally passed in response to a problem. A statement of purpose may appear in a preamble, or may be gleaned from various provisions within the statute. Note the clearly stated aim of the Class Action Fairness Act, passed in 2005 in response to the fear that mass litigations were injuring plaintiffs and defendants alike:

---

2. Regardless, later in the year, the ban was struck down as "arbitrary and capricious" by a New York state court judge. *See* Benjamin Mueller, *Judge Strikes Down New York City's Ban on Foam Food Containers*, N.Y. Times (Sept. 22, 2015).

Section 2 (a)(1) Class action lawsuits are an important and valuable part of the legal system when they permit the fair and efficient resolution of legitimate claims of numerous parties by allowing the claims to be aggregated into a single action against a defendant that has allegedly caused harm.

(2) Over the past decade, there have been abuses of the class action device that have—

(A) harmed class members with legitimate claims and defendants that have acted responsibly;

(B) adversely affected interstate commerce; and

(C) undermined public respect for our judicial system.[3]

That umbrella statement shapes your reading of the Act's numerous, varied provisions: Each subsequent section seeks to either shield defendants from abusive suits, to make recovery more transparent (to aid the plaintiffs), or to protect the overall integrity of the litigation.

Unless you have ascertained the full range of a statute's attributes (i.e., its definitions, scope, effective date, exceptions and purpose), you still need to look outside of the text to ensure your full understanding of the measure.

B. Extrinsic Evaluation (i.e., Looking Beyond the Statutory Language)

Often, the truest statement of purpose of a statute is found during its deliberation, which is codified in the legislature's daily sessions. Witness the weight of the following passage, excerpted from the Congressional Record. The debate concerned proposed reforms to the federal EB-5 program, a controversial naturalization measure established by the Immigration Act of 1990. The program affords foreign nationals an American visa in return for their investment in domestic companies that employ U.S. citizens. One Senator commenced declaring his position in this fashion:

Mr. LEAHY. Mr. President, I have championed the EB-5 Regional Center Program for many years. I have done so because I have seen its ability to generate investment and create jobs in distressed communities. But the program is facing some pressing challenges. Reports of rampant fraud and abuse raise serious concerns and threaten to cripple

---

3. Class Action Fairness Act, Pub.L. 109-2 (109th Cong., Feb. 18, 2005), §2(a).

the program's integrity. The incentives Congress established to invest in high unemployment and rural communities are also routinely abused, undermining a core objective of the program—to spur growth and create jobs in underserved areas. The Regional Center Program is set to expire on December 11. It should be reauthorized, but we should not extend it blindly....[4]

In the above opening remarks, the Senator has clarified his position (support for an amended program) while shaping the discussion (retain key elements, while eliminating fraud and abuse). Such aspirations, of course, do not guarantee that the final statutory language shall meet these goals, but a clear indication of the impetus for the measure helps the Reader to understand clauses appearing later in the legislation that may seem disjointed or draconian.

Thus, the extrinsic words of the legislature can provide legal guidance. Note also that *regulations*—which carry the force of statutes within the Hierarchy of Authority—are often contemporaneously and publicly described in detail by the agency that promulgated them:

The Securities and Exchange Commission today adopted final rules to facilitate smaller companies' access to capital. The new rules provide investors with more investment choices.

The new rules update and expand Regulation A, an existing exemption from registration for smaller issuers of securities. The rules are mandated by Title IV of the Jumpstart Our Business Startups (JOBS) Act.[5]

In the above excerpt, the agency has quickly (and quite triumphantly) declared the purpose of the updated regulation. A lawyer reading the passage can instantly answer a client's question of the "why" behind the new rule. Further, a lawyer/law student researching the topic learns whether reading updated Regulation A would be productive.

If the legislative record or adopting agency fail to inform on the purpose of a measure, access the relevant press attending the law's adoption. While newspaper accounts may be slanted, they at least awaken you to the issues on the table. To correct the political bias of a publication, it is useful to actually write

---

4. Congressional Record of November 19, 2015 (114th Cong., 1st session), *available at* https://www.congress.gov/congressional-record/2015/11/19/senate-section/article/S8151-1.

5. SEC Press Release, *SEC Adopts Rules to Facilitate Smaller Companies' Access to Capital* (March 25, 2015), *available at* http://www.sec.gov/news/pressrelease/2015-49.html. An eager Legal Writer should note the optimal efficiency of the Release. The 4-sentence excerpt included herein—by itself—conveys the regulation's mission, benefactor, and origin (and each of the sentences numbers less than 20 words).

yourself a 2-sentence history of the events leading to the law (e.g., "families clamoring for new deductions for multiple children in private schools under a local education relief act; editors believe the measure only provides superficial assistance for the middle class").

With these varied tools, you should be able to answer the questions of *what* was adopted, *why* it was adopted, and *when* it takes effect. To gauge your own ability to engage in a thorough reading of legislation, try the Exercise below, which offers several statutes working in tandem.

Exercise One: Reading a Statute

The Exercise relates to a notorious New York insurance fraud a few years ago, wherein a child falsely reported (to the police and others) a father's death by drowning. In the hypothetical, imagine the following facts:

- the daughter was 16 years old at the time of the fictitious report of the drowning,

- she telephoned the missing persons report to the police and faxed a claim form to the insurance company,

- the hoodwinked townspeople spent two days volunteering their time searching for the "victim," and

- the insurance policy, valued at $100,000, was offered for payment, but the crime was discovered before the actual check was cashed.

Read all of the New York Penal Law provisions appearing below. Then decide which provisions best apply to each of the two hypothetical defendants. Naturally, the prosecutor is seeking the broadest possible set of the most serious charges against each individual. Accordingly, be able to explain why you believe the provisions not selected were inapplicable. Additionally, be able to answer the question of why there are varying degrees of each crime (i.e., the "why" of the question).

———————

ARTICLE 240.50 *Falsely reporting an incident in the third degree.*

A person is guilty of falsely reporting an incident in the third degree when, knowing the information reported, conveyed or circulated to be false or baseless, he:

1. Initiates or circulates a false report or warning of an alleged occurrence or impending occurrence of a crime, catastrophe or emer-

gency under circumstances in which it is not unlikely that public alarm or inconvenience will result; or ...

2. Reports, by word or action, to an official or quasi-official agency or organization having the function of dealing with emergencies involving danger to life or property, an alleged occurrence or impending occurrence of a catastrophe or emergency which did not in fact occur or does not in fact exist; ...

Falsely reporting an incident in the third degree is a class A misdemeanor.

ARTICLE 176

A fraudulent insurance act is committed by any person who, knowingly and with intent to defraud presents, causes to be presented, or prepares with knowledge or belief that it will be presented to or by an insurer, self insurer, or purported insurer, or purported self insurer, or any agent thereof:

1. any written statement as part of, or in support of, an application for the issuance of, or the rating of a commercial insurance policy, or certificate or evidence of self insurance for commercial insurance or commercial self insurance, or a claim for payment or other benefit pursuant to an insurance policy or self insurance program for commercial or personal insurance that he or she knows to:

(a) contain materially false information concerning any fact material thereto; or

(b) conceal, for the purpose of misleading, information concerning any fact material thereto; or....

176.10 Insurance fraud in the fifth degree.

A person is guilty of insurance fraud in the fifth degree when he commits a fraudulent insurance act.

Insurance fraud in the fifth degree is a class A misdemeanor.

176.25 Insurance fraud in the second degree.

A person is guilty of insurance fraud in the second degree when he commits a fraudulent insurance act and thereby wrongfully takes, obtains or withholds, or attempts to wrongfully take, obtain or withhold property with a value in excess of fifty thousand dollars.

Insurance fraud in the second degree is a class C felony.

Article 105.00 CONSPIRACY

105.00 Conspiracy in the sixth degree.

A person is guilty of conspiracy in the sixth degree when, with intent that conduct constituting a crime be performed, he agrees with one or more persons to engage in or cause the performance of such conduct.

Conspiracy in the sixth degree is a class B misdemeanor.

105.05 Conspiracy in the fifth degree.

A person is guilty of conspiracy in the fifth degree when, with intent that conduct constituting:

    1. a felony be performed, he agrees with one or more persons to engage in or cause the performance of such conduct; or

    2. a crime be performed, he, being over eighteen years of age, agrees with one or more persons under sixteen years of age to engage in or cause the performance of such conduct.

Conspiracy in the fifth degree is a class A misdemeanor.

105.13 Conspiracy in the third degree.

A person is guilty of conspiracy in the third degree when, with intent that conduct constituting a class B or a class C felony be performed, he, being over eighteen years of age, agrees with one or more persons under sixteen years of age to engage in or cause the performance of such conduct.

Conspiracy in the third degree is a class D felony.

Overall, resign yourself to the fact that a disciplined review of a statute may foremost result in your thorough understanding of what the measure does not define, clarify, or state. All the more reason to develop a consistent approach to how you translate what has actually been articulated by a piece of legislation. And such diligence affords all the more reason for a Professor or supervisor to trust your Legal Writing.

III. Analyzing Cases

Another analytical tool that may be all too often taken for granted is the ability to effectively summarize cases. Note the striking difference between the two case summaries below, both variations centering on a famous Supreme Court pronouncement concerning libel damages in cases against newspapers:

WEAK:

> In Gertz v. Robert Welch, Inc., 418 U.S. 323 (1974), the Court ruled against a periodical that had labeled a plaintiff's attorney part of a "Communist" plot. The Court ruled that the constitutional protection afforded public figures in New York Times v. Sullivan, 376 U.S. 254 (1964), did not shield a publisher from comments concerning a known trial attorney who had litigated a claim by the family of a man shot and killed by a police officer. The plaintiff, a lawyer who had been labeled a "Leninist" by a national periodical, had lost at the trial and appellate levels. The Supreme Court did, however, invoke a balancing test to exclude the possibilities of presumed or punitive damages.

BETTER:

> Gertz v. Robert Welch, Inc., 418 U.S. 323 (1974), was a libel case concerning a fatal shooting by a Chicago police officer. The victim's family sued the policeman for damages. Contemporaneously, Gertz, the lawyer for the family, was labeled by a Conservative periodical as part of a political plot to discredit law enforcement. Gertz sued the owner of the periodical.
>
> The jury awarded Gertz $50,000 in damages, but the district court judge declined the award, citing the actual malice standard of New York Times v. Sullivan, 276 U.S. 254 (1964). That standard asserts that the First Amendment protects defendants in comments on public figures. The Seventh Circuit Court of Appeals affirmed the judge's ruling on a theory that New York Times shielded all discussion of matters of public interest. However, the Supreme Court held that the States may decline to extend the New York Times actual malice requirement to discussion of private individuals (such as the attorney), as long as those State interpretations do not impose presumed or punitive damages. The case was thus reversed and remanded.

The second example tells a story and thus propels the reading through the last sentence. The first example itself resembles a news item by appealing to alarming language; such meandering tales can be avoided by adhering to a sequential pattern of recapping conflict-legal positions-outcome.

That sequential pattern is best introduced as a list of five steps, described in detail below. These steps will guide you when summarizing a case, prioritizing a fact pattern, or simply relating a legal "story" to a Legal Reader. Just as is the case with every good piece of legal fiction or television drama, the first step involves making plain the parties and the conflict.

A. Explain the True Nature of the Dispute

Imagine that, in the jurisdiction of X, a breach of contract claim requires 1) a failure to perform specified services, 2) with such failure brought to the attention of the court within six years from the signing of the contract. The Partner in charge of your department has asked for a summary of the passage below that highlights the facts relevant to a contract claim:

> The Plaintiff contends that he **signed the contract with the industrial exterminator in January of 2009.** The contract asked whether the Plaintiff had retained an exterminator in the past, and the source of the referral to the Defendant. **The contract specified that the Defendant would spray each corner of the Plaintiff's office space no less than four times a year.** In 2008, the Defendant suspended services with all customers because of a series of workplace injuries. In January 2009, the Plaintiff referred three other customers to the Defendant. **In February and May of 2009, the Defendant visited the Plaintiff's place of business and sprayed each corner; there were no other sprayings that year, or any year thereafter.** In 2010, the Defendant transferred his business to a family member. In 2013, the Plaintiff retained the services of a new exterminator; that contract also called for sprayings four times a year. **In December 2014, the Plaintiff brought suit, alleging that the Defendant's spraying was 1)** too noisy and invasive, 2) **not completed four times a year during the contract period,** 3) a cause of decreased business, 4) failed to eliminate all insects and pests, and 5) conducted in a manner that posed an ecological hazard.

Only the facts in bold are relevant right now. Some of the above facts (e.g., the transfer of the business to a family member) are readily "backburnered": They may be relevant later on, but, at the moment, they do not answer the Partner's question. Likewise, some of the above facts (e.g., the past experiences with an exterminator) are possibly relevant to a defense, but a listing of possible defenses is not the present task.

Thus, the emphasis on details must always be tempered. Include the facts relevant to the issues being analyzed. To guarantee that the Reader knows that other facts exist, simply include "inter alia."

B. Follow the Life of the Litigation

The well versed Legal Writer does not attempt to express familiarity before knowing how the plaintiff fared at every level of the litigation. In a sense, law school spoils students. You are asked to read the last decision on any issue, usually in the form of a Supreme Court or Circuit Court opinion. While that high level of decision-making provides a model caliber of Writing to unconsciously absorb, it concurrently diminishes the role of the opinions preceding final resolution of the dispute.

Therefore, work backwards towards the commencing of every case you would summarize. Be able to explain which party prevailed at each level, as well as how the issues morphed as the matter moved on. In the *Gertz* example above, there were actually four decisions: those of the trial jury, the District Court judge, the Seventh Circuit Court of Appeals, and the Supreme Court. The Writer's unwillingness to engage in such a thorough procedural recap can unintentionally convey a superficiality that undermines credibility.

C. Identify the Specific Holding (and Its Ramifications for the Parties)

The following passage (concerning a fictitious *Lussbender* case) contains much information:

> A claim of illegal diesel fracking (i.e., drilling via fracturing processes) resulted in a November 2013 jury verdict against Lussbender and his company. That verdict exceeded $3.4 million in compensatory and punitive damages. Upon review in December 2014, the Second Circuit questioned 1) whether joinder of the CEO was proper, and 2) whether the calculation of punitive damages was proper in light of the 2008 holding of the Supreme Court in *Exxon Shipping Co. v. Baker.* The *Lussbender* oral arguments have been scheduled for the Spring 2015 term.

The summary above details much of the legal reasoning and includes a healthy chronology of dates, but it omits the ramifications of the story: Has the company stopped fracking? Is Lussbender still in charge? Have any damages been paid? It is likely that the punitive damages sanction has been placed on hold until the next (and highest) level of appellate review; nonetheless, despite the inclusion of all those dates, the summary generates a disturbing lack of closure for the Reader. And note that, even if such details are not disclosed by the case decision, your disclosure of such non-available answers gains you credibility. An example of such diligence is detailed below:

EXAMPLE:

> The decision indicated that the fracking enterprise has filed appeals on other issues germane to the litigation, but it did not offer judgment on any of these ancillary issues.

In general, your case summary should follow a comprehensive and consequential progression. Parties are in conflict, so they go to trial. They maintain respective positions, and the judge/jury decides. Then one of the parties appeals (perhaps maintaining a new position in the process), and the appellate court rules. Someone gained from the process, while someone else did not. The litigation shall continue, or it is over. While there are multiple purposes for a case summary, its successful design is universal and should thus be memorized and practiced early on. Think conflict, positions and ramifications.

That progression is what the Legal Reader most craves. Names of witnesses are a distraction; save such data for when strength of evidence is in dispute (e.g., "The third witness was Admiral Horatio Levy, a man with 30 years of experience in naval maneuvers."). Identification of additional charges, claims, and consequences are, again, what prompted someone very wise a long time ago to employ "inter alia" in Legal Writing. Avoid aimless travel logs—tell a story that travels from accident/crime to checkbook/jail time (much like the successful dramas on television).

IV. Miscellaneous

Two final notes on case summaries:

First, the parenthetical explanation[6] provides a shorter, more efficient alternative. However, care must be taken to conform the explanation to the varieties permitted by the *Bluebook*. Specifically, a summary of moderate length (e.g., less than 3 lines) is permitted if it a) includes a direct quote, b) provides a short term of art, useful in the present context (e.g., "176 lbs. of marijuana"), or c) includes only a clause commencing with a present tense verb. Concerning the last and most popular of these 3 alternatives, see the examples below. The samples attempt summaries of the *Gertz* case described above:

---

6. The Bluebook calls these explanations "parenthetical information regarding cases." Rule 10.6.

NOT ALLOWED:

> Gertz v. Welch, 418 U.S. 323 (1974) (This case found that the actual malice standard set forth by Times v. Sullivan did not apply when the libel victim is a private citizen).

ALLOWED:

> Gertz v. Welch, 418 U.S. 323 (1974) (finding the Times v. Sullivan "actual malice" standard to not apply when the libel victim is a private citizen).

"Finding" is a permissible word with which to commence a parenthetical explanation, as is "ruling," "holding" or determining." "This case found" makes grammatical sense but is not acceptable. Rather than question the Bluebook or legal tradition on this point, recognize that acceptance of that simple dictate generates a healthy amount of respect for the Legal Writer.

The second final note is to remember that the case summary should always be phrased in the past tense, with one exception: The resulting principle of law.

WEAK:

> However, the Supreme Court generally held that the determination of punitive damages violated the balancing test and thus the First Amendment protections.

BETTER:

> However, the Supreme Court generally held that the determination of punitive damages violates the balancing test and thus the First Amendment protections. The States may decline to extend the New York Times actual malice requirement to discussion of private individuals (such as the attorney), as long as those State interpretations do not impose punitive damages.

To fail to shift to the present to distinguish facts (which already occurred) from resulting principle (which shall apply to other cases in the future) places too much work on your Reader, who is not only hearing a story for the first time but also learning a number of other unrelated stories in the document. If need be, add an explanatory sentence to clarify that you have not haphazardly changed verb tense, as the second example above clarifies.

As is the case with all Legal Writing, organization precedes actual prose. In the Exercise below, you are asked to eliminate items and then organize the remaining items into a summary that is helpful to the Reader on the most immediate issue.

Exercise Two: Outlining a Case Summary

<u>Background:</u> The issue of college athlete amateurism has significant consequences for the athletes, for the schools, for the NCAA, and for the businesses that would contract with any of those three groups.

In *O'Bannon v. NCAA* (2014), a federal judge in the Northern District of California ruled in favor of a group of former NCAA athletes whose names had been used in a video game. The video game had utilized the names of the famed athletes pursuant to a license from the NCAA. The former athletes sued for unpaid royalties.

Your firm counsels a sports league akin to the heralded NCAA. Your supervisor has thus asked for a 1-page summary of the decision. From the lengthy list below, pick the 8–10 items that best form the outline for your concise summary. Then place these items (in sequence) within a 5-point outline in order to effectively convey case summary information. Note that, while all of the 20, random items below play a part in the court's decision, the Board is extremely busy and needs to quickly be brought up to speed on the landmark case (i.e., a considerable number of points noted below are not relevant, for now).

1. The NCAA was founded by the presidents of 62 colleges and universities. A school seeking to change rules does so by submitting a proposal to the current Board, comprised of the heads of eighteen schools.

2. At trial, the NCAA argued that its restrictions on athlete compensation a) serve its educational mission, and b) "protect the popularity" of college sports.

3. In July 2015, the case was partially settled while on appeal.

4. Television networks, advertisers and other third parties need not notify pictured NCAA athletes of the time and place of their image's distribution.

5. The court found that the NCAA's restrictions on amateurism, which cap compensation, were not justified by the association's bylaws.

6. The plaintiffs recovered their costs from the NCAA, and post-trial motions were greatly limited.

7. The 20 plaintiffs brought an antitrust action against the NCAA in 2009 to challenge the rules restricting compensation for the association's top tier basketball and football players.

8. The court noted that commentators have long suggested that the NCAA hold compensation in trust for the NCAA athlete.

9. A non-jury trial was held in California between June 9, 2014 and June 27, 2014.

10. An expert testified that the top tier NCAA football conferences "almost always" defeated schools from lesser conferences in sporting contests.

11. The court found that college sports "generate a tremendous amount of interest, as well as revenue."

12. For varied reasons, the Court found that there are no professional football or basketball leagues "capable of supplying a substitute for the bundle of goods and services" that the top tier NCAA conferences provide.

13. While the court wished that the conflict could be addressed by other means, it ordered an injunction against the current NCAA compensation cap.

14. The plaintiffs argued that the bar against athletes receiving revenues from video game makers that used their names violated the Sherman Antitrust Act.

15. One expert argued that there can be no anti-competitive violation unless consumers (i.e., video game purchasers) were harmed.

16. Most schools ignored the NCAA's compensation cap rules, until 1948.

17. The NCAA was founded in 1905 and currently has 1,100 schools playing approximately 25 regulated sports.

18. A survey of NCAA sports fans disclosed that 47% said they would be less likely to watch games if the athletes were paid $50,000 a year.

19. The NCAA President has no authority to override the association's bylaws.

20. One expert testified that the existing NCAA compensation cap could be satisfied by the fashioning of a "stipend" or grant-in-aid by the schools.

V. Conclusion

Writing a Rule is not overwhelming. We see Rules every day—online when returning a purchase, at the DMV when registering a car, in the papers when we hear someone violated a bribery statute. Further, in your first month of law school, you read countless examples of Rules in cases.

However, creating your own, effective Rule that inspires confidence requires a concentrated effort at understanding and summarizing legal source materials, chief among which are statutes and cases. Likewise, the ensuing Rule Application is, theoretically, a simple science of "plugging" Facts into your Rule. Stated otherwise, having the benefit of a test, the Writer need merely list where elements have been met. But that simple science can go wrong if the Application does not address all the considerations raised by the Rule. Accordingly, you will often have to backtrack and adjust either expectations or resolutions to deepen your analytical approach. Such editing in tandem is a precursor to penning a Formula that not only conveys information but also impresses, the subject of the next Chapter.

Chapter V

Elaboration and Variation: More Effective Rules and Rule Applications

Chapter Objectives:
- Revisiting the Creation of Formula Parts (Rule and Rule Application)
- Enhancing Rule Preparation Through the Use of Inferred and Translated Rules
- Enhancing Rule Application by Including Counter-Analyses and Policy Considerations
- Adding Citation Where Necessary
- Opting for the Most Effective Formula

Substantive Takeaways:
- Federal Common Law on Punitive Damages Assessed Against Corporations
- Tolling of Statutes of Limitation in IRS Matters
- "Right of Publicity" under State law
- Little League Baseball Rules on Commercialization
- Section 43(a) and the "*Polaroid* Test" for Adjudging Confusion Over Trademarks

---

I. Introduction

Neither a Rule nor a Rule Application need be a certain length. An effective Rule can be a series of short sentences (with cites); a successful Application "plugs" the present facts into those sentences as necessary. Thus, in developing the relevant skills, avoid the collegiate approach of burying the reader in detail. Concurrently, avoid the temptation to equate brevity with meaningful analysis.

Such a dual task can seem a bit impossible, at first. But the conflict is easily resolved. Forget the length of the Rule/Rule Application and strive foremost to answer the Legal Reader's overriding question, "Has this case ever been decided before?" When you understand that this question is never truly answered with a "Yes," then seek to provide the most information possible.

II. Writing a "Rule"—Revisited

The Rule is a collection of the principles that are used to resolve a legal dispute in a particularized area. In a sense, it simply relays standards, supported by authorities. It commences by identifying a jurisdiction:

WEAK:

> As *Polaroid* held, there are at least eight factors that courts employ to establish consumer confusion over the origin of a product. *Polaroid Corp. v. Polarad Elecs. Corp.*, 287 F.2d 492 (2d Cir. 1961).

BETTER:

> In the Second Circuit, there are at least eight factors that courts employ when evaluating consumer confusion over the origin of a product. *See Polaroid Corp. v. Polarad Elecs. Corp*, 287 F.2d 492 (2d Cir. 1961).

The Rule is ideally limited to 1–2 paragraphs, and it serves as the introductory part to the Legal Writing "Formula." The Rule could occasionally be summed up in a sole statute, but legal analysis is rarely that simple. Statutes are drafted for the broadest possible set of circumstances; further, statutes are not religiously updated by legislatures. Significantly, many statutes lack definition sections, and many more have been subjected to repeat instances of judicial interpretation/limitation.

The statute nonetheless often serving as the starting point, a Rule on any topic is the result of a challenging process law schools call "Synthesis." In essence, students are asked to rationally combine cases, statutes, secondary materials and any other applicable authorities to provide the best possible guidance on a client's specific problem. In Chapters I and II, this book offered a short list of suggestions for preparing an effective Rule. In sum, the student should account for all relevant authorities, present a sequential test, and address the Reader's concerns. The example below, centering on the prosecution's task in proving insurance fraud in a case against a minor, reiterates the goals of these three laudatory aims:

WEAK:

> A "fraudulent insurance act," according to the statute, is committed by any person who knowingly prepares a "false report" and submits it to an insurance agent. Such reports also cannot be submitted to government officials. Cases add that the report must contain "material" information. Commentators generally feel that the law could be better defined.

BETTER:

> In New York, insurance fraud is defined by statute. Articles 240.50 and 176 collectively define "insurance fraud," "false report," and "fraudulent insurance act." Overall, these statutory provisions provide for five degrees of the crime.
>
> The five degrees are largely distinguished by the amount of money sought, as well as by the party to whom the false report was submitted. The cases have clarified that all five variations will be strictly enforced by the courts. There are no known cases involving a minor as a defendant.

The stronger example—in addition to presenting much more specific details—indicates a jurisdiction, proceeds "down" the Hierarchy of Authority (discussed in Chapter I), and eventually explains that there is no relevant case. The second passage thus indicates at once a breadth of research and a direct utility to the problem at hand.

To refresh all of these lessons on Rules, complete the review Exercise appearing below.

Exercise One: Spotting Poor Rule Practices

In 2008, the Supreme Court limited punitive damages imposed under federal common law. The related Rule offered below, while theoretically providing guidance, actually creates work for the reader. Re-write the attempted Rule, adhering to proper "top-down" order, eliminating distractions, inserting necessary language, and generally striving to help the Reader understand a new area of the law.

> Until 2008, maritime law, largely created by federal courts, allowed for punitive damages in civil judgments. The Exxon case established that punitive damages are no longer allowed under the federal common law. Exxon Shipping Co. v. Baker, 554 U.S. 471 (2008). The Court did not discuss whether its holding, which stated that a 1:1 ratio

between compensatory and punitive damages was advisable, applied to a cause of action accruing under a statute. Class actions would be held to the ratio. Id. at 491. The Court's rationale relied in large part upon the Due Process Clause of the U.S. Constitution, U.S. Const. amend. V, but, of course, that provision does not speak to punitive damages (because Constitutional provisions are generalized in nature), nor does any state or federal statute.

Additional suggestions for Rule drafting concern enhancement and research recapture. Specifically, upon review, a Rule can nearly always go deeper; further, what gets initially edited out can likely help elsewhere in the Formula. These suggestions are detailed below.

A. Proceed from the Test to the "Flavor"

Consider the following Rule, which attempts to educate the reader on the statute of limitations in criminal investigations for tax fraud:

> The Department of Justice has 6 years from the tax code violation to bring a criminal action. 26 U.S.C. §6531. This period begins running upon the first act of malfeasance. This 6-year period can be extended if the government files a Complaint within the last nine months of the statutory period. Although the government can extend the time period for offenses of a "continuous nature," tax violations are generally considered to be outside of this exception.

The above passage commences with the standard (i.e., the most important and universally applicable of the proffered information). The passage then continues to educate the Reader by adding "flavor," or those considerations not always called into play but nonetheless beneficial to a Reader desiring a fuller understanding of the relevant guidance. "Flavor" can include factors (i.e., considerations not required), secondary commentary on the standard, or the necessary proof at trial.

In short, save all the non-essential revelations about the subject area as additional information. But be sure to place such information *after* the test invoked by the courts.

B. Add the "Elaboration"

The *Elaboration,* a concept introduced in Chapter IV, expands upon the Rule in one of various ways. The Legal Writer can add case summaries to explain how the cases within the jurisdiction have interpreted the statute as a whole. Alternatively, the Writer can select some of the more challenging terms within the statute and explain how these are defined.

Witness the efficiency of adding Elaboration to the Rule from above:

> The Department of Justice has 6 years from the tax code violation to bring a criminal action. 26 USC §6531. This period begins running upon the first of a series of violations. However, this 6-year period can be extended if the government files a Complaint within the last 9 months of the statutory period. Although the government can extend the time period for offenses of a "continuous nature," that doctrine has undergone changes in recent years.

> Traditionally, the "continuous nature" doctrine advised that, where violative acts are repetitive in nature, the statute of limitations does not begin to run from the first act. For example, in <u>Hodgeson v. Ragnone</u>, 217 N.W.2d 395 (Ct. App. Mich. 1974), a landowner brought an action sounding in nuisance and trespass against the county drainage district ...

> However, the significance of the doctrine appears to be diminishing. In <u>Robert L. Kroenlein Trust v. Kirhchefer</u>, 357 P.3d 1118 (Sup. Ct. Wy. 2015), a bar owner brought an action for conversion against a former employee ... The court held that the doctrine is not a "tolling mechanism." Rather, it allows each subject act to be considered separately for statute of limitation purposes ...

> Overall, the 6-year period is strictly enforced more often than not ...

In the above passage, the Writer has chosen the likely vexing term ("continuous nature") as the subject of the Elaboration. Note that simple transitions propel the passage (e.g., "traditionally," "appears to be diminishing"). Note also that each case summary commences with a phrase more designed to fit the story of how the legal principle being advanced (than to instantly begin the storytelling of a case).

Of perhaps paramount importance, the Elaboration commences and ends with a simple statement summing up the overall effect of the included case summaries. Such a "scorecard" usually conveys one of three themes: the cases comport, the cases conflict, the cases provide little guidance. Whatever is the outcome of your comparative analysis, share the conclusion with the Reader; few things distract more than the littering of a Formula with random case summaries, thus revealing disparate stories with no introduction, combining to no ultimate resolution.

C. Add the Corollary or "Inferred" Rule

Law students enjoy a luxury that inspires envy among practitioners: Being presented with *some* relevant authority in legal problems. Conversely, my own first, "on the job" research assignment concerned adverse possession, a controversial doctrine owing its roots to neighboring farmers governed by the Napoleonic Code. There were no precedents to be located (not surprisingly, not many Brooklyn landowners had acquiesced to use of their property by strangers in the 1980s). Likewise, a colleague once had to fashion a criminal appeal around the sole fact that the jury room door had not been locked during deliberations (he located a sole case).

The rules of elementary research instruct that, in situations where direct authority does not exist, the Writer needs to look to other jurisdictions. The next alternative is to spread out from the subtopic to its overarching field of law. Thus, a dearth of cases on the "right of publicity" leads to the umbrella topic of "privacy" and its hearty selection of authorities.

Perhaps the more interesting solution lies in simply examining the unavoidable facts and/or practical results in interpretative cases. In such an approach, the goal is to actually identify two Rules: a) the explicit test used by the courts, and b) the inferred test recognized by any researcher. The *inferred* test is unstated but nonetheless educates what practicality demands in terms of results. In other words, identify the prohibition in the Rule (normally strict), and then explain its enforcement (sometimes less strict). Examples of introductory language to such inferred Rules appear below:

- *In practice, the courts tend to impose solely compensatory damages. See, e.g., ...*

- *Despite the strict language of the statute (e.g., "parents" and "siblings" only), cases allow claims by all family members ...*

- *Regardless, no case surveyed added the theoretically possible but highly rare conspiracy charge to the underlying indictment.*

In the Exercise below, there are three brief summaries of hypothetical criminal insider trading cases, all stemming from violations of S.E.C. Rule 10b-5. Imagine these are the only insider trading cases in the jurisdiction in recent years. In 1–2 sentences, state the additional Rule that may be inferred on the topic.

Exercise Two: Inferring a Rule

- In *U.S. v. Nesbit*, the Second Circuit upheld a sentence of five years in prison for an insider trader. The defendant, a bank manager, had earned over $1 million from his wrongful trading.

- In *U.S. v. Coston*, the Second Circuit modified and reduced the trial court's imposition of a 3-year prison sentence. The defendant, a nurse, had earned less than $15,000 from the improper trading. No fine was imposed.

- In *U.S. v. Lepresham*, the Second Circuit unanimously affirmed the penalty of 6 years in prison (and a fine of $1.2 million) for a convicted insider trader. The defendant, a brokerage firm compliance officer, had earned over $5.5 million from his trading activity.

D. Where Principles Vary Greatly, "Translate" a Rule

Sometimes, a variety of cases on point does little to explain a jurisdiction's approach to the Reader. Perhaps the courts use terms interchangeably; perhaps the courts arrive at seemingly random or conflicting results. Whenever a test does not naturally evolve from the case law, look to "translate" the varying results into a new vocabulary that focuses the reader on a novel (but previously unnamed) element.

EXAMPLE:

> ... The courts of the Fifth Circuit tend to emphasize different parts of the Limited Liability Company statute. Nonetheless, it can safely be said that all of the Circuit's approaches foremost value the actual business conducted by the subject corporation ...

Therefore, "translation" is the lawyer's default whenever encountering a split among the Circuits. The Writing tool permits the analysis to proceed while conveying that the authorities are not ideally aligned.

E. Account for Trends in This Area of the Law

The most recent pronouncement on a topic is always the most vital.

For example, between 2010 and 2014, motions for vacatur of an arbitration decision in the Second Circuit (pursuant to Federal Arbitration Act sections 10(a)(1–4)) failed over 90% of the time.[1] Thus, a Memo opining on the chances of vacatur would, empirically, predict a low chance of reversing the arbitration decision.

However, in September 2015, a Southern District of New York judge took the unlikely step of vacating the discipline imposed by the National Football League upon a star quarterback via an arbitration before the League Commissioner.[2] To leave this latest decision out of the Rule would almost seem dishonest; a supervisor would wish to be informed of the hint of a burgeoning counter-trend, while the court or an adversary would cite your research as one-sided. The uncommon finding is thus elevated, and the Rule is improved by its inclusion. To the extent that a Reader craves more details on this potential "outlier" case, a subsequent, optional part of the Formula called *counter-analysis* provides opportunity for Elaboration (and will be discussed later in the Chapter).

There thus exist varied means of expanding and fortifying a Rule. There similarly exists a ready list of means by which Rules grow weaker.

III. The Pitfalls

A. Leaving Out the Outliers

Such self-interested editing is wrong. No area of law is governed by principles that are utilized in the same manner 100% of the time, and no two students (or lawyers) draft the exact same Rule. Evaluate the effect of the concluding sentence in the hypothetical below:

> To register a luxury car in Missouri, one must do three things: 1) offer documentary or testamentary proof of a clean driving record, 2) forward a certified copy of the title, and 3) pay a fee of $1,000 to the Secretary of State. At least one lower court has waived the Title copy requirement where the other two requirements were readily met.

In the above example, the exception actually serves to strengthen the Rule. Like the old saying goes, you never know what your house looks like until you step outside.

---

1. *See The "Manifest Disregard of Law" Doctrine and International Arbitration*, Report of the NYC Bar Association (2012).

2. *NFL Management Council v. NFL Players Association*, 15 Civ. 5982 (S.D.N.Y. Sept. 3, 2015).

B. Including Too Much Text

Students tend to take the college essay approach to drafting a Rule (i.e., when in doubt, throw it in, and, if it seems important, say it twice). Such an approach succeeds primarily in irritating the Legal Reader. Say things once, with force.

C. Including Unnecessary Subjectivity

There are always sections in which the soundness of an authority may be questioned. Do not criticize an authority as you reveal it.

Witness the relative effectiveness of the two passages below, both based off of the immediately prior example in this Chapter:

WEAK:

> To register a luxury car in Missouri, one must do varying, seemingly unrelated things: 1) offer documentary or testamentary proof of a clean driving record (e.g., a low number of moving violations, based upon apparently ever-changing standards), 2) forward a certified copy of the title, and 3) pay a fee of $1,000 (regardless of annual income or means) directly into the coffers of the Secretary of State. At least one lower court has waived the dubious Title copy requirement where the other two requirements were readily met.

BETTER:

> To register a luxury car in Missouri, one must do three things: 1) offer documentary or testamentary proof of a "clean" driving record, 2) forward a certified copy of the title, and 3) pay a fee of $1,000 to the Secretary of State. At least one lower court has waived the unnecessary Title copy requirement where the other two requirements were readily met.

The first passage—in attempting to rapidly inject some perspective—does more harm than good. Namely, it mentions the likely adversarial debates while previewing answers that may or may not later arrive.

The second passage reserves the right for later subjectivity by simply placing quotes around the potentially problematic language appearing in the statute.

By now it should be evident that solid Rules require frequent re-drafting. Ultimately, the Rule must include all the principles that you shall later apply in order to furnish a prediction to a legal problem. Thus, a sole attempt at a Rule will not suffice, and the varied segments of the Formula will have to be adjusted accordingly.

Overall, aside from incorporating this expanded list of considerations, the best Rules build exponentially upon them. In the exercise below, begin to utilize more of this book's Rule guidance on the topic.

Exercise Three: Drafting a Thorough Rule

Sylvia "Cash" Huggins, a star Little League pitcher, has come to our firm for possible assistance. A 12-year-old baseball phenomenon, Ms. Huggins has gained national recognition in recent months for her 82 m.p.h. fastball. Nonetheless, she was ejected from this year's Little League ("LL") championship in Williamsport, Pennsylvania for refusing to wear the official LL cap. The ejection cost her family endorsement deals valued at over $750,000.

The tale is unprecedented. After the singing of the National Anthem, and as Sylvia was completing her warm-up pitches, the umpires noticed that she was not wearing her usual blue and white team hat. Instead, she was wearing a similarly colored hat with one small change: The addition of a *GoFarther* corporate logo (as part of a deal with the brash, highly publicized web site creator). Sylvia's parents have been coy about revealing all the terms of the *GoFarther* sponsorship; it suffices to note that Sylvia and her parents adamantly refused to change back to the original hat for the big game.

The umpires immediately ejected Sylvia from the game, citing the LL handbook. When Sylvia's team refused to take the field without her, the game was promptly canceled. While not directly addressing the present fact pattern, the handbook contains several relevant provisions:

- Article XVII, LL Constitution: Disqualification from Tournament (adopted in 1989):

  Once the Tournament has begun, a player may only be disqualified upon hearing at LL Headquarters in Norfolk, Virginia ...

- Rule 9.01—Umpires (adopted in 2001):

  (d) Each umpire has the authority to eject a player for unsportsmanlike conduct or language during a game in progress. The player shall leave the field immediately upon ejection.

- Article XIII, LL Constitution: Commercialization (adopted in 1991):

  Exploitation of Little League in any form or for any purpose is prohibited.

The client would like to argue that LL procedures were not followed. I thus need your help in evaluating the likelihood of a federal court intervening to overturn the suspension and game cancellation, and allow a makeup game to go forward. Please draft a Rule utilizing the above three authorities. We shall later use your Rule to argue that Sylvia Huggins was wrongfully ejected. Be sure to reveal authorities in "top-down" format, and to elevate principles over their authors.

IV. Writing an Effective Rule Application

Ever read a bad mystery novel? You probably resented the introduction of a prime suspect in the waning pages, or an ending that was completely unforeseeable. The Rule Application (i.e., the end to the legal novel you have constructed) is held to the same critique.

Above all other sections, the Rule Application needs to be blunt and forceful. Because of the mere amount of information that has been imparted by the time the Legal Writer begins an Application, the Reader needs both reminder and resolution. Stated otherwise, you may have to resort to much more straightforward, assertive language on page six of your Memo than you would employ on page two.

For example, the "right of publicity," a subtopic of privacy law, concerns the unlawful use of another's image and is governed by widely varying State authorities. The Right is often exercised by celebrities. Consider these excerpts from a hypothetical Brief arguing against recovery by the estate of a comedic actor. The actor's legendary pratfalls and gestures were used without permission by a corporation in its training videos:

> RULE:[3] In New York, a statute protects a person's right of publicity by outlawing the unauthorized use of certain personal attributes. N.Y. CIV. RIGHTS LAW §50 (McKinney's 2014). Specifically, section 50 guards against the use without permission of a plaintiff's name, picture, portrait or voice. *Id.* "Portrait" has been liberally construed to include those traits or accessories that connote an individual's persona. *Onassis v. Christian-Dior, Inc.*, 122 Misc. 2d 603 (Sup. Ct. N.Y. 1984).

> RULE APPLICATION: In the present case, the defendant, Delvado Corp., cannot be said to have run afoul of the statute. While the company may have mimicked the Plaintiff's gestures and mannerisms in

---

3. Note that "Rule" and "Rule Application" are never so labeled in Legal Writing.

a training video, without express consent, section 50 does not protect the rights of parties who are deceased. *See* N.Y. Civ. Rights Law §51 (describing actions that may be maintained by a "living person or holder of such right"). Since the plaintiff is deceased, there was no violation.

You can almost hear the Reader throwing the Brief down in disgust. A character has not only been introduced at the climax at the story: He is much stronger than everyone else in the tale. What is most regrettable is that this particular surprise ending can easily be avoided through editing (i.e., returning to the Rule to add the dispositive section 51 provision). Such misplacement of a key factor illustrates the first principle of Rule Application: *Make sure it aligns with (but does not add to) the Rule.*

A. Meticulously Align Your Rule with Its Application

There are two favored manners of aligning the Rule Application with its Rule. One way simply obligates the Legal Writer to present all relevant principles and then apply each in turn. Let us call this sequential block presentation the "Traditional Approach." This approach is used most often and dovetails nicely with a simple, multi-part test. Note the ease of use below in a sample based upon section 10(a) of the Federal Arbitration Act, a provision that governs the aforementioned federal court intervention in confirming or vacating a private arbitration decision:

> RULE: Under section 10 of the Federal Arbitration Act, there are four bases for a federal court to reverse an arbitration decision. The courts will act to upset the award if the arbitrators 1) engaged in corruption or fraud, 2) evidenced partiality, 3) engaged in misconduct by refusing to postpone the hearing or hear material evidence, or 4) exceeded their authority.

> RULE APPLICATION: In the instant case, Johnson will likely be able to overturn the arbitration decision against him. While both parties acknowledged in their briefs that subsections 1 and 2 are not in dispute, the arbitrators refused a reasonable request to postpone the arbitration by three days to accommodate Johnson's request to attend a close relative's funeral. Further, regarding element 4, the chair of the arbitration panel was quoted on the record as saying "Today, I am the law." Such statement clearly indicates authority being exceeded. Since two of the four statutory bases for reversal are present (i.e., elements "2" and "4"), Johnson is likely to have the arbitral decision upset on appeal.

The Traditional Approach thus works best where elements are short and sweet and clearly resolved in one party's favor. Note that such a paradigm shines only when strict attention is paid to both the order of the elements as initially presented and the precise vocabulary employed within those elements.

B. Vary Your Application Format When Necessary

A variation on the Traditional Approach permits the reader to instantly resolve the question of whether a Rule element has been met in the present case. The Application simply accompanies the revelation of the Rule element. In essence, the Legal Writer employs a "decide as we go" approach that resolves sub-issues the moment such are raised. Let us call this variation the "Instant Gratification Approach."

Such an approach may work better when a test weighs factors (instead of elements), is disjunctive (i.e., not requiring all elements to be met), or is a bit complicated. Consider these two examples, both relating to the vexing question of whether a corporate officer's personal calendar qualifies as a "corporate record" (and thus not able to be protected by the Fifth Amendment, which only protects individuals):

EXAMPLE OF A TRADITIONAL APPLICATION:

> The Second Circuit has developed a 4-part test to determine whether a desk calendar is a corporate record. *See Witness 81 v. United States*, 657 F.2d 5 (2d Cir. 1981). The test is designed to identify whether the record is "overwhelmingly corporate." *Id.* at 11.

> The test first asks whether the defendant witness prepared the document and had sole access to it. Next, the test asks the nature and purpose of the calendar. Additionally, the test requires a determination of whether the document was necessary to the corporation's business. Finally, the test inquires as to whether the witness had written about personal matters on the calendar (i.e., was there an expectation of privacy).

> In the instant case, at most two of these four factors are clearly satisfied. The witness herein created the desk calendar in response to a suggestion in an official corporate Memo, but he also entrusted the calendar's daily upkeep to two assistants. Moreover, although the corporation sent a second memo stressing the importance of both privacy and punctuality (and their achievement through desk calendars), the witness also reflected his children's dental appointments reflected on the calendar. The overriding

goal being an answer to the question of whether the document is definitively "corporate in nature," the likely answer is "No."

EXAMPLE OF AN "INSTANT GRATIFICATION" APPLICATION:

The Second Circuit has developed a 4-part test to determine whether a desk calendar is a corporate record. *See Witness 81 v. United States*, 657 F.2d 5 (2d Cir. 1981). The test is designed to identify whether the record is "overwhelmingly corporate." *Id.* at 11. The test first asks whether the defendant prepared the document and had sole access to it. In the instant case, the defendant delegated upkeep of the calendar to two subordinates, thus indicating a joint, corporate responsibility for maintaining the record.

The test next asks the nature of the calendar (i.e., its purpose and use). In the instant case, all parties testified that the calendar contained both corporate and personal data. Therefore, the record cannot be said to be "overwhelmingly corporate" based on this factor.

In turn, the test asks whether the document was necessary for the corporation's business. While its use was certainly encouraged (for development of personal skills), the calendar was by no means on a par with a trading ledger or payroll schedule. Thus, again, the calendar is not decidedly corporate.

Finally, the test asks whether the calendar contained personal information. In the instant case, it was undisputed that unique items such as folded pictures were housed in the calendar, which also listed family dental appointments. The "personal information" element is thus satisfied.

Overall, the instant facts more often not satisfying the relevant test, it is unlikely that the record would be found to be "overwhelmingly corporate."

In the above example, the Instant Gratification model might work better. The Reader would easily become confused while familiarizing himself first with four elements, then their four applications, then being reminded that no one element is dispositive. Conversely, moving immediately from exposure of the element to its relevance in the instant case gives the passage a momentum that best serves the general goal of engaging the Reader, as well as the particular challenge of educating the Reader in this area of the law (i.e., a scorecard for "corporateness").

Whichever model you become most adept at, strive to utilize it with purpose. And resolve the questions posed by an element in determinative language. "Likely" and "unlikely" (or their harsher cousins "probable" and "improbable") are the customary choices. As is true with case summaries within a Rule Proof, your Rule Applications should have a predictable rhythm that hints at finality—much in the way that pop tunes fade out after three minutes, and chapter books tend to move on after approximately 20 pages. Foremost, make the style selection invisible: If the reader has to re-read for assurance that you previously explained an element, you have succeeded primarily in slowing reading.

C. Add a Counter-Analysis

While you are preparing a Rule Application, you undoubtedly encounter the consideration that almost succeeds in convincing you to change your argument. That tempting notion is your *counter-analysis*, which serves as the most likely attack on your reason. It is normally commenced with clear introductory language, such as "One could argue that."

Both the contrary argument[4] and its refutation require support from an authority—if there is no authority for the contrary argument, then it is not much of an argument at all. In toto, a successful counter-analysis has 4 parts:

(i)   The opposing proposition

(ii) Its citation

(iii) Your refutation

(iv) Its citation

EXAMPLE (based upon the "corporate record" example from above):

> One could argue that satisfaction of any one element is enough to find a document "overwhelmingly corporate" in nature. *Witness*, 657 F.2d at 7. In the present case, there is undoubtedly a corporate purpose (among other purposes) for the desk calendar. However, such a micro-focus on the occasional use of the record to memorialize meeting times or project deadlines counters the spirit of the instructions of the lead case. What is paramount is the intention of personal privacy inherent in the maintenance of the document, thus triggering a Fifth Amendment right. *See Witness*, 657 F.2d at 8 ("the issue is whether by requiring [the personal records'] production, the witness is being compelled to testify against himself").

---

4. Within an Office Memorandum, the counter assertion is phrased as a contrary *prediction*.

Note that the requirement of two authorities within a counter-analysis does not require separate authorities; in the example above, different rationales within a sole case are offered. Note also that the entire counter-analysis can be completed in several lines. Indeed, writing too much counter-analysis poses the danger that the Reader will favor the contrary thought to your own argument/ prediction. Likewise, a second counter-analysis is discouraged; one is enough.

D. Consider Evaluating Policy

In tennis championships, a player struggles mightily to win six games before his or her opponent, by a margin of two games. Often, the two elite players reach six game victories by a slim margin, prompting a new mode of scoring: The Tiebreak.

Policy arguments are the tiebreak for Legal disputes. They normally avoid Legal authorities (i.e., statutes and cases) and thus are only permitted to the extent that statutes and cases fail to declare a winner. Nonetheless, a Policy argument needs support (from virtually anywhere) and ideally provides the incentive for the judge to rule in your favor.

Policy arguments seek to open the courthouse windows to current events, sociological norms, and psychological studies. They draw upon both cultural traditions and current trends. They advance the cause of your client, a larger group of people, or society as a whole. With such loose boundaries, they are favored by 1L students. But do not make the mistake of assuming they are always relevant. Indeed, a strict set of proscriptions cabins this extremely loose art form.

First, Policy Arguments are made by invitation only. In oral argument, the invitation is clear to discern (e.g., "Why should we rule for your client, counselor?"). In Legal Writing, the invitation is less clear. Often, the Legal Writer ensures a Policy Argument's relevance by including it last, where page limitation permits.

Second, recognize that a test constructed by a court may elevate a Policy consideration to become part of that legal test. Imagine that the excerpt below concludes a motion requesting court intervention to prevent the EEOC from enforcing its 150-year old interpretation when the corporate defendant spent over $1 million in legal fees. Is the holding below according to statute, or according to policy considerations?

> Courts intervene in EEOC matters in a great many situations. The statute in play encourages a 3-part test that asks 1) whether the agency has violated its own statute of limitations, 2) whether the respondent has suffered irreparable injury, or 3) whether items on a generalized

list of equities warrant court intervention. Element three has enough flexibility in the joints to allow us to rule that the agency here wasted enough time, money and energy to warrant a reversal. Legal fees have become the bane of a civilized society. Dated interpretations need to be stricken from the books. And in these times of government mistrust and budgetary nonsense, someone has to speak for the little people.

The answer is that the decision offers a *Legal* (not Policy) rationale. While the "little people" language echoes the introduction to countless Policy arguments, the statutory standard expressly asks the court to consider a list of equities; hence the court never veered away from Legal considerations.

To fine tune your abilities to distinguish Legal from Policy arguments, complete the Exercise below.

Exercise Four: Policy Arguments

An Occupy Wall Street-like group enters Comesetti Park at 10:00 p.m. While in the Park (which is privately owned), the protesters play music and chant slogans. There is debris, but the attentive group is well-stocked with garbage bags and shovels; a leader proclaims that "cleaning up" corporate America starts with cleaning up after each other. Tenants of neighboring apartment buildings lodge complaints with the local police about the noise.

Between 11:00 p.m. and 1:00 a.m., the police make 37 arrests for violations of a City ordinance prohibiting trespassing, which is defined as "knowingly entering the property of another without permission." The trespassing statute provides no guidance on defendants who assume that a park is public (and who are not facing a complaining witness). The judge later takes note of both the unstated mission of land preservation and the disruptive, after-hours noise created by the group. The local jail is completely filled with protesters when the judge asks for short, written arguments as to why the charges should be upheld or dismissed.

In a concise, one-half page argument, explain why—for Policy reasons—the arrested individuals should be charged/released.

V. Conclusion

Recognize that lawyers provide value through analysis. The answer "We just don't know" or "We need more facts from the client" very rarely satisfies a supervisor or court.

Moreover, in college, we all raced to complete the shortest part of an assignment first (e.g., the Table of Contents; the Introduction; the Conclusion). Such time-efficiency is useless in Legal Writing. In fact, one of the most alarming facets of the craft is the amount of work that underlies even the briefest of passages. The Rule and Rule Application may be the shortest sections within your Legal Writing, ranking well behind Facts and procedural history sections in terms of length. Yet, paradoxically, these Formula parts may require the most work. To maximize your efforts, remember that an effective Rule satisfies at least 6 bits of guidance:

- Gather all relevant principles
- Prioritize authorities and offer a test
- Proceed from the "test" to its "flavor"
- Support each and every assertion
- Answer the ultimate (often unspoken) question
- Account for outliers and trends

Likewise, in completing a strong Rule Application, remember the following points:

- Strictly align with your Rule
- Choose between a Traditional and Instant Gratification mode of presentation
- Add a counter-analysis (always) and a Policy argument (where space permits)

In the Exercise below, utilize all of the book's guidance in preparing a robust Formula of a Rule and Rule Application. The Exercise, a hypothetical updating and varying an actual case, concerns the Lanham Act's private cause of action for trademark infringement.

Exercise Five: Writing an Effective Formula

<u>FACTS:</u>

During Super Bowl 48 at Giants stadium in New Jersey, Paul Sentsdale was arrested for selling "throwback" Giants jerseys from the trunk of his car. The jerseys featured the names and numbers of three somewhat obscure players from the 1980s: "McClustney," "Savaro," and "Landum." Sentsdale was arrested less than 100 yards from the front entrance to the stadium; Giants jerseys were not on sale during the game, which featured the Seattle Seahawks and the Denver Broncos.

The criminal charges were later dropped, but the owners of the Giants brought a civil action in the jurisdiction of its headquarters. The action alleges violation of federal trademark law under Section 43(a) of the Lanham Act. That provision states as follows:

15 U.S. Code § 1125—False designations of origin, false descriptions, and dilution forbidden

(a) Civil action

(1) Any person who, on or in connection with any goods or services, or any container for goods, uses in commerce any word, term, name, symbol, or device, or any combination thereof, or any false designation of origin, false or misleading description of fact, or false or misleading representation of fact, which—

(A) is likely to cause confusion, or to cause mistake, or to deceive as to the affiliation, connection, or association of such person with another person, or as to the origin, sponsorship, or approval of his or her goods, services, or commercial activities by another person, ...

shall be liable in a civil action by any person who believes that he or she is or is likely to be damaged by such act.

At a preliminary court hearing in New Jersey last month, the following facts were established by the testimony:

1. The three major jersey manufacturers in the United States do not sell (and have no plans to sell) jerseys bearing the names of such former Giants players.

2. Two purchasing fans testified to having firmly believed that the Giants were affiliated with the jersey sales.

3. Three purchasing fans testified to the poor quality of the jerseys (one irate fan stated, "The numbers start to fall off after one wash!").

4. Sentsdale believed he was "filling a need" among true Giants fans, particularly thosed strapped for cash. He made a profit of approximately $600 on Super Bowl Sunday.

5. Five of the purchasers of the jerseys understood that Sentsdale was selling "knockoffs" (one fan testified, "Reebok wouldn't sell a Savaro jersey!").

6. The Giants did not conduct a formal survey of fans regarding any possible confusion caused by the sales; however, a handful of fans sent e-mails or faxes on Super Bowl Sunday asking if the Giants were behind the sales.

7. The jerseys sold by Sentsdale display the same color scheme on officially licensed Giants jerseys (i.e., royal blue, red and white). However, the Giants logo is replaced by a short catchphrase, "Giants Among Men."

8. An expert testified that over $50 million a year is earned by sellers of "bootleg" football jerseys.

KEY CASES:

1. *Polaroid v. Polarad*, 287 F.2d 492 (2d Cir. 1961) (contributing the eight factors that help a court adjudicate claims of confusion among consumers). These eight factors include:

   • Bad Faith (e.g., misleading statements by the seller)

   • Customer Sophistication (i.e., a customer's awareness that he is purchasing an imitation)

   • Actual Confusion (most often evidenced by customer surveys)

   • Desire to enter the field by the trademark holder

2. *NFL v. New Jersey Giants*, 637 F. Supp. 507 (D.N.J. 1986) (finding that a seller's bad faith and a customer's actual confusion predominate among the *Polaroid* factors).

OTHER AUTHORITIES:

1. Darren Rovell, *NFL cracks down on fake jerseys* (Feb. 3, 2013), *available at* http://espn.go.com/espn/otl/story/_/id/8900519/nfl-us-government-score-record-bust-fake-jerseys.

2. Darren Rovell, *Nike raises NFL jersey prices* (April 9, 2014), *available at* http://espn.go.com/nfl/story/_/id/10752520/nike-raises-prices-two-types-nfl-jerseys ("The Elite jersey, which is the closest to what the players wear on the field and boasts being water repellent and has a tighter, tailored fit to the body, went up nearly 20 percent to $295, up from $250.").

Chapter VI

Walking Like a Duck and Locating the Proper Language

Chapter Objectives:
- Identifying an Audience
- Further Identifying Meaningful "Legalese"
- Using Word Choice as a Means of Achieving Brevity
- Adhering to a List of Style Conventions

Substantive Takeaways:
- Federal Law on Labor Unionization
- Presidential Messages on Business Regulation
- Tortious Interference with Contract per *Pennzoil*

I. Introduction

All of us are share a common disadvantage: The English language came from too many sources, and thus now has simply too many similar terms. Witness the confusion occasioned by such redundancies. "Flammable" and "inflammable" mean the same thing, as do "till" and "until," "though and although," and "toward and towards."

Likewise, there are untold problems caused by the present race to informality. A student volunteering for a class trip can realistically proclaim both "I'm *down* with that" and "I'm *up* for that." In general eager participants go "all *out*" and are also said to be "all *in*." A valuable idea both "has legs" and "will fly." A project that has stalled has been both "tied up" and "tied down." A bad idea is alternatively "full of hot air" and "a lead balloon." An "*ingrate*" is someone "*ungrateful*." And it was never quite clear to me why it is that we teach our children to avoid both "the shifty" and "the shiftless"—are both *shift* and its absence equally detrimental? Further, nowadays the best periodicals print sentence fragments, and the newscasters use slang.

As discussed in Chapter I, law students are universally apprehensive about Legal Writing. They come from vastly differing undergraduate courses of study, such as Philosophy or Chemistry. They also have heard widely varying tales of the eccentric focal points of the Legal Writing course (e.g., learning "CREAC"; writing within merciless page limits). They are also coming of age at a time when people are increasingly communicating through electronic pictures and symbols.

This book has suggested that the craft of Legal Writing should remain focused on a sole goal: The identification of the relevant law, and its application to specific facts. This goal becomes blurred if excessive attention is devoted to widely varying forms of communication and nuanced semantics. Concurrently, it is suggested/repeated that, in choosing professional vocabulary in this difficult language and in these difficult linguistic times, the student need foremost follow a simplified guidance adhering to three steps:

1. Write for an educated (but newly initiated) audience,

2. Write in short sentences and numerous paragraphs, using necessary legalese, and

3. Adhere to a list of conventions stressing universal formalities.

As I tell my students, nowhere other than in law school and places of legal employment shall these dictates be rewarded. In short, walk like a duck, and learn to quack like the rest of us. The first obligation is thus to identify the ducks you are addressing.

II. Identifying the Audience

One of my favorite exercises I offer students asks them to describe the first Legal Writing assignment, in writing, to a fictitious listener. The "listener" for half of the class is a teenage cousin pre-occupied with his cell phone. The listener for the other half is a favorite college professor. All students have 10 minutes to jot down their thoughts. The exercise is usually offered within the first two weeks of class.

Students instantly recognize that word choice is key. The teenage cousin would need to pause to construe a phrase such as "summary judgment." Likewise, even the sage college instructor may not grasp the import of a customary remedy such as "vacatur."

The students often rise to the challenge, "dumbing down" the language for the teenager, while retaining more mature vocabulary for the college professor. Both halves of the class are somewhat humbled, as each slowly realizes the tremendous advantage enjoyed by those who write for an educated audience. Then the students, naturally, wish to know which of them adapted the best.

In truth, the exercise may have no genuine answer. A problem centering on theft of computer secrets via an e-mail might involve terms and notions equally incomprehensible to both the teen and the learned muse; conversely, a writing problem simply describing a criminal assault might require the same fundamental language for both listeners. The exercise's true utility thus lies in compelling the writer to picture a listener throughout the writing process.

The listener who should be pictured is a hypothetical seasoned attorney who knows nothing of the subject at hand. If I assign a First Amendment issue, I tell my students that they should assume that I (as Legal Reader) am a real estate attorney. If I assign an intellectual property problem, then I am family rights advocate. In short, assume the Reader knows how to grasp a new field of law, if the document explaining that field meets the profession's requirements. Atop the list of such requirements is the range of acceptable language.

III. Using Permissible Legalese

As was also noted in Chapter I, warnings on the complexity of legal language are legendary. The medieval tale of the court lawyer ordered to wear his burdensome document as a hat permeates law school. To similar effect are aged comedy routines lampooning such formalities as "the party of the first part and the party of the second part." The choice of language can be confounding to first year law students, who are asked to instinctively trust a portable law dictionary, while concurrently avoiding the use of such uncomfortable language in everyday speech.

But that law dictionary has hidden value. *Legalese* is easy to memorize and effective. Additionally, when used in moderation, it communicates a sincere desire to join the profession. Consider the utility of the following two passages, both centering on foreign regulation of mergers:

WEAK:

> The defendant argued that the European Union's antitrust analysis, if that body of law were to apply, would still produce the same outcome, because the EU would ultimately employ the same analysis.

BETTER:

> Assuming, arguendo, that this matter were in a European Union court, the result would be the same.

Lawyers understand "arguendo." Thus, the second passage is easier on the eyes.

Simply put, legalese can often be the best choice. I am always reminded of the debate inspired by a past employer's attempt to streamline the vocabulary of the legal department. Instructors from a company specializing in the use of direct language sent representatives to our workplace to offer a day-long seminar on the means of writing more directly. By mid-morning, the department's contracts wordsmith had heard enough. He bellowed from the back of the room, "I CANNOT REPLACE THE WORDS 'FORCE MAJEURE'—I WILL GET FIRED ONCE WE ARE SUED!"

While that protest was perhaps an overstatement, the point was (and is) well taken: The rush to dismiss all verbiage peculiar to the legal profession is not ultimately useful. Some of the terms of art carry unique meaning, and the author of a contemporary replacement runs the risk of undermining the intended legal effect of the document. As has been aptly noted, "last will and testament" may sound redundant, but it is what courts and parties have come to agree should govern disposition of the estate.

Further, some legalese—possessing a unique connotation—actually shortens writing. Consider the efficiency of the following phrases, each listed before its commonly accepted definition:

- *Inter alia*: among other things
- *Ex post facto*: a law passed now to cover things that happened in the past
- *Gravamen*: the gist of the lawsuit

Stated otherwise, sometimes a duck need walk like a duck.

What is thus perhaps more useful is a reference point for a modest amount of legalese. It is suggested that Legal Writers generally avoid terms requiring the Reader to turn to a law dictionary but most definitely consider utilizing the terms included as "Appendix B" at the end of this book. To see the distinction in context, try your hand at the Exercise appearing below.

Exercise One: Separating Useful from Non-Useful Legalese

Upon hearing that the first assignment for his Contracts class had to number less than 500 words, Aldus took it upon himself to save space (and impress his Professor) by utilizing a bevy of Latin phrases. In correcting the jargon-laden opening paragraphs of his submission, translate the unnecessary phrases, while retaining the few terms that actually propel the passage:

The notion of *de facto* undue influence is a vexing one. According to the relevant *corpus juris*, a party who has coerced an outcome from a party *compos mentis* may not later enforce the agreement for an economic advantage. Examples of such *inter vivos* violative relationships include, *inter alia*, executor-testator, attorney-client, and employer-employee (when the latter is not *sui juris*).

The doctrine has undergone a number of significant changes. *Seriatim*, at *lex communis*, a *de minimis* amount of influence was found to be insignificant. The modern trend is the *de jure* prevention of the *actus reus*, evidenced *ipso facto*. *Exempli gratia*, doctors are often precluded from serving as witnesses to a last will and testament. *A fortiori*, an insurance company may not serve as beneficiary from a policy it has issued, the agreement being null and void *ab initio*. Further, even those companies obtaining additional witnesses may find themselves declared by a magistrate to have acted *ultra vires*.

A judge seeking to reform the violative agreement has a number of options. He can simply, *sua sponte*, restore the *status quo ante*. Of course, even if the agreement survives *in camera* inspection and a subsequent hearing, an appellate court may order a trial *de novo* to rectify a perceived injustice. The *ratio decidendi* in such written decisions appears to be, *sub silentio*, the advocacy of fairness in all contractual dealings.

Note that some local rules (and employers) demand that terms borrowed from Latin be italicized. While this book generally opposes the use of italics in formal Legal Writing, the Legal Writer should learn whether such a rule is in effect—and follow it religiously.

IV. Employing Fifteen Useful Style Conventions[1]

To similar end, the Legal Writer should become conversant with a set of Writing guidelines and not look back. "Appendix C" of this book warns of eas-

---

1. For purposes of this book, a Writing "convention" is commonly utilized but not universally accepted.

ily confused words, while "Appendix D" provides a starter kit for formatting and grammar. The suggestions below will hopefully assist with the adaptation of your style.

A. Avoid Contractions and Slang

Excessive informality succeeds foremost in earning the Reader's contempt. Display some respect for the wisdom of the ages by dressing up speech to a minor extent. One way to sufficiently "dress up" your language is to imagine you are defending someone in traffic court. You would likely refer to the levied fine as "unreasonable" (and not "bogus") and the ticketing police officer as "mistaken" (and not "lame"). Some other examples of wise choices appear below:

WEAK:

> The appellate court, at its own sweet pace, ultimately decided that the practice was weak but in no way insider trading, a bizarre view given the *O'Hagan* decision.

BETTER:

> Two years later, the appellate court held that the misguided practice did not constitute insider trading, a ruling that seemed questionable in light of the *O'Hagan* decision.

To further help you ease everyday speech out of your Writing, "Appendix B" provides 10 euphemisms accepted within the profession.

B. Never Use Questions

If the Reader agrees with your point, the question is unnecessary. If he does not agree, then you have placed him on the defensive. The invitation to personal investment is superfluous, particularly when—as is demonstrated below—all questions can be converted to declarative statements making the same point.

WEAK:

> Would the court wish that future such members of management similarly invoke privilege at every turn?

BETTER:

> To be sure, a decision rendering the defendant's actions de minimis may very well invite countless unsubstantiated claims of privilege in the future.

C. Avoid Attempts at Humor

Here is where Legal Writing differs from storytelling, newscasts, and dinner speeches. Irony is often lost in print, and puns can be misconstrued as a lack of seriousness of purpose. Of course, this rule becomes more flexible as the law student graduates to more specific forms of writing (e.g., a law school Note, discussed in Chapter X). For those who fear that successful Legal Writing stultifies creativity, rest assured that mastery of multiple styles of writing is common, as evidenced by Francis Scott Key and countless other attorneys.

D. Use Only Metaphors and Rare Words You Have Previously Seen in Print

In my first year as lawyer, I prolonged a debate with a supervisor by mispronouncing "vehemently" (properly pronounced "VEE-A-MENTLY") as a strange, 4-syllable creation ("VEE-HEM-MENT-LY"). My former co-workers still swap stories about the supervisor's robust laughter. After my shame settled, I swore to never again speak a word or phrase I had not heard, and never to use a word or phrase when Writing that I had not seen in print; such is a pretty good rule.

E. Use No More Than Three Phrases/Clauses in Your Sentences

If you see three or more commas in a paragraph, you have likely gone on for too long. Again, the remedy is quite painless:

WEAK:

> Surely, the plaintiff will cite to the defendant's lack of quarterly Board meetings, a formality required by statute in the majority of States and presently under consideration in many others, but such aged prerequisites speak more to the corporate structure than its actions.

BETTER:

> Surely, the plaintiff will cite to the defendant's lack of quarterly Board meetings. But that formality, while required or soon to be required by a majority of States, speaks more to corporate structure than deeds.

F. Use No More Than Eight Sentences Per Paragraph

Many lawyers would agree that, on average, a shorter paragraph is more informative (and less off-putting). Also, command of sequential words such as "Moreover" and "Likewise" universally impress the Legal Reader.

G. Use at Least Two Full Paragraphs on Each Page

The sequential words highlighted above crave for the start of a new paragraph.

When in doubt, simply hold a pen (point facing down) over the middle of a long paragraph, and drop it. The resulting mark is surprisingly effective as an indicator of where the new paragraph should commence.

H. Only Interrupt Text in One of Two Ways: "i.e., ...", or "e.g., ..."

The Reader is helped along by rapidly recognizing your entrance into digressions; do not ask the Reader to register multiple entry points.

EXAMPLE:

> The court ultimately sided with ExxonMobil (i.e., found no need for treble damages), although the issue of precise damage calculation remains in need of specific guidance.

On a related note, ellipses—those lines of dots signifying the exclusion of quoted text—can be extremely interruptive if inconsistently used. Form a habit of using three dots to communicate the removal of a remainder of a sentence, and four dots to communicate the removal of more than part of a sentence.

I. Likewise, Consistently Introduce Identifiers

Legal Writing often requires the introduction of an acronym or shortened term for a party. Generally speaking, choose one method of doing so, and use only that formation.

EXAMPLE:

> The Securities Litigation Uniform Standards Act (hereinafter "SLUSA") remains the primary mechanism by which State securities fraud actions are removed to federal court.

J. But Do Not Always Use Identifiers

Remember: The first rule of Legal Writing is to not slow reading (Chapter 1). Thus, identifying the "Public Investors Arbitration Bar Association" as "PIABA" is helpful. Slowing reading to clarify that "Travelers" shall stand for "The Travelers Company" is of far less utility.

K. Avoid Exclamation Points and the Use of Bold/Italics

One of my more popular anecdotes relates the feedback I once received from a supervisor on a short memo. The memo was to explain the company's potential liability for a problem; in conclusion thereof I wrote—in bold—"over a million dollars." The supervisor was insulted by the memo, and immediately told me so. "So you placed 'a million dollars' in bold because I do not otherwise pay attention when I read?" she asked in half-jest.

That was a valuable lesson for me. Superficial distinctions confess (and possibly encourage) the Legal Reader's inattention—if you become known as the intern who places all key facts and conclusions in bold, your Readers will only scan your Writing in search of such highlighted parts. Litigators will agree that a deposition witness who answers "I *really* don't know the answer to that one" may previously have provided some flawed answers. Likewise, the Legal Writer needing to italicize or place in bold acknowledges that other parts of the passage are less vital or sincere.

On an even more basic note, Legal Writing is filled with cites that utilize italics and bold; leave such tools out of the text.

L. Spellcheck, Both Automatically and Manually

The computer can inform the student that the typing error "trual" is not a word. But only a manual read discloses that "trail" has been typed where "trial" was intended. It bears noting that all errors (i.e., whether in substance, grammar, or formatting) erode credibility. A Supreme Court Justice has stated that, when encountering a "sloppy brief," he is "inclined to think that person is a sloppy thinker."[2]

---

2. Bryan A. Garner, *The Psychology of Credibility*, ABAJ. (May 2015), at 24 (quoting Supreme Court Justice Antonin Scalia).

M. Limit Direct Quotes

Lawyers are paid to add value; "lifting" passages rarely helps to educate the Reader. A good rule of thumb is to use no more than one direct quote per paragraph. Remember always that a direct quote of 50 words or more requires special treatment.[3]

N. Always Italicize/Underline Case Names

The only time that you do not italicize or underline is when referring to the party itself.

EXAMPLES:

The *Chevron* case ended in 1984.

The *Chevron* Court established a test for agency deference.

Chevron stands as a barometer for court intervention.

Chevron decided against further appeals, as the company had won its case.

O. Add a Proofread for Word Choice

Legal Writers inevitably develop a word bank of reliable terms and phrases (e.g., "Moreover"; "Consequentially"). As will be discussed throughout this book, repetition is fine for critical standards of law; when it come to style, routinely repeating words appears slothful. To alleviate the chance of over-inclusion of your crutch phrases, engage in one more proofread. Simply "Find" within your word processing program to check for your usual transitions and phrases to ensure a rational amount of use thereof.

———

Those tips aside, recognize that a certain amount of trial and error is inevitable in a 1L Legal Writing course. The top five mistakes I have seen are (in order of frequency) 1) long sentences, 2) unparallel structure, 3) dangling participles, 4) improper pronoun usage, and 5) shifting verb tenses. With those five frequent errs in mind, correct the language that follows, which attempts a summary of State of the Union addresses in the last 100 years.

———

3. Namely, indentation on both sides, single spacing, and the elimination of quotation marks. Bluebook Rule 5.1.

Exercise Two: Streamlining a Summary of Inaugural Addresses and the Regulation of Business

American Presidents have been surprisingly consistent in choosing to announce their philosophies on business regulation in their inaugural addresses. For each of the 10 passages below, correct the summary sentences.

1. Teddy Roosevelt, 1905: President Roosevelt speaks against the "anxiety inseparable from the accumulation of great wealth in industrial centers," and, never fearing the good fight, the country ultimately came around to his suspicion of the large trusts of the day.

2. Woodrow Wilson, 1913: Years before fighting the world war no one wanted, his speech spoke in favor of "the genius of individual men and the limitless enterprise of groups of men" (i.e., he catered to both his supporters and detractors in a conciliatory gesture aimed at calming hostilities caused by its differences).

3. Calvin Coolidge, 1925: Initially promising not to impose legislation that "destroys those who have already secured success," that legislation or its administrative counterparts in the form of agency regulations dominated the years prior to the Great Depression.

4. Herbert Hoover, 1929: Although initially speaking of constitutional limits to federal regulation of business and his preference for State regulation, the Hoover Presidency was marked by his failed efforts at government stimulation of business, and its resulting failure to win re-election.

5. Richard Nixon, 1973: In his inaugural address, it was said that "... the time has come to turn away from the condescending policies of paternalism—of 'Washington knows best,'" and it did indeed subsequently focus on cutting back on government-funded programs, as such actions were a prime example of "paternalism" at its worst.

6. Jimmy Carter, 1977: The 39th President speaks of equal treatment under the law "for the rich and the poor," but circumstances played its ugly hand, resulting in hard times for American businesses that feel the sting of embargo, such as oil and grain.

7. Ronald Reagan, 1981: President Reagan boldly declared, "In the present [economic] crisis, government is not the solution to our problem," but, ironically, it would both play a large role in the lives of Americans, either through his tax reform bill, or—more directly—his having intervened in the air traffic controllers strike.

8. <u>George H.W. Bush, 1989</u>: The father of the future 43rd Commander-in-Chief, the address harkened back to the days of Nixon when he states, "The old solution, the old way, was to think that public money could end our problems," perhaps foretelling his impending problems of difficult relations with foreign power, the economy sinking into a recession, and that he failed to muster enough votes for re-election.

9. <u>William Clinton, 1993</u>: An era of change, President Clinton declared, "It is time to break the bad habit of expecting something for nothing, from our government or from each other," while also reminding that Washington, D.C. needed to be responsive and was the greatest form of representation.

10. <u>Barack Obama, 2009</u>: The 44th President cautiously reminds that "... this [financial] crisis has reminded us that without a watchful eye, the market can spin out of control, and that a nation cannot prosper long when it favors only the prosperous," and added, "Together, we discovered that a free market only thrives when there are rules to ensure competition and fair play."

Three other specific problems recur among first year Legal Writers, as evidenced by the following frequent questions:

- *Is "the Court" singular or plural? I thought "The Court issued their opinion" made more sense. The same for "The Board of Directors expressed their concern that the stock price was unsustainable."*
- *Isn't the goal to vary your language? I wrote "manifest disregard of law" twice on the previous page.*
- *Can't I just provide a list of "bullet points"?*

The first of the above questions (re. pronoun usage) focuses on implied meaning. If the Writer is intending to convey the thought that each member of the Supreme Court majority eventually came around to a position, both "its" and "their" appear to be correct. However, the best solution is to consistently follow the norms of grammar: "The Court changed its position." (i.e., treat "the Court" as a singular noun, replaced by the singular pronoun).

The second of the above questions (re. balancing variety and clarity) addresses a more stylish concern. Students often balk at repeating generic words— indeed, college professors rewarded their employment of variety in vocabulary. But a proper focus on the needs of the audience cures that conflict. The Legal Reader is endeavoring to acquire a rudimentary education on a new topic. At that moment, he cares little about the Writer's skill in finding substitute words.

Witness the difference between the following two passages, both attempting to introduce the Reader to the notion of efforts at labor unionization:

WEAK:

> The National Labor Relations Act of 1935 prohibits an employer from interfering with employee attempts to join or form unions. The law favors labor organizations in various ways. Collective bargaining, concerted activity, and certification of a union representative are all protected. The NLRA specifically prohibits interference with one or more of these rights.

BETTER:

> The National Labor Relations Act of 1935 prohibits an employer from interfering with employee attempts to join or form unions. Chief among the guarded rights is the shielding of "concerted activity." Concerted activity is defined as group action by employees seeking mutual protections. In deference to such activity, the NLRA guarantees the employee's entrance into a union, and the employer's duty to bargain with such union as the employee's representative.

The words "concerted activity" and "union" permeate (if not dominate) the second example. But it is doubtful that any other synonyms would adequately introduce the field of law or signify its key terminology.[4] The lesson? Repeat terms of art when connoting a key definition or standard; save collegiate wordsmithing for less vital sentiments.

Finally, the last question (re. suggesting "bullet points" as a cure) bespeaks an unwillingness to transfer a skill set. Specifically, many business students and law students drawn from the workforce feel more comfortable conveying information in a list of facts, factors, or elements. But such a format signals expedience, and possibly superficial analysis. Legal Writing demands more formal prose, evidencing both a diligence in presentation and an earnest desire to enter the legal profession. Unless a "list of bullets" is expressly requested, utilize that approach solely as an outline for a more substantive piece of work.

---

4. The actual statutory provision reads as follows:
Section 7—Employees shall have the right to self-organization, to form, join, or assist labor organizations, to bargain collectively through representatives of their own choosing, and to engage in other concerted activities for the purpose of collective bargaining or other mutual aid or protection ...
Labor Management Relations Act of 1935, 29 U.S.C. § 157 (2012).

Exercise Three: Perfecting Parallel Structure

In the 1980s, a titan battle between Texas corporations vying to acquire Getty Fuel resulted in landmark rulings on the claim of "tortious interference with contract" and resultant punitive damages. For each of the related descriptions below, correct the compound sentences/notions on defenses or damages (highlighted in bold) to employ correct parallel structure within a single sentence. As a hint, strive to consistently use the active voice.

1. In 1985, in *Pennzoil, Co. v. Texaco, Inc.*, a Texas state court had to decide the value of a lawsuit seeking damages for Texaco's alleged "tortious interference" with Pennzoil's contract to acquire third party Getty Oil Company. **After the Texas jury found liability, Pennzoil was awarded compensatory damages of approximately $7.5 billion. The court also determined that punitive damages of approximately $3 billion were necessary. An amount close to $600 million in interest is also deemed proper.**

2. Subsequently, Texaco filed a federal suit in New York seeking an injunction against enforcement of the Texas jury verdict and its awards. Texaco argued that the Texas requirement of a sizeable bond during appeal violated its rights. **Specifically, that federal petition argued violations of the Civil Rights Act, the federal court also had to decide whether various amendments of the Constitution precluded the bond requirement, and even the Securities and Exchange Commission weighed in on a preemption issue (involving the Securities Exchange Act).**

3. In 1987, the Second Circuit Court of Appeals upheld the federal District Court decision. **That court ruled that the Constitutional and Civil Rights Act claims were likely to succeed. The Texas bond requirement is nullified. Also, Pennzoil's claim that the Second Circuit Court should abstain was denied.**

4. Finally, in late 1987, the Supreme Court reversed, stating that both lower federal courts "failed to recognize the significant interests harmed by their unprecedented intrusion into the Texas justice system." **It was also noted that the key issues could have been determined by the Texas courts. The decision also noted that the principle of comity supports deference.** Shortly thereafter, Texaco filed for Bankruptcy.

V. Conclusion

To be sure, there are few allies in the war on poor Writing. Pop culture seems to introduce new terms on a monthly basis. Our society's attention span is now measured in milliseconds. One constant is that to be thought to write like a lawyer remains an insult.

But Legal Writing is a distinct art. It seeks a durability that promotes stability in business. It requires its champions to behave differently (I encourage all my 1L students to immediately commence sending texts and e-mails comprised of complete sentences, and they usually thank me years later).

Further, recognize that the layman's term is no stronger because of its popularity. News outlets like comforting listeners by parroting such phrases as "There are no known threats to disrupt train service." Can there ever be an unknown *threat*? By definition, a threat must be "known" to cause harm. "There are no known *surprises* to disrupt train service" may actually work better. Yet the cryptic phrase "known threat" lives on.

Of course, examples can become too numerous to document, and word choice itself can become an obsession. However, in the final analysis, law as a profession focuses on words. Students arrive at law school believing they shall deliver great oratories or unearth rare cases. They promptly learn that the profession demands and rewards something else. The "day's work" of a lawyer entails writing something a bit better than someone else can; the raw materials for that work starts and ends with a vocabulary. To aid with your short term vocabulary, Appendix C offers guidance on words commonly confused with their counterparts or homophones.

Fortunately, law students begin to effortlessly absorb terms they read repeatedly, growing to instinctively employ language such as "evidence adduced at trial" and "vetted choices." Such is a collateral benefit of reading Supreme Court opinions nearly every night. Likewise, in the long run, what you read in general largely determines your word choice. You will quite naturally possess a proper and expanded vocabulary years from now. In the interim, use this Chapter to begin to cling to some phrases and to discard others.

In college, we all used $10 words (to show we had consulted a Thesaurus), wrote the theme several times (to ensure it would sink in), and buried the contrary approach in a footnote (to ensure it did not sink in). Legal Writing presents a series of new strategies. Specifically, mechanical choices on sentence length, paragraph coherence, and use of legalese may result in Writing that appears to conflict with your collegiate tastes. You are in a new pond. Walk like a duck, and be proud about it.

PART TWO

Chapter VII

That Old Frame:
The Office Memorandum

Chapter Objectives:
- Learning the Six Components of a Basic Legal Memorandum
- Appreciating the Strict Rules of Formatting Attending Such Writing
- Becoming Conversant with "Predictive" Vocabulary
- Distinguishing Between Short and Long Form Conclusions

Substantive Takeaways:
- Statutes of Frauds and Required Writings, Generally
- Federal Regulation CC and Bank "Holds" on Deposited Checks
- Treasury Department/FinCEN Anti-Money Laundering Guidelines
- California's "Transformative Test" as a Defense to Copyright Infringement

---

I. Background

Perhaps no law school assignment inspires the dread attending the "Office Memorandum." Often distributed within the opening week of 1L classes, the task involves reviewing a short set of materials and producing a formal legal analysis of moderate length (e.g., five pages). The Memo serves as the introduction to Legal Writing. The new first-year student is required to analyze a short list of authorities (e.g., three state court cases) and offer a prediction on a fictitious problem in a specified jurisdiction (e.g., covenants not to compete in Virginia). Thus, even before becoming familiar with a fraction of the syllabus topics underlying their substantive classes, 1L students must opine with confidence on a contract, a potential tort, or a pending criminal charge.

Further, nearly all State Bar examinations now include at least one "MPT" ("Multistate Performance Test"), a practical module of approximately 90 minutes within the strictly-timed testing day. The module provides a hypothetical legal library and client file and requests the preparation of a final product (e.g., a Memo, a Brief, a contract, or a Will & Testament). This trend to include such "real time" lawyering as part of a jurisdiction's licensing requirements only serves to heighten the ability to create an effective Office Memo.

Although such Memos can mean a great many things to a great many lawyers, this storied communication of short term research is actually surprisingly consistent in terms of components. This Chapter shall both provides examples and instruction on the appearance and content of the most universal of Legal Writing course documents.

II. Formula Parts/Structure

The required Components of an Office Memo can range, but, collectively, seek to impress upon the student the need for delayed subjectivity within segmented writing. The segments are easily learned; the need to remain objective proves a bit tougher to grasp. I teach my students that, in revealing and explaining the applicable legal principles, regrettably, there are countless opportunities to lose credibility. The first such opportunity appears in the task of formulating the proper heading.

A. The Heading

The Heading serves as the "inside address" of the Office Memo. It also memorializes the subject matter and date of creation, two vital details that assist the employer with, among other things, file management. Overall, great care should be taken from the outset of typing to create the perfect document (remember the industry's caveat: sloppy Legal Writing reveals sloppy minds). To that end, review the two examples below:

WEAK:

TO: Senior Partner

FROM: Junior Associate

Re: Silvester Fische

Date: 11/3/15

BETTER:

TO: Senior Partner

FROM: Junior Associate

RE: Our client, Mr. Silvester Fische

DATE: November 3, 2015

It took but seconds to "tab" the entries of the second sample and to make the all-capitals format uniform, thus providing a better cosmetic appearance. Further, the spelled out date speaks of effort and formality, whereas "11/3/15" not only reeks of familiarity but is also prone to numerical error. Above all, recognize that a primary goal of the Memo—which is the shortest assignment of the Legal Writing class—is cosmetic perfection. Spelling errors are to be eliminated via "Spellcheck" or similar tool, and inconsistencies in font and spacing simply are not tolerated. Such mishaps are easily rectified through the addition of an additional proofread to your Writing process. The next component involves far more mentally challenging revisions.

B. The Issue Section

The "Issue" of a matter represents a sole basis for resolution of the conflict. It takes the form of a single-sentence question. The Issues section of a Memo serves as a reference point for every Reader who shall handle the Memo, as well as a subtle reminder for the Writer of the focal point(s) of the project.

I instruct my class that framing the Issue properly has far-reaching consequences. By way of example, an Appellate Brief[1] that errs in this regard may result in an appeal being denied (or, even worse, the wrong issue being granted an appeal). Accordingly, this section perhaps requires the most practice by the 1L student. To commence this learning curve, three guides are hereby offered:

1. Begin Each "Issue" with "Whether," "Does," or "Is"

To be sure, there are additional means of starting an Issue. But initially opting for one choice among this limited subset gets the Writer writing while re-

---

1. Although striving to provide a practical starting point for the creation of various legal documents, this Book intentionally excludes the Appellate Brief from the mix; that document is normally reserved for seasoned or specialized attorneys. Indeed, in teaching Legal Writing to hundreds of 1L students over the course of eight years, I have heard of only one of those students being asked to prepare such a Brief for an employer prior to completing law school.

minding that the goal is a single sentence, concluded with terminal punctuation (i.e., a period or question mark).

2. Combine Law and Facts, and Get Specific

Students naturally phrase the issue as a problem caused by generic authority, but rarely specify the exact facts that have triggered the legal dispute. Consider the relative effectiveness of the following two Issue sections, both centering on a popular common law defense to copyright infringement claims:

WEAK:

Issue Presented

Does the transformative test provide relief for our client?

BETTER:

Issue Presented

Does the transformative test, as defined by California case law since 2005, provide a defense to a claim of infringement under the Copyright Act of 1976 (as amended) where, by the artist's own testimony, the "creative elements" do not predominate the work?

The second example specifies the governing authority while conveying the *direct* problem (i.e., the client's admission) as well as the *indirect* problem (i.e., the dated statute). Rather than blandly educating the Reader, "This is a copyright case," the second example offers a body of relevant precedent, and the terms by which such precedent could be researched (i.e., "Copyright Act of 1976," "transformative test," and "creative elements"). I often remind my students that, if potential search terms are not included in the Issue, revision is necessary.

3. Write a Complete Question, Limited to Four Lines

An Issue that is too short appears to have not been properly focused, while one that is too long appears to have not been re-drafted. Either way, the Legal Writer appears slothful. A good rule of thumb is to set a target of 3–4 lines.

More pointedly, a short Issue needs more law and facts; a long Issue needs to eliminate extraneous concerns. Review the examples below, both referencing the statutory bases for federal vacatur of a private arbitration discussed in Chapter V:

WEAK:

Whether under Section 10 of the Federal Arbitration Act, the courts will upset the award if the arbitrators 1) engaged in corruption or fraud, 2) evidenced partiality, 3) wrongfully excluded evidence or refused to postpone a hearing or 4) exceeded their authority when they denied a reasonable request for an adjournment made by the plaintiff's counsel, and they repeatedly mocked the plaintiff's counsel by curtailing his questions?

BETTER:

Whether under Section 10(a)(4) of the Federal Arbitration Act, a court would find that arbitrators "exceeded their authority" where the arbitrators 1) denied a request for an adjournment based upon a family death, and/or 2) repeatedly curtailed the plaintiff's questioning?

In addition to its verbosity, the first example echoes the four statutory bases without hinting at the client's best chance of recovery. The second example indicates the best statutory choice for analysis ("exceeded their authority") while also streamlining the facts ("reasonable request" is explained; "mocking" has been eliminated as a basis for appeal). Note that the second example at once provides search terms and fulfills its task in a minimal amount of lines.

Note also that the Issue can always be phrased in terms of the current client (e.g., "Whether Mr. Jones can have the decision against him vacated ...") or in terms of all parties similarly situated (e.g. "Whether a party losing an arbitration can have the decision vacated ..."). Such distinction has little meaning, but the Writer should clarify and consistently adhere to the Reader's preference in this regard.

A faulty or improperly focused Issue sets the Memo on a very dangerous path. To commence practice at writing effective Issues, try the Exercise below.

Exercise One: Perfecting Issues

Highlight the weak points in the following five passages (all drawn from prior Chapters). Additional authorities/facts for your corrected answers are included in parentheses after each passage. If necessary, split the Issue into 2 new Issues.

1. Why a court shouldn't dismiss a tort claim filed by a guest on corporate headquarters property when the guest was "bit" by the CEO's dog and that dog had not bitten anyone in the past and the injuries were minimal? (case law within the State defining extraordinary negligence as requiring "known aggressive tendencies"; dog weighed 2 lbs).

2. Does Gertz v. Welch dictate a dismissal for our client? (alleged libel of a private citizen; knowing offense; punitive damages sought).

3. Whether Mr. Jones will likely be charged with insurance fraud or conspiracy thereof when he and his daughter staged his death? (Article 176;

phony report of a drowning death; phone call to police; phone call to newspapers; phone call to insurance company).

4.   Why a plaintiff cannot use newly amended Securities and Exchange Commission Regulation A, which was adopted pursuant to a Congressional Act and designed to assist smaller companies, with the costs and intricacies of legal stock offerings to the public? ($6 million in annual revenue).

5.   Whether the client will be found guilty of insider trading (Section 10(b) of the Securities Exchange Act; only $1,200 in profits; defendant bragged of learning earnings announcement "ahead of the fools in the crowd").

The next series of Memo Components are undoubtedly more substantive; still, strict attention must be paid to cosmetic appearance.

C. The Brief Answer

The Brief Answer responds to the Issue. The Component provides the user friendly solution to the Issues addressed in the Memo. The section is universally embraced by young Legal Writers, for it requires no citation and, consequentially, most clearly resembles non-Legal Writing. If written correctly, it is likewise uniquely appreciated by the Legal Reader.

The sole guidance for this component is to avoid lapses into informality. Sentence fragments and slang do not make the Memo any more appreciated; conversely, the disruption caused by a change in style either puzzles the Reader or makes him/her desire a complete departure from the structure. Evaluate the effectiveness of the two passages below, each continuing the Issue example from above:

WEAK BRIEF ANSWER:

Issue Presented

Whether under Section 10(a)(4) of the Federal Arbitration Act, a court would find that arbitrators "exceeded their authority" where the arbitrators 1) denied a request for an adjournment based upon a family death, and/or 2) repeatedly curtailed the plaintiff's questioning?

Brief Answer

No. There were not enough wrongful acts here.

BETTER BRIEF ANSWER:

Issue Presented

Whether under Section 10(a)(4) of the Federal Arbitration Act, a court would find that arbitrators "exceeded their authority" where the arbitrators 1) denied a request for an adjournment based upon a family death, and/or 2) repeatedly curtailed the plaintiff's questioning?

<u>Brief Answer</u>

A court would likely not intervene in the present case. Although both the denial of an adjournment and curtailing of questioning seem harsh, there is no precedent for such discretionary acts by an arbitrator forming the basis for vacatur of an otherwise proper proceeding.

D. The Facts Section

As described in Chapter III, the Facts section is vital. Its significance within your legal analysis is tied directly to your ability to tell the "story" of the dispute. This Chapter offers an additional three tips for effective storytelling, as described below.

1. Create a Clearly Demarcated Timeline

Every story has a beginning and an ending. Your Facts section similarly needs starting and ending points.

Start with the beginning that comports with your overall approach. For example, a bank examiner writing a report after auditing a branch will tell a limited story, with starting and ending points close in time. The theme is simply that a branch was examined on a certain day, and the bank branch was in violation of a regulation. Conversely, the lawyer penning a Memo to her supervisor regarding the allegation may start her story six months prior (e.g., when the head of a department went on leave, thus placing pressure on the staff).

Regarding the end of the story, end with the most recent event in the life of the Issue (e.g., "The bank received the regulatory report alleging a violation last week."). Such consistent use of this termination point rewards Reader expectations (while reminding the Legal Writer of deadlines and obligations).

2. Endorse a Mental State (or Lack Thereof)

Every Facts section contains a theory. The Theory impliedly endorses the prediction to follow in the Memo. "Theories" represent Legal Writing at its highest level, at once integrating fact, law, conclusion, and motive. For the purpose of preparing an efficient Legal Memo, recognize that the Facts Section only needs to provide the Reader with the events, statements, or determinations that will support the prediction to follow. However, the Reader still needs to know if alleged failures by the defendant were willful, negligent, accidental, or something else altogether.

Continuing with the bank examination example, note the differences in Theory announced below.

EXAMPLES:

A. The examiner noted that the bank appeared to have inadequate capital on three successive Fridays in August. When questioned on these apparent lapses, the Vice President did not provide a meaningful answer.

B. The examiner initially noted that, during the review period (50 weeks), the bank appeared to be undercapitalized on three occasions. The Vice President, who oversees the capital department and four other departments, responded that his staff would examine the historical records.

The first example above would likely appear in a Memo suggesting that the bank agree to the regulatory finding and negotiate a small fine. It endorses an *intentional* mental state. The second example presents a somewhat different picture of events—amidst the blizzard of bank computations and paperwork, errors might have been made on a handful of occasions. The second example thus endorses, at worst, a *negligent* mental state.

In all areas of litigation (i.e., civil, criminal, or administrative), distinctions in mental awareness are critical. The coloring of a case begins with the initial research thereon; thus the Office Memo needs to reflect your impressions of the degree of mental culpability.

In a larger sense, as discussed in Chapter III, the key is not avoid ugly Facts but to amplify/condense facts in view of your Memo's ultimate conclusion. Again, elimination of Facts is never an option, as the next tip clarifies.

3. Incorporate All the Facts Necessary for the Subsequent Analysis

The inclusion of Facts late in the analysis signals, at best, analytical ambivalence. Accordingly, once you have completed the Memo, proofread for the revelation of key Facts. Stated otherwise, it is permissible to expand upon a previously disclosed Fact late in a Memo (i.e., within Rule Application). While Facts may sometimes be revealed in a "preliminary statement" or other Memo section detailing purely procedural history, it is not advisable to initially disclose a new Fact after the Facts section.

E. The Discussion

The "Discussion," which contains your Formula, serves as "the guts" of the Memo. It presents, in order, the Rule (perhaps with an Elaboration[2]) and the Rule Application. These basic Formula parts were described in detail in Chapters I–V of this book.

Regarding the preparation of the Rule, it is worth adding that model Rules do not mention the client. You are normally asked to identify the relevant law and apply this law to a present case. While completing the first of these two tasks, there is no need to even mention the client's name—such a detail would belong in the "Issue" or "Brief Answer" components, or the Rule Application section of the ensuing "Discussion" component.

Regarding the preparation of the Rule Application, it is worth adding that signal words aid the Reader greatly. Simply commence your Application with the words "In the instant case." Further, repetition should trump style. Many students exhibit a hesitancy to mimic an outline in applying a Rule when such a rigid approach is exactly what the Reader craves. Witness the efficiency of the following example, which expands upon and concludes the arbitration vacatur examples from earlier in the book:

EXAMPLE:

> In the instant case, it is not likely that the facts meet any of the statutory standards contained within the Federal Arbitration Act.
>
> Regarding the first option (i.e., engaging in corruption or fraud), there is simply is no evidence of such outrageous conduct. This standard is set by the case of ...
>
> Regarding the second option (i.e., evident partiality), there is only scant, unrelated evidence of rudeness towards the parties ...
>
> Regarding the third option (i.e., wrongfully excluded evidence or wrongfully denied postponement), the case law from our jurisdiction affords the arbitrators much discretion ...
>
> Finally, regarding the fourth option (i.e., exceeding authority), Mr. Jones comes closest to satisfying the standard. But, again, precedents simply set the bar too high ...

The language "likely/unlikely" signals to the Reader the precise nature of the prediction. Depending upon the strength of the Legal Writer's prediction,

---

2. The Elaboration, or expansion of the Rule, is discussed in Chapters IV and V.

the words "probable/improbable" may be utilized. Note that the words "Rule Application" do not appear in the writing (nor the term "Rule"). However, experienced lawyers employ trigger terms such as "In the instant case" to overtly signal the commencing of an Application. Conversely, the last section of an Office Memo is clearly announced via a title.

F. The Short and Long Form Conclusion

The "short form" Conclusion is easily learned and embarrassingly commonplace. The succinct variation of the Component simply states, "For all of the foregoing reasons, X...," thus serving foremost as a bookmark for the Writer (and, at times, a reward for the Reader).

Far more satisfying is the "long form Conclusion," which both adds a new consideration and summarizes prior legal analyses. For example, the following passage—centering on a hypothetical petition asserting that an IRS tax evasion case was brought late—subtly ties the present conclusion to the words of an icon from 80 years ago:

> In conclusion, the defendant has not shown the factors necessary under case law interpreting §6531(2) of the U.S. tax code to toll the IRS case. Essentially, those factors seek a determination of whether there was sloth and resulting prejudice, which was clearly not evident in the present case.
>
> It was Oliver Wendell Holmes, Jr. who wrote that "The life of the law has not been logic; it has been experience." And experience instructs us that, in the present matter, a trial at any point between 2000 and 2007 would have yielded the same result: the Defendant simply refused to file a federal return in 1999. For all of the above reasons, the judgment against the defendant must be affirmed.

The reference to a popular judge from decades ago serves to both support the prediction and provide a healthy departure from pages of legal analysis— some "mental sorbet" for the Reader, if you will. The caveat here is that quotes and consideration too far removed from the present case facts appear to reveal a pretentiousness on the part of the Legal Writer. I advise my students to simply "open the conference room windows" to the news in the streets. Such a focus on current events naturally leads to a consideration that is both timely and relevant.

Note that the long form Conclusion (like the short form) ends with the reminder that the Reader base the prediction on all of the offered analyses. Some boilerplate is simply too efficient to ever excise from variations.

III. The Pitfalls to Memo Creation

A. Failing to Meticulously Align Your Rule with Its Application

Students often fear one part of the Formula being much longer than another. Much more fatal to an analysis is a Rule Application that does not neatly align with the Rule. The latter shortcoming is extremely disappointing. The Writer has offered the specific test for a jurisdiction, and it logically follows that the exact test needs later to be applied. Witness the effectiveness of the below passages, both relating to the Lanham Act's "likelihood of confusion" analysis discussed earlier in Chapter V:

EXAMPLE:

> In the instant trademark case, our client, East Coast League Baseball, will be unlikely to prevail on its Section 43a claim. Regarding the first element of the test, there is some evidence that, in light of the similar color schemes and fonts, purchasers of the inexpensive baseball jerseys were confused at the time of sale. However, regarding the second element, as numerous depositions established, the defendant sports apparel retailer acted in "undeniable good faith." One purchaser went so far as to send the retailer a donation to assist with future inner city projects. The relevant test having two conjunctive parts, any claim failing to satisfy either part would fail.

The passage above succeeds simply because it exhibits organized thought. The Legal Writer becomes familiar with the "template" allowing for such presentation; to the (grateful) Legal Reader, the template is invisible.

B. Forgetting Formula Component Purpose

To a lesser extent, errors can be linked to a simple misunderstanding of the various Formula parts. Again, the Rule offers principles, possibly explained via an Elaboration. The Rule Application joins those principles to the present case, and thus first mentions the client and other items in the case file. To randomly switch between precedent and present case causes an uneasiness in the Reader that may never be effectively quelled.

Here is a tip on reiterating the distinctive purposes of Formula parts: When referencing any precedent, use the words "In that case." However, when referencing the present matter, use only the words "In the instant case." Again, the Reader will appreciate the repetition for this purpose.

C. Failing to Consistently Format

Each Component title must be treated the same way (e.g., underlined, capitalized, and/or italicized). Further, each paragraph must be indented the same amount of spaces, and paragraphs must uniformly follow the same spacing routine. For better or for worse, sloppy formatting is interpreted as indicative of sloppy reasoning.

IV. Conclusion

As has been consistently stressed by this Book, the goal of Legal Writing is generating credibility—through proper grammar, correct citation, and, overall, valuable analysis. Of course, all of these worthy aims lose their "punch" if residing within an ineffective structure. It can be thus said that all Legal Writing seeks to offer new thoughts in an old frame. That old frame has withstood the test of time and still has much to showcase. Treat it well and throughout your career, it will glamorously display your insights and hard work.

To conclude this Chapter, try your hand at completing a short Office Memo (i.e., less than three pages). Remember to follow the Formula, keep present case facts and names out of the Rule, keep the respective Formula parts true to their purposes, strictly align Rule with Rule Application, and keep formatting consistent.

Exercise Two: Writing a Strong Office Memo

Hypothetical Facts:

In early 2016, the Indoor Football League suspended a star player nicknamed "Touchdown Thomas" for 6 games (without pay) based upon his screaming obscenities during a nationally televised press conference. Thomas protested, and—pursuant to the League's Collective Bargaining Contract ("CBC")—an arbitration was held at League headquarters in New York. The sole arbitrator upheld the suspension, issuing a statement reading as follows:

> I care little for the dictates of the CBC. This case is governed by common sense. An IFL player deserves discipline when he embarrasses the League on a national basis. The degree of that penalty is solely up to the league or the arbitrator.

The CBC suggests limiting suspensions for off-field behavior to 3 games. In the written decision, the arbitrator, while acknowledging that the CBC was the "law" for purposes of the arbitration, opined that its limitations on types and degrees of penalties were "for advisory purposes only."

Your firm has been retained to lodge an appeal under the doctrine of "manifest disregard of the law" ("MDOL"). That doctrine has been interpreted in the Second Circuit as synonymous with § 10(a)(4) of the Federal Arbitration Act (as is described below). You are to write the Memo predicting the likelihood of Thomas getting the IFL decision vacated by a court in the Southern District of New York. Note that Thomas is 35 years old, and may not have many more full seasons ahead of him. As Mark Twain once commented, "We chase phantoms half the days of our lives. It is well if we learn wisdom even then, and save the other half."

Background Materials:

1. Federal Arbitration Act ("FAA"), 9 U.S.C. § 10(a)(4) (2012) (providing a basis for vacatur by a federal court where the arbitrator has "exceeded his authority");

2. Hall Street Associates, L.L.C. v. Mattel, Inc., 548 F.3d 85 (2d Cir. 2008) (stating that MDOL is simply "judicial gloss" for FAA § 10(a)(4));

3. Stolt-Nielsen S.A. v. AnimalFeeds Int'l Corp., 130 S. Ct. 1758 (2010) (casting uncertainty on the continued use of MDOL); and

4. Goldman Sachs Execution & Clearing, L.P. v. Unsecured Creditors' Comm. of Bayou Group, 758 F. Supp. 2d 222 (S.D.N.Y. 2010) (finding that MDOL "survived" as a basis for vacatur in the Second Circuit despite any confusion caused by the Hall Associates case. To successfully assert the doctrine as a means of vacating an arbitration award, the petitioner must demonstrate 1) that there was a clearly applicable standard, and 2) that it was intentionally ignored by the arbitrator).

Components to Include:

Issue(s), Brief Answer, Discussion, and Long Form Conclusion.

Note that there are several means of analyzing the arbitrator's determination. Be sure to offer a clear prediction that ultimately addresses all Legal and Policy considerations.

Chapter VIII

What Readers May Really Want: The E-Memo

Chapter Objectives:
- Converting the Office Memo into an E-Memo
- Modifying Content for a New Audience (While Avoiding Excessive Informality)
- Drafting an Informative Subject Line
- Including Sufficient Language Protecting Confidentiality and Privilege

Substantive Takeaways:
- Introduction to Attorney Work Product Privilege
- FDA Regulations Covering "E-Cigarettes"
- State Common Law Governing the "Right of Publicity"

I. Introduction

The most recent technological revolution has naturally spread to law schools and law firms. Legal Readers now often desire the same ease of use and portability that accompanies all other aspects of their life. Consequentially, the obsolescence of some Legal Writing assignments is often bemoaned by practicing lawyers and other law school alumni. Specifically, the contemporary, fast-paced environment is described by the modern practitioner as requiring a more succinct form of communication than the Office Memo. Thus the E-Memo, formerly a luxury of high tech offices, has become a commonly preferred means of communicating research within the legal business.

Further, an E-Memo is thought to offer the simultaneous advantages of confidentiality and ease of storage. Arguably, a legal staff adept at communicating the result of its analysis offers the legal employer lower costs per document, as well as the discretion to design a remote law practice. Additionally, the E-Memo—notoriously short in length—provides for quicker, more intimate responses to client concerns, while affording the expedient ability to deliver underlying documents as attachments.

As has been the case since Pandora's famed box, there are concurrent disadvantages to this apparent cure-all. This Chapter shall both explore the variations on the new legal art form and provide the Legal Writer with a list of checkpoints to review prior to hitting "Send."

II. The Moving Parts

Of course, as a means of expediting communication, a traditional Office Memo can be readily attached to an e-mail or text. But such attempts may be hindered by technological snafus such as incompatible computer systems and outdated conversion software. Research results and attendant predictions can be more predictably shared within the body of an e-mail itself, affording greater likelihood of confidentiality and ease of use at once. While there is no textbook E-Memo format, such communications lend themselves to a short list of commonalities, five of which are discussed below.

A. The Subject Line

Imagine you work in a law office. You and others in the "intern pool" are assigned research on whether client Chadley Johnson may sue his bankrupt former employer for his pension under the ERISA statute. Consider your supervisor's reaction to receiving e-mails with the following subject lines:

- "Call me on the Johnson research"
- "Bad news for Johnson"
- "Follow-up to our talk yesterday"
- "ERISA claims against former employers; client Chadley Johnson"

The first three of the above examples would all disappoint your supervisor. The first example gives no indication of the research's results (and simply creates more work for the Reader in the form of a telephone call). The second example conveys an inappropriately lighthearted tone; moreover, such confessing commentary would be disastrous if the work product were later deemed not privileged. The third example is so vague that it could have been penned by anyone from the firm's senior partner to the building's manager.

The last example (i.e., "ERISA claims ...") exhibits the most professionalism. A topic of law is identified, as well as a category of claimants (i.e., former employees). The additional, specific reference to the client at once jogs the Reader's memory and goes a long way towards establishing the work product privilege.

The lesson is simple: Time and care must be expended in titling research communicated by e-mail. Loss of privilege and/or confidentiality create consequences to the firm, the client, and your reputation. More importantly, your e-mail's title rests all day on your supervisor's screen, potentially serving as a harrowing reminder of your inattention to detail. Thus, for the sake of the case and your credibility, become conversant with the jurisdiction's demands for a successful assertion of work product privilege.[1] Further, your titling of the e-mail should be your last step in the process, so as to align the subject matter with its terse description. Finally, consider adding "CONFIDENTIAL" to the title line, a suggestion that may become repetitive in this Chapter that is nonetheless important.

B. The Greeting

Like the subject line, the opening words of an E-Memo are not subject to completely individualized interpretation. Consider the following opening lines, all received at one time or another in my years as an intern coordinator:

- How ya' doin'?
- Hi Scott
- Felicitations!

Such greetings set the wrong tone and connote a less than diligent effort. To make things at once simple and more professional, adopt a uniform standard e-greeting: "Dear Mr./Mrs. X." Such an abundance of formality ensures that your E-Memo will never cast doubt about your very best efforts.

Those best efforts can likewise be undermined by a communication that is carelessly addressed and sent. Many are the tales of e-mails sent to too large an

---

1. For example, in Illinois, an attorney work product privilege is established when the attorney prepares material that, if discoverable, would disclose the "theories, mental impressions, or litigation plans" of the attorney. *Fischel & Kahn, Ltd. v. van Straaten Gallery, Inc.,* 189 Ill. 2d 579, 591 (Sup. Ct. Ill. 2000).

audience (by mindlessly pushing the "Reply All" button) or to the wrong party (via address book mis-entries). Computer errors happen. To ensure you have adequately minimized the consequences of such an error, consider adding of the following standard phrases to your greeting line:

- "This is a confidential e-mail"
- "E-Mail Intended Solely for Use by X"
- "To be read only by the Addressee"

Such additions do pose the risk of your gaining a reputation for an abundance of caution, but such may be the best reputation to garner at a new place of legal employment.

C. The Discussion

The Discussion section replicates the Formula (described at length in Chapters I–V), providing both structure and meaning to the Office Memo. The key difference is the tone, which seeks to serve the Reader's overriding goal of immediacy.

Thus, the E-Memo essentially becomes the Formula adapted for a broader audience. That audience is normally comprised of either a supervisor, or the client himself. Witness the conversion process demonstrated by the two passages below, the second one intended for receipt by the client:

OFFICE MEMO VERSION:

> Under section 10 of the Federal Arbitration Act, there are four bases for a federal court to reverse an arbitration decision. The courts will act to upset the award if the arbitrators 1) engaged in corruption or fraud, 2) evidenced partiality, 3) engaged in misconduct by refusing to postpone the hearing or hear material evidence, or 4) exceeded their authority.

> In the instant case, Johnson will likely be able to overturn the arbitration decision against him. While both parties acknowledged in their briefs that subsections "1" and "2" are not in dispute, the arbitrators refused a reasonable request to postpone the arbitration by three days to accommodate Johnson's request to attend a close relative's funeral.

> Further, regarding element "4," the chair of the arbitration panel was quoted on the record as saying "Today, I am the law." Such statement clearly indicates authority being exceeded. Since

two of the four statutory bases for reversal are present, Johnson is likely to have the arbitral decision upset on appeal.

E-MEMO VERSION *(for the Client):*

There is a federal statute that allows parties who lose an arbitration to appeal to a federal court. The reasons for such appeal range from outright fraud (such as when an arbitrator has been bribed) to where the arbitrators refuse requests to postpone a hearing. Another basis for appeal occurs when arbitrators appear to ignore all rules governing their behavior (a situation closer to your case). Arbitrators who create their own standards in such fashion are said to have "exceeded their authority."

In your case, as the Record plainly shows, some unfortunate comments were made by the arbitrators. These comments were often made in direct response to your request for reasonable accommodations. Further, your request for an adjournment was denied, without much discussion. This hasty decision seems unreasonable, as the request was for a brief recess, and the death in your family was surely cause for a break.

Overall, for at least two reasons, it appears that you have valid grounds for an appeal to change the outcome. I will be in touch within the week. At that time, please let me know how you wish to proceed.

Note that the "Legal tenor" of the Office Memo yields to the practicalities of the E-Memo. Words such as "evident partiality" and "reversal" have been replaced by, respectively, "unfortunate comments" and "change the outcome."

In the next example, written for a supervisor, some authority has been added (the boss might require more assurance of your position). Still, the Discussion prioritizes immediacy and the E-Memo avoids polite chatter:

E-MEMO VERSION: *For the supervisor*

The Federal Arbitration Act allows aggrieved parties to appeal to a federal court (Sections 10(a)(1–4)). The reasons for such appeal range from outright fraud/bribery to where the arbitrators refuse requests to postpone a hearing. The most relevant basis reverses arbitrators who create their own standards (i.e., "exceeded their authority").

In the client's case, some ill-advised comments were made by the arbitrators (see attached transcript, pp. 145–149). These comments may reveal a predetermined intent to disregard the law (most of the Circuit's case law reversing arbitration decisions finds such questionable statements to be "mistakes"). Further, a request for an adjournment due to a family member's death was denied, without much discussion. Thus, for at least two reasons (re. 10(a)(3) and (4)), it appears that we have valid grounds for an appeal. I've asked the client for direction; his deadline is Friday.

Note the flexibilities, in both text and cites. Note also that, in both of the above examples, the E-Memo concludes with a clear delineation of the next step: The Legal Writer has requested of the client an answer by a date certain (i.e., if the client wishes to continue the litigation). This specifying of the next step is itself a vital consideration in preparing the E-Memo, as discussed below.

D. The Call for Action

The request for follow-up by the Reader (or client) is a basic requirement often overlooked by Legal Writers. Such request should be taken seriously and made as concrete as possible. The outlining of future conversations or actions communicates that the law firm shall not work again on this case until so notified (a proactive move to avoid billing disputes). Such outlining also brings finality to the questions at hand (a necessary move to lock in the firm's best advice as of the date of the E-Mail).

This weighty requirement can encompass much more than a request for further contact. The E-Memo—like the Office Memo—attempts the best Legal analysis based upon presently known facts. Examine the differences between the two examples below, both concluding an E-Memo to a (hypothetical) client evaluating whether the FDA's regulation of "E-Cigarettes" and related nicotine products will damage his "vape shop"[2] business:

WEAK:

> In conclusion, the FDA rule targets "tobacco products" but not accessories. The regulation becomes effective two years after finalization of the rule. The measure also empowers the FDA to set a minimum age, require health warnings, and prohibit vending machine sales. Once you have reviewed this E-Memo, please give me a call.

---

2. It is estimated that there are over 10,000 "vape shops" in the country, and approximately 1,000 suppliers of "vaping" equipment. Laurie Tarkan, *How new rules could kill the vaping boom*, FORTUNE (Sept. 29, 2015), *available at* http://fortune.com/2015/09/29/vaping-fda-rules/.

BETTER:

> In conclusion, the FDA rule targets "tobacco products" but not accessories. The regulation becomes effective two years after finalization of the rule (which occurred in May 2016). The measure empowers the FDA to set a minimum age for the user, require health warnings by the manufacturer, and prohibit vending machine sales (with oversight running to several parties).
>
> In our conversations to date, you have indicated that you did not know the ages of the E-Cig users within your establishment. As you can see, the FDA regulation extends to various responsibilities and parties. I urge you to carefully review this E-Memo, and then give me a call no later than June 5th so that we can discuss the regulation's relevance to your business more fully.

To be sure, the first example satisfies the need to "place the ball in the court" of the Reader. However, the second example serves this purpose and others. First, it informs the client that he needs to share more facts for a fuller analysis. Second, it clarifies for the benefit of future third parties that final legal advice has not been rendered. In short, the second example better summarizes the present state of the attorney-client relationship. Heightened clarity in all forms of Legal Writing is cherished.

E. The Preservation of Confidentiality

Even when prepared with the utmost seriousness and care, e-mails are too often lost, crashed, and misdirected. Accordingly, they pose a danger to client and firm confidentiality. Professionals and clients alike accept that mistakes and accidents happen; nobody accepts the professional's failure to anticipate imperfection.

The best confidentiality agreements serve a very short and easily discernible list of goals, as detailed below:

(i) Advise the recipient that the subject matter is confidential;

(ii) Warn that legal action may be taken against reckless or intentional re-communication of the subject matter; and

(iii) Provide a name and telephone number for someone who can be contacted to report the misdirection of the subject matter. Add a date/time for such remedial communications.

There is no universal language to establish and protect confidentiality. Indeed, some Legal Writers utilize the confidentiality disclaimer as a means of lightening the mood. Meanwhile, some law firms grasp an opportunity to publicize the firm name, or to impress third parties with their professionalism (or snazzy logo). But all successful variations do tend to satisfy the three goals exhibited above. Some suggested language appears below:

- "The sender of this e-communication is a ..."
- "This communication includes privileged and confidential data ..."
- "Intended for the sole use of ..."
- "If received in error ..."

It has been said that a "classic" is a book everyone owns and nobody reads. Well, lawyers always read the boilerplate, but not everybody knows how to create it. Before continuing in this Chapter, try your hand at styling your own confidentiality boilerplate in the Exercise below.

Exercise One: Perfect the Boilerplate

Correct the following draft confidentiality clause, inserting full sentences to complete budding thoughts where necessary. Remember to keep language sufficiently formal, expect routing error, and provide a date and time for remedy.

THIS E-MAIL IS PRIVILEGED. END OF STORY. IF YOU'VE RECEIVED IT AND YOU'RE NOT THE RECIPIENT, DESTROY IT. THERE ARE LEGAL CONSEQUENCES FOR YOUR INACTION. THIS IS A LAW FIRM AND WE TAKE THESE MATTERS QUITE SERIOUSLY. GOVERN YOUR ACTIONS ACCORDINGLY. HAVE A NICE DAY.

III. The Pitfalls

To be sure, there are drawbacks to the creation of E-Memos. Four chief arguments against their usage are explained below:

• First, E-Memo retention may be cumbersome. Most workplaces adhere to a strict e-mail retention policy (e.g., one year in an active mailbox; subsequently stored in archive folders). Employees are sometimes oblivious to these policies, even where such are clearly communicated.

• Second, the Legal Writer's depth of research (and sincerity of sentiments) may be misconstrued. Read the passage below, and then attempt to answer the question of whether the Legal Writer conducted a targeted review of relevant case law, or simply read a few Blog postings:

It seems there's a Florida case finding for the petitioner (as the Eleventh Circuit cases often do). Whether or not a present case will follow this precedent is highly speculative. Further, the attention garnered by the Supreme Court's granting cert just last week over a different kind of business issue casts doubt on appeals of this type.

• Third, E-Memos can seem to promote uninformed legal opinions. Citation may pester all of us to one degree or another, but the strict requirement of its presence does ensure a diligent survey of current law.

• Finally, formats (and thus expectations) vary greatly. One man's E-Memo is another's glimpse at research before going to lunch.

For all of these reasons, some workplaces simply demand that all formal Legal research be communicated in either hard copy format or as an attachment to an e-mail or text (or via link to an e-repository). However, when E-Memos are requested (in law school or place of employment) remember the dual goals of exhibiting a flexible tone and adhering to confidentiality-driven formalities.

IV. Conclusion

Whenever I teach 1L students the attributes of the budding art form known as the E-Memo, it is with a great deal of trepidation. Foremost among my concerns is what new development shall supplant e-mail. It does not require a great stretch of imagination to predict that in the near future some Legal Writer shall be explaining, "Oh, the 'X Memo'? That's like the E-Memo, just not as formal."

Further, there is the very real concern of theft. It would seem that if a firm's recordkeeping system has been hacked twice, its employees may be waiving privilege or confidentiality by continuing to use it.

Regardless, alumni and legal employers are asking whether law school graduates can write E-Memos. Accordingly, if the art form has taken root and is required by your employer, strive to follow these dictates:

- Provide for a meaningful title/subject line,
- Commence the E-Memo in a manner that conveys respect and an ongoing concern for confidentiality,
- Communicate meaningful analysis in a more concise style (accompanied by little or no legal citation),
- Keep the tone consistent but perhaps less formal,

- Include a meaningful "call for action" by the Reader, and
- Formally preserve confidentiality through boilerplate.

To put these varied goals to practice, try the Exercise below. The problem centers on varying State approaches to the "right of publicity," a protection described in Chapter V that is owned by us all, but mostly enforced by celebrities.

Exercise Two: Write an E-Memo

Based upon the instructions and research appearing below, prepare an E-Memo addressed to a law firm partner. Your prediction itself is inconsequential, as long as the analysis remains consistent and is consistently supported. Cases should be referenced, but not cited; additionally paraphrase (and do not simply copy) the provided parenthetical explanations. Remember, inter alia, to maintain a professional tone, and to repeatedly account for confidentiality.

Instructions

TO: First Year Associate
FROM: J. Scottsantis, Litigation Partner
DATE: January 29, 2016
RE: The Lapp City Council, New Innovations, Inc., and
               Darlene Drudgins

Pop music star Darlene Drudgins (also known as "Debra Danger") has sought advice on her rights. In sum, for months the Lapp City Council has been operating a "Rock and Roll Pavilion," in New York's famed City Park. The entrance to the Pavilion features a 90-second holographic movie that resembles Danger and her vocal stylings. The Pavilion, which features a modest amount of licensed photos and donated memorabilia, charges public patrons a $15 admittance fee and has been a huge success.

Danger believes that the appearance, mannerisms and stylings of the anonymous female singer portrayed in the movie clearly identify her. Since she was never contacted for her consent, Danger is suing to halt the display of the movie and for compensation for the use of her image. Danger possibly alleges a violation of her right to publicity. She does not wish to cause ill will by threatening legal action against the City, so any lawsuit would be filed solely against the production company. That company, New Innovations, Inc., is headquartered in New York and conducts business in both New York and California.

This is apparently a case of first impression for the State of New York. While the State is home to numerous celebrities, apparently the question of whether displaying a moving, 3-dimensional image depicting the performance style of a living public figure requires the consent of the party depicted has not been addressed. As I recall, the States have varying views on the right of publicity (it is all laid out in several famous cases I have seen in the last 10 years).

In New York, as I recall it, all relevant rights are statutory and can be traced to the legislative response to the 1902 case involving a flour package. Those rights are limited and often deemed secondary to the rights of the press. There is that famous case of the mid-'80s wherein a male model in a bomber jacket sued the publisher for unauthorized use of his picture, and he lost. And of course the famous football player sued *Sports Illustrated* and lost when they ran his picture in advertisements without obtaining his consent (the court called the use of his picture "coincidental advertising," or something to that effect).

Conversely, California acknowledges an expansive "right to publicity," which affords the depicted party more protections (statutory and otherwise). The statute itself provides for both a statutory and common law claim. Moreover, the press sometimes loses the First Amendment battle. There was some case from the 1980s where a pop singer won a case against the truck company that refused to meet her price for a jingle and then resorted to using a sound-alike. And there was a surprising victory for a game show co-host who said a robot in a commercial was dressed like her. In sum, California seems to want to protect its celebrities from exploitation, even if that unauthorized use does not go so far as to borrow someone's name, picture, portrait or voice.

Please review the authorities and prepare an E-Memo of no more than 300 words in length. The E-Memo should include a title line, greeting, and analysis (labeled "Discussion"). Please address the E-Memo to me; if need be, I will adapt it and send it to the client.

Research

(i)   N.Y. Civ. Rights Law §§ 50–51 (McKinney 2008) (collectively protecting the plaintiff's "name, picture, or portrait" and/or voice);

(ii)   *Roberson v. Rochester Folding Box Co.*, 171 N.Y. 538 (N.Y. 1902) (finding the unauthorized use of a picture of a stranger on a box cover to not violate her right of privacy);

(iii) *Stephano v. News Group Publ'ns,* 64 N.Y.2d 174 (N.Y. Sup. Ct. 1984) (finding the model's consent to one photo to justify continued use by the magazine);

(iv) *Namath v. Sports Illustrated,* 80 Misc. 2d 531 (Sup. Ct. N.Y. 1975) (holding that a photograph of the New York Jets star quarterback, initially publishable without the subject's consent as news, could lawfully be re-published by the weekly magazine as "incidental advertising");

(v) Cal. Civ. Code § 3344(a) (West 2012) (protecting, among other things, "likeness in any manner");

(vi) *Midler v. Ford Motor Co.,* 849 F.2d 460 (9th Cir. 1988) (finding a common law claim for singer Bette Midler based upon the defendant's use of a sound-alike for a jingle);

(vii) *White v. Samsung Elecs. Am., Inc.,* 971 F.2d 1395 (9th Cir. 1992) (finding a common law violation where a commercial advertisement placed a faceless robot in the same attire and game show context of the plaintiff, Vanna White).

Chapter IX

Into the Fray:
The Trial Motion

Chapter Objectives:
- Learning to Draft Effective Point Headings and Subheadings
- Appreciating the Formal Structure Attending a Court Document
- Distinguishing the Trial Motion from the Office Memo
- Arranging Presentation Within a Sentence for Maximum Persuasive Effect
- Applying Nuanced Skills of Persuasion to Various Documents

Substantive Takeaways:
- The Debate Over Unlicensed Taxicab Service
- "Remote Tippees" and Insider Trading Liability
- Voiding Debtor "Preferences" Under the Bankruptcy Code
- "Fracking" Regulation by the States

I. The Trial Motion

The Trial Motion requires a much more structured and label-intensive format than the Office Memorandum. In short, a module is dictated by the profession, and the Writer learns to use the module to showcase the strengths of his/her case. The creation of this "court document" entails a high degree of care. Whereas internal documents such as the Office Memo and E-Memo will be read by allies, a Trial Motion[1] is read by the court and your adversary. Sim-

---

1. The term "Trial Motion" is used in this book in the broadest sense, connoting a memoranda of law served before, during or after trial in hopes of securing a full or partial rul-

ply put, it is a public document. It is therefore even more imperative that, in substance and form, the document adhere to universal standards and reflect precise planning.

The Trial Motion is the most basic of researched court pleadings. The Writer seeks to convince the court that specific relief is appropriate in view of the present law and the dispute's facts. It normally numbers less than 20 pages but requires a host of new formalities.

A. Issue(s) Presented

The proper drafting of Issues was discussed in Chapter VII. In sum, Legal Writers should identify a position within a sole question that balances Facts and law. Within a Trial Motion, the positioning of the Facts and law are significant. Here is a phrase you shall hear throughout law school: When attempting to persuade, proceed "strong-weak-strong." The adage is also sometimes conveyed as "start strong and end strong." The strategy is true of panel presentations, oral arguments, and Legal Writing—perhaps nowhere more true than in the targeted weapon of a Trial Motion.

Witness the comparative effects of the two Issues stated below, both utilizing the same Fact pattern, and both centering on a Circuit split on the requirements of insider trading by a remote "tippee" of nonpublic information:

PROSECUTION EXAMPLE:

> Whether, per the decision in *Newman v. United States*, a defendant who learned of confidential information that had originated in an investment banking department engaged in securities fraud as prohibited by Section 10(b) of the Securities Exchange Act of 1934 and S.E.C. Rule 10b-5 promulgated thereunder.

DEFENSE EXAMPLE:

> Whether, a fourth generation tippee of allegedly inside information violates S.E.C. Rule 10b-5, per the Second Circuit decision in *Newman v. United States*, when he learns of the information from an acquaintance who suggests that many other parties have already traded upon the information.

The first example "wraps itself in the American flag," as the saying goes. To wit, the facts are bookended by the official words of an appellate court and the

---

ing for the client. Some examples are motions to exclude evidence, for dismissal, and for summary judgment.

U.S. Congress. The words that echo in the Reader's ears speak of authority and a mandate to protect investors.

Conversely, the second example stresses the defendant's plight, details of which bookend a trimmed down reference to that government mandate. The words that echo suggest that the defendant is an everyman, and that the prosecutor may have over-reached.

In sum, recognize that Issues do provide the leeway to commence persuasion, an opportunity that grows within the ensuing "Statement of Facts" section.

B. Statement of Facts ("Statement")

In general, the Statement of Facts within a Trial Motion follows the same guidance for Statements within other Legal Writing documents. That guidance is offered in Chapter III.

Additionally, the "strong-weak-strong" guidance applies within a Statement. Consider the following concluding sentences, which expand upon the insider trading hypothetical above:

PROSECUTION EXAMPLE:

> … In sum, the defendant was subpoenaed for information on his conversations with insiders at a public company. When specifically questioned about his after-hours trading in the subject stocks, the defendant exercised his Fifth Amendment privilege from self-incrimination. The defendant was thus charged and surrendered to authorities on December 12th. This hearing followed.

DEFENSE EXAMPLE:

> … In sum, having fully cooperated with all government requests for testimony, Mr. Jones was nonetheless charged with a sole violation alleging his receipt of non-public information. The charging instrument includes no details that would educate when or how he engaged in insider trading. He thus makes this Motion to Dismiss.

Apart from the selected names for the accused, the difference in effect is attributable solely to the "ending note" of the Facts, again emphasizing the importance of the positioning of Facts.

C. Summary of Argument

The Summary of Argument is free of citations ("This is my time!" as one of my students described it). It also poses new structural concerns, as it simply requires a layman's translation of an existing argument. Witness the conversion process below, which focuses on the debate over the illegality of unregistered taxicab drivers:

ARGUMENT:

> BECAUSE MOBILE, INC. EMPLOYS UNREGISTERED DRIVERS, THE COMPANY IS IN VIOLATION OF VEHICLE & TRAFFIC LAW SECTION 112-49.

SUMMARY:

> For centuries, livery companies (i.e., taxicab companies) have been legally compelled to register with the government. In very recent years, a handful of enterprises have attempted to circumvent registration requirements under claims that they operate as "transportation network companies." The court must not be taken in by these misleading semantics, for both legal and policy reasons. The State statute clearly contemplates coverage of all vehicles providing public transportation. One could argue that Mobile, Inc. (and other similar enterprises) are meeting a need for services, but the data do not support altering the legislative scheme in the presence of hundreds of licensed taxicabs.

Note that the Summary addresses, in turn, the facts, and the Legal and Policy arguments. It even includes the counter-analysis, perhaps lessening that contrary argument's sting when it appears in full a few pages hence.

D. Argument

An "argument" within Legal Writing is made possible by two conventions. These conventions are discussed in sequence below.

1. The Point Heading

The Argument commences with a one-sentence conclusion. That conclusion is phrased as a "Point Heading," which is supported by two or more "Subheadings." The Point Heading is the focal point of litigation documents such as the Trial Motion and the Appellate Brief. It is an affirmative sentence requesting ultimate relief. It ultimately serves as the subjective statement of your argument. It is normally single-spaced and typed in all capital letters to connote its significance; it is the conclusion wished upon the reader which all other parts of the document support.

The Point Heading is thus the central assertion of the Motion. Below are listed the major attributes of this key structure:

(i) The Point Heading is a Mixture of Law and Fact

Successful Point Headings effectively combine detailed law and fact. Just as in the creation of the "Issue," the goal is to reveal the identifying elements of the case. A general "WE SHOULD WIN" Point Heading lacks persuasion and, more importantly, signals a lack of effort on the part of the Legal Writer.

Below are two examples of Point Headings, each attempting to convey the argument that, under Pennsylvania common law, the owner of a small corporation should not be subject to personal liability for a corporate debt (a.k.a. "piercing the corporate veil"):

WEAK:

> BECAUSE IT CANNOT BE SHOWN THAT FRAUD WAS PER-PETRATED, THE PETITION MUST BE DISMISSED.

BETTER:

> BECAUSE IT CANNOT BE SHOWN THAT THE MULTIPLE-OWNER, CORPORATE FORM OF SINGULAR SENSATIONS, LLC WAS USED TO "PERPETRATE FRAUD" AS EXPLAINED IN THE *LUMAX INDUSTRIES* DECISION, THE PETITION MUST BE DISMISSED.

Note that the second passage does more than just convey details. To wit, it identifies the standard as well as the reason the Writer believes that relief will ultimately be deemed unnecessary. Perhaps equally important, the second passage provides a self-contained heading that fits well into a Table of Contents, an explanatory tool that serves as an Argument's summary in varied forms of court documents (the importance of the Table of Contents as an immediate presentation of Argument becomes readily apparent to skilled Legal Writers).

(ii) The Point Heading States an Independent Basis for Relief

In sum, the Point Heading states a proposition that, if agreed with, provides the totality of the remedy desired by your client. Further, the specific relief requested is described. Some examples appear below:

> BECAUSE MR. JOHNSON'S ARTWORK SATISFIES THE TRANS-FORMATIVE TEST, HE CANNOT BE HELD LIABLE FOR COPY-RIGHT INFRINGEMENT, AND THE COMPLAINT MUST BE DISMISSED.

> THE DEFENDANT'S TEXT MESSAGES QUALIFY AS WIRE COM-MUNICATIONS FOR PURPOSES OF A WIRE FRAUD CONVICTION AS DEFINED BY SECTION 1343 OF THE UNITED STATES CODE.

Whereas the Legal Writer delays revelation of the conclusion in the "Discussion" section of an Office Memo, the Writer would trumpet it via a Point Heading in a Trial Motion. The significance of this assertion thus calls for a set of rigid formalities, as is described below.

(iii) The Point Heading Needs to be Stated in a
Sole Sentence, Concluded by a Period

There simply are no two-sentence Point Headings. Further, as is the case with a statement of an "issue," a good limit to length is four lines. Witness the two examples below, which vary the unlicensed taxi debate introduced above:

WEAK:

> BECAUSE THE JONES LIVERY COMPANY EMPLOYS DRIVERS NOT ADEQUATELY REGISTERED WITH THE STATE, IT IS IN VIOLATION. THE RELEVANT STATE STATUTE IS CONNECTICUT'S UNFAIR TRADE AND PRACTICES ACT, WHICH PROHIBITS ACTS THAT ARE "IMMORAL, UNETHICAL, OR OPPRESSIVE" AND THUS THE COMPANY SHOULD BE FINED.

BETTER:

> THE DEFENDANT'S EMPLOYMENT OF UNREGISTERED TAXICAB DRIVERS CONSTITUTES AN "IMMORAL. UNETHICAL AND/OR OPPRESSIVE" ACT UNDER CONNECTICUT'S UNFAIR TRADE PRACTICES ACT, TRIGGERING LIABILITY.

The second example above at once adheres to the one-sentence rule and reveals a fact pattern that violates the relevant statute. Moreover, the tighter passage is easier on the eyes and, as will be seen later in this Chapter, ends by ringing "words of authority" in the Reader's ears.

(iv) Subheadings Support the Point Heading

Subheadings follow nearly all of the formatting rules for Point Headings. These art forms are contained in a single sentence written in declarative fashion. They are distinguished from Point Headings in that, while the latter state a claim for relief, the Subheading states a premise that helps to support the Point Heading.

For example, below are detailed three Subheadings in support of a Point Heading seeking relief for a defendant under the above-referenced Wire Fraud Act:

BECAUSE MR. MILES CANNOT BE SHOWN TO HAVE ENGAGED
IN A SCHEME AS DEFINED BY THE <u>MAXWELL</u> CASE, THE IN-
DICTMENT AGAINST HIM MUST BE DISMISSED.

A. *In the D.C. Circuit, the <u>Maxwell</u> case educates that a defendant must
    be shown to have both engaged in a scheme and used the wires to fur-
    ther it.*

B. *Other Circuits have utilized the <u>Maxwell</u> test to set a clear standard
    governing prosecutions.*

C. *Mr. Miles did not engage in a "scheme," and also did not undertake
    any violative wire communications.*

Collectively, the Point Heading and the Subheadings serve as the focus of the
structured outline (discussed in detail below). Before proceeding with the
Chapter, practice the guidance offered thus far by completing the drafting Exercise below. It centers on voidable preferences under Bankruptcy Law, a favorite topic for law students craving "black-and-white" rules.

Exercise One: Drafting Point Headings

Section 547 of the Bankruptcy Code reclaims for the Trustee's coffer of assets most conveyances made within 90 days of the filing of a bankruptcy petition (the period is lengthened to one year for transfers to "insiders"). In the
hypothetical below, fashion sole-sentence Point Headings based upon the Facts
provided. Create one Point Heading for the bankruptcy trustee seeking to
"avoid the transfer," and an opposing Point Heading for the third party creditor seeking to maintain the transfer (i.e., keep the money).

FACTS:

To generate goodwill, the debtor, Wildlife Farms, paid its chief supplier
110% of its outstanding debt 85 days before filing its bankruptcy petition.

NOTES:

Courts generally exempt routine creditors from classification as "insiders,"
defined as including relatives, partners, and corporate officers.

The check to Wildlife Farms was actually authorized 105 days before its
delivery.

Once familiar with Point Headings and Subheadings, a formatting question predominates. There is little room for creativity here, as the "formal outline" dictates the placement and style of these pivotal structural marks.

2. The Formal Outline

The second convention serving to shape the delivery of an argument within a Trial Motion is the Formal Outline. This structure is characterized by strict adherence to rigid rules of formatting. These rules can be summarized by the following points of guidance

• Alternate between letters and numerals. If making a sole Argument, no letter/number is required; however, its subdivisions are still numbered as if that Argument had been numbered.

EXAMPLE: Two—Argument Motion

    I.   POINT HEADING

        A.   SUBHEADING

        B.   SUBHEADING

EXAMPLE: One—Argument Motion

    POINT HEADING

        A.   SUBHEADING

        B.   SUBHEADING

• If including a sub-division, there must be a companion (i.e., always divide into two, and never divide into one).

• Distinguish each set of subdivisions through indentation, and keep all attendant indents consistent.

• Maintain parallel structure in subdivision titles.

Headings and Subheadings are always phrased as single sentences. The question thus arises whether a *sub*-subdivision must also be a complete sentence. It is doubtful that many practitioners would endorse that level of inflexibility. Among other considerations, a sub-subheading (by necessity, thrice-indented) would defeat its primary purpose of clarification if extending onto a second or third line. It is thus suggested that sub-subheadings (and further subdivisions) simply remain consistent in structure.

EXAMPLE:

    (i)   Because the plaintiff could not prove his possession was notorious, open, or hostile, he fails at asserting adverse possession.

        1.   No "notorious" possession

        2.   No "open" possession

        3.   No "hostile" possession

These three bits of guidance should help you assemble any possible string of Arguments. Hence, a Formal Outline converting the Discussion section of an Office Memo into a Trial Motion offering two Arguments could be outlined as follows:

ARGUMENT

   I. POINT HEADING

      A. SUBHEADING [RULE]

      B. SUBHEADING [ELABORATION]

      C. SUBHEADING [RULE APPLICATION]

         (i) SUB-SUBHEADING

         (ii) SUB-SUBHEADING

  II. POINT HEADING

      A. SUBHEADING [RULE]

      B. SUBHEADING [RULE APPLICATION]

This tight structure actually liberates the Legal Writer: It assures that the product conforms to industry standards, while allowing for the freedom to prioritize authorities, amplify assertions, and avoid pointless repetition of notions or assertions. As I like to tell my students, the formal outline is the holiday display upon which countless and varied baubles and ornaments may be strewn.

Before so strewing, practice creating the framework by completing the Exercise below, which centers on the legal debates attending extracurricular high school activities and qualifications for college.

Exercise Two: Outlining a Trial Motion

Imagine that a high school unilaterally changes the requirements for membership in its national honor society. A friend asks you to champion her cause. You write a letter to the school principal advising that the change is illegal, but the letter is not heeded. The friend now needs an emergency motion to halt implementation of the new service requirement (a requirement that would force her son out of the honor society, damaging his college applications). In less than one page, create an outline for your intended Trial Motion based upon the authorities and fact pattern appearing below.

FACTS

The national School Invitation Great Honor Society ("SIGHS") has a Constitution, Bylaws, and over 2,000 member high schools. New inductees are admitted each June, upon completion of their Sophomore year. One local high school, Tempest High, has altered the formula, deciding in December 2014 that existing members should have to also perform 200 hours of community service (such requirement was not communicated at induction in June 2014).

Amanda Fields, a family friend, is quite concerned. Her son, who was inducted in June 2014, simply does not have the time to fulfill the new community service requirement. Amanda fears that her son's college application will be found lacking if he is expelled from SIGHS.

LAW

The three relevant authorities (and their most vital excerpts) are as follows:

(i)   ***Maintaining standards*** *(Article 7, Section 1). Once selected and inducted, all members are expected to maintain the standards by which they were selected.*

—Article 7(a), SIGHS Constitution of 2012

(ii) *Congratulations! Based upon your exemplary grades and overall academic achievement, you have been selected for inclusion in SIGHS, a national honor society. In the upcoming year, you shall be expected to maintain these academic credentials in order to sustain membership in our SIGHS chapter.*

—SIGHS Invitation Letter to Jonathan Fields, June 2014

(iii) *As a member in good standing of SIGHS, the High School strictly adheres to all of that organization's rules and principles.*

—Tempest High School Handbook, October 2014

Finally, the "long form" Conclusion explained in Chapter VII is suggested as the ending section of the Trial Motion. When advocating on behalf of a client, the naked, "short form" Conclusion should be reserved solely for instances where the page limit is looming.

II. Additional, Optional Motion Components

Three extra Components sometimes appearing in Motions are addressed below:

A. The Statute Implicated

This section simply provides the reader, as a courtesy, with the cite (and, occasionally, the full text) of the statutory provision at the center of the dispute. An example appears below:

The parties in the current dispute assert the application of S.E.C. Rule 10b-5, 17 C.F.R. part 240 (West 2012). That Rule provides in relevant part that ...

While seemingly a harmless Component to add, the Component is of little utility where there are multiple authorities at issue, or where one party disputes application altogether (in which case the mere reference to the statute/rule actually lends credence to the opposing argument).

B. The Preliminary Statement

This pointed section seeks merely to include the procedural history of the case. It normally includes pleadings, dates, and court orders.

In its more advanced state, the Preliminary Statement involves a timeline, more details on court-related proceedings, and the respective positions of the parties. Witness the effectiveness of the example below, which indirectly communicates the argument that the prosecutor may have engaged in an abuse of process:

> The instant matter commenced with a Grand Jury indictment dated March 13, 2005. That Indictment was held in abeyance by this court while a superseding Indictment was prepared. In May 2006, a superseding Indictment was served upon the defendant; that Indictment was dismissed upon the motion of both parties in November of that year. In June 2008, a civil action was commenced by the plaintiff Securities and Exchange Commission based upon the facts alleged in the prior two criminal indictments. In June 2009, an Amended Complaint was filed.

Conversely, the government's Preliminary Statement would read as follows:

> The present action was commenced by a civil Complaint from 2008 based upon several years of investigation and pleadings.

C. The Tables

A Trial Motion may sometimes include a "Table of Authorities" (for all sources cited therein) and a "Table of Contents" (for all Components included therein). Most of the details of the Table can be automatically formatted by word processing programs available to law students and law firms alike. A quick checklist for effective Tables is included below:

(i)   Proofread for errors in citation and page numbers

(ii) Copy Point Headings and Subheadings exactly as they appear in the document itself. Indeed, judges and many Legal Readers first scan the Table of Contents for a survey of the Arguments being offered.

(iii) Number these pages with small Roman Numerals. Overall, the Tables should be limited to 3–4 pages.

III. Conclusion

Many students enjoy the more impassioned vocabulary attending the creation of documents of advocacy. The somewhat stultifying predictive language of "likely" or "unlikely" yields to the more demonstrative "should" or "must." A new company is "fledgling"; an unhelpful case is "misguided"; and an opposing position is "ill-advised."

But understand that, on the whole, these language choices are very minor considerations; indeed, I have often shown my students that, with very few alterations, an effective Office Memo can become an effective Trial Motion. The Trial Motion is actually a more decided Office Memo, with the predictive language strengthened, the conclusion appearing earlier, and a host of formalities added.

The true means of producing your best possible court document is through depth of analysis. In short, accord more effort and time to re-writing and re-organizing than to checking the Thesaurus. An actual legal fray may prove to be wildly unpredictable, but one consistency is that ostentatious word choice rarely decides the victor. To allay any lingering fears of this new type of document, a sample Trial Motion shell is attached as "Appendix E." To conclude the Chapter with such emphasis on organized diligence, try your hand at the Exercise below. It centers on the perplexing State debate over the legality of "fracking" (i.e., oil drilling though underground bombardment). Once again, the parties are fictitious, but the Legal authorities are genuine.

Exercise Three: Writing a Trial Motion

Background

Hydraulic fracturing (a.k.a. "fracking") enables natural gas extraction from underground areas bordered by shale formations. Conventional fracking involved the injection of water or chemicals; a more recent (and controversial) variation calls for the injection of diesel fluids.

Per the 2005 amendments to the federal Safe Water Drinking Act, fracking with diesel fluids is permitted, with a State license. A company named Hydrosoil Gas has lawfully fracked in Pennsylvania for a year, but has now commenced storing the requisite machinery and chemicals in New York, where fracking was recently outlawed.

POLICY FACTORS:

- The first fracking patent was issued in 1949.

- As of 2013, over two million oil and gas wells had been hydraulically fractured in the United States.

- Fracking with diesel fluids has been linked to water contamination and the deaths of livestock.

- In two of his State of the Union addresses, the President called for renewed interest in natural gas drilling as a means of combating dependency on foreign oil.

- Congress refused to outlaw diesel fracking in 2005.

- Over 20 states have delayed final rulemaking defining the grounds for a State diesel fracking license.

- Pennsylvania ranks in the top three states in terms of fracking revenue. The practice is said to employ over 500 Pennsylvania companies and, in turn, 7,000 employees.

- In 2014, the White House finalized measures that aim to ultimately curtail the underground injection of **diesel** during hydraulic fracturing.

- About 2% of all fracked wells involve the use of diesel.

- In November 2010, the New York State assembly voted 93 to 43 (30 abstentions) to place a moratorium or freeze on hydraulic fracturing to give the State more time to undertake safety and environmental concerns. In early 2015, the Governor banned all types of fracking in New York. No other State has gone as far as New York in this regard.

- In late 2015, the border city of Suffrenville, N.Y. passed an ordinance ("Order No. 1212") banning the storage of fracking-related chemicals and equipment within its territory.

- As a matter of Constitutional law, one State may not limit the commerce of another sovereign entity. *See, e.g., McCulloch v. Maryland,* 17 U.S. 316 (1819) (finding, inter alia, that a State may not "impede" lawful actions via taxation).

Instructions

Based upon the factors listed above, create a Trial Motion seeking an injunction against Suffrenville's ban. Offer a sole, Policy-based Argument. Be sure to include detailed sub-headings.

Suggested Point Heading

THE TOWN OF SUFFRENVILLE'S BAN ON FRACKING-RELATED STORAGE SHOULD NOT BE PERMITTED BECAUSE …

———————

Chapter X

The Law School Note: Having a Story to Tell (Instead of Having to Tell a Story)

Chapter Objectives:
- Identification of a Proper Note Topic
- Organization of a Note/Scholarly Piece
- Review of Fundamental and Universal Tools
- Employing Deepened Analysis

Substantive Takeaways:
- Online "Crowdfunding" as Capital Formation
- Executive Orders and Labor Law Disputes
- Elder Law and Related Penal Code Sections

I. Background

I am often approached by students wishing to be published by law school journals and thus requiring faculty supervision of the process. Further, many young attorneys enhance their careers by co-publishing scholarly articles with lawyers at their first employer, a noteworthy opportunity made possible only by prior experience in organizing ideas into a product comprised of lengthy legal commentary. Whenever I advise the student author on that first piece of legal scholarship, I urge adherence to a short checklist:

- Find your spark.
- Diligently learn the subject area.

- Follow a standard, industry outline
- Write until a solution comes to you.
- Follow your heart. And your outline.

Students normally object to such a form definite, parroting a list of questions such as:

Aren't I setting myself up as an expert?

Won't I be going out on a limb?

Will I get preempted along the way?

The answer to all of these questions is a resounding "Yes." You are most definitely defining yourself as an expert; if not, the Note is not worth reading (much less publishing). And you are most definitely risking opposition to your theme. But that is true of every piece of Legal Writing you shall ever produce.

The third question raises a specter that is equally disposed of but likely more tangible. All students encounter "preemption checks" by their journal editors, and some will face that ugly possibility that another law student in a distant locale has been pursuing the same research. It is the position of this book that all Note topics overlap a bit with existing research but are ultimately salvageable through adjustment of the working premise, a practice common to all scholarship that will be reinforced later in the Chapter.

All topics being fair game, and all Note authors being a tad egocentric, the process remains one of creativity, hard work, and persistence. In other words, find your spark, diligently learn your subject area, and write until a solution comes to you.

II. Finding the Spark

If Hollywood can posit that everyone has a screenplay inside, surely each member of the vastly educated ranks of law school can summon a meritorious notion. Often, a valid contribution comes from the most instinctive and basic of everyday questions. Why was the city council's ban on sugary drinks struck down by the appellate court? Why did the President say Congress is to blame for the immigration stalemate? What exactly is the process by which the Supreme Court grants certiorari?

Follow your hunches rather than conclude that valid Note ideas fall only on the lucky. Commonplace questions lead to learned solutions. Surely, after a year of varied and demanding law school courses, some thorny issues have clung to you. The challenge, therefore, lies not in finding worthy pursuits, but in linking them to areas of productive research.

Such a linking is done by lawyers and law firms every day. Clients inquiring about an IRS case are directed to the tax department. Relatives who have lost their driving licenses are put in touch with a criminal court litigator. A songwriter who seeks to know the effect of a Library of Congress copyright is forwarded to the firm's intellectual property guru.

Closely related is the law student's search for an area in which to ground a budding inquiry. The aforementioned city council ban on sugary drinks connotes administrative law (albeit on a localized level). The immigration debate—of this or any age—speaks to the legality of the President's executive order authority as defined by/hinted at in Article II of the Constitution. Even a question as amorphous as locating the legal authority for the Supreme Court's cert process is readily tied to a concrete source.[1] Indeed, with the "open courthouse" American common law system, it would be quite difficult to locate a topic that does *not* link with an area replete with both primary and secondary authority.

The quest for a successful Note next asks for a crystallized working premise. By the beginning of second year, students recognize that topics are like fireflies on an August night: Easy to surround but never quite sparkling when you want them to. That process of fine tuning your notion can only be effectuated by first becoming conversant with the accompanying body of law.

III. Diligently Learn the Subject Matter

Once comforted that you have a notion worth pursuing, a formal organizational outline serves as a prod for your own education on the topic. Someone once said that all popular films follow one of 36 plots. Further, experts on screenplays advise that every successful movie adheres to a pattern of acts, set off by three "plot points." Whether you agree with these blanket statements or not, the fact remains that there is a great deal of structure behind any lengthy work.

---

1. The quick Internet search of "Supreme Court cert procedures" yields the URL http:// www.uscourts.gov/about-federal-courts/educational-resources/about-educational-outreach/ activity-resources/supreme-1 ("The Supreme Court has its own set of rules ...").

And a Note represents your lengthiest Legal Writing to date. An outline is no longer a strong suggestion—it is the required starting point. The typical Note outline proceeds along the following five parts:

A. Introduction Section

The Introduction requires a working title that makes the Note stand apart. Selective editors truly enjoy a departure from classic rhetoric. I have titled my own pieces with inspiration from a song from a Broadway show, a quote from Mark Twain, and a country western movie. Such unconventional titles provide an allure to your Note that is difficult to quantify (and best left to your journal editor to fully explain). Separately, the Introduction normally houses the terse listing of each subsequent section within a Note, a useful roadmap readily evidenced within any sample Note you choose to read.

More importantly, the Introduction needs to point out the harm occasioned by the status quo—whether that status quo be attributable to a statute, a case decision, a regulation, or simple inaction. My years as a litigator taught me that every case requires a victim, for few triers of fact care to point the finger of blame for purely technical violations. Likewise, scholarship requires the identification of somebody in peril. Thus, before traveling too far down the road of writing a Note, ask yourself, "Will people care about this problem?" Life is full of logical inconsistencies and human foibles; effective scholarship clamors that a specifically harmful inconsistency needs to be immediately addressed.

In this regard, the example provided by journalism is of great assistance. Note how the newspapers wrap stories around people, and introduce such stories with a call for reform. Few people would read an article titled "Price Gouging Statutes Repose Too Much Discretion with the Attorney General." However, many would find their attention provoked by "Attorney General to Investigate $5 Gas Sales as Price Gouging." Likewise, a Note needs to (concretely) reveal someone harmed by the status quo.[2] Evaluate the two examples below:

WEAK:

THE AMERICAN ANTI-TRUST LAWS:
WHY CONGRESS MAY NEED TO REFORM

---

2. Many students seek to alter the status quo via their scholarship. However, there is nothing wrong with using the structure and tools described within this Chapter as a means of *preserving* the status quo to prevent harm.

BETTER:

THE SHERMAN ANTI-TRUST ACT OF 1890 AND THE
$5 GALLON OF GAS: THE CALL FOR CHANGE

The second example clearly entices and informs in superior fashion. How a law from 1890 can be blamed for skyrocketing fuel costs in 2015 is a legitimate question, to be answered by the subsequent *Background* section within your Note.

B. Background Section

The Background section is often the easiest to both plan and write: It serves primarily as a recap of the current law. Indeed, the biggest obstacle to completion of this section will be knowing when to *stop* providing background.

Another pitfall to be avoided when writing the Background section is the employment of subjectivity. Recall that when learning to draft an ideal Rule (Chapters I and II), you were cautioned against adding subjective commentary. Likewise, remain neutral when providing the status quo. Your Note will afford you plenty of time later on to editorialize. Note the differences between these two examples, both dealing with the problems caused by billions of dollars presently being donated to online entrepreneurs via "Crowdfunding":

WEAK:

> State Crowdfunding statutes, passed by nearly 25 states in a matter of months, ironically cite section 3(a)(11) of the Securities Act of 1933, an aged provision known more for its disuse.

BETTER:

> Many of the states that have passed Crowdfunding statutes have cited section 3(a)(11) of the Securities Act of 1933. That statutory provision was first interpreted in 1961; in recent years, the Securities and Exchange Commission has refused requests for a formal re-interpretation of its 1961 ruling.

The second passage still succeeds in conveying the author's ultimate opinion (that existing law is outdated). But the second passage maintains an air of deference and formality more aligned with what the "academic academy" labels scholarship; stated otherwise, the second author is more likely to generate credibility.

The first passage identifies three potential culprits: A rush to legislation, rampant State defiance of federal regulation, and a dated federal standard. Such a shotgun blast slows the development of the Note. Thus, a lapse into subjectivity—while feeling good—not only erodes credibility, but also blurs the focus on the proper Issue. And the Issue section drives the scholarship.

C. Issue Section

The Issue poses the specific problem to be addressed by the Note. It must always be foremost in the Writer's mind, although its precise wording may be worth postponing until other sections have crystallized.

The most ready way to identify the key Issue is to focus your Note on one of three ills: a) inadequate statutes, b) improper enforcement of existing statutes, or c) inconsistent judicial decisions involving those statutes. By focusing on the biggest of possible problems, you arrive at the clearest statement of the Issue.

For example, the Federal Sentencing Guidelines can be said to have set penalties for white collar crimes too high. Conversely, the Department of Justice can be said to have too often utilized the high end of the guidelines in its sentencing requests. Moreover, judges may be the cause of the alarming sentences, as the data may indicate that white collar crimes tend to draw stiffer penalties in more populated regions of the country. Any one of these possible themes is acceptable; the use of three themes allocates blame to all (and thus, ultimately, to none).

D. Resolution Section

Closely related to a specific identification of the problem is the identification of the cure. The Resolution section is where the author earns his/her praise, for lawyers are expected to pose a remedy. Ask the Legal Reader to join you in amending the statute or urging a case's reversal. But do not stop there: Provide the actual statutory language that needs to be included in an amendment, or expressly state what the outcome of the test case needed to be.

This task is universally resisted by young Writers, who feel that they lack the experience to cure an ill (and have grown accustomed to learning Issues from collegiate courses that do not always require an exact solution to a discovered dilemma). But you are already an expert on the topic, if for no other reason that few lawyers have the time to personally research fine points at great length. Recognize also that, while preparing your Note during the customary four–six month process, there is nothing wrong with saving the proposed solution for the last section to be written.

E. Conclusion Section

Finally, the Conclusion offers the opportunity to sum up, reiterate the theme, and leave the Reader with some food for thought. It is also a great place to come back to that Broadway show lyric or novelist quote that started the piece.

At this point, I normally suggest to the student that he/she discuss his Note topic with others. While I would not always endorse a budding author's advertising an idea on the Internet (and thus universally sharing a unique idea), each student surely has a partner or law school colleague who can act as a sounding board. Often, merely the act of voicing the issue aloud—like a screenwriter's "pitch"— can serve to streamline a message and eliminate noise (i.e., those metaphors and anecdotes that, while enjoyable to write, do little to advance the theme).

To test your familiarity with the 5-point Note outline, try the Exercise appearing below.

Exercise One: Creating an Outline for a Note

Please read the three introductory paragraphs below in preparation for stating a theme via an outline. The topic is executive power under the Constitution.

In 2015, President Barack Obama issued several Immigration Accountability Executive Actions. In the main, these Actions would shift resources to the southern U.S. border, limit deportations to felons (and not families), and encourage greater background checks on aliens present within the geographical boundaries of the United States.

In 1981, President Ronald Reagan reacted to a widespread strike by over 11,000 air-traffic controllers by terminating their employment. President Reagan relied upon a prior Executive Order greatly limiting the controllers' right to strike.

In 1952, the Supreme Court struck down President Truman's seizure of the steel mills via Executive Order 10340. In a decision conveyed via five differing opinions, the Court effectively ruled that the President had no inherent wartime power to seize property absent express Constitutional or Congressional authorization. *Youngstown Sheet & Tube Co. v. Sawyer*, 343 U.S. 579 (1952).

Using these examples, write five topic sentences that would guide you through a Note similarly evaluating the legality of the most recent White House pronouncements. Be sure to weigh factors such as presence of foreign conflict, Congressional inaction, or urgent circumstances (i.e., the same factors that steered prior analyses of swift executive action). Note also that, in the wake of mass shootings in 2015, some commentators have urged use of the Executive Order to legislate gun control of automatic weapons.

IV. Writing Until an Answer Comes

Armed now with the requisite structure, there is no excuse for not writing. Employ full sentences, paragraphs, and sections in an early attempt at a piece in full. Realize that your initial goal is not to write a 40-page Note, but to author three sections (i.e., Background, Issue, Resolution), each approximately ten–twelve pages long. Sections 1 and 5 (the "Introduction" and "Conclusion," respectively) will ultimately write themselves.

Remember throughout the process that a Note is expected to engage in deep analysis; as one maxim states it, Notes "go an inch wide but a mile deep." The two chief ways to thus elevate your writing are to effectively describe precedent cases and to accurately summarize statutes. Meaningful statutory and case analysis is discussed in Chapter IV. Two points within that Chapter require reiteration.

First, recognize that even after diligently dissecting the verbiage of a codified law, accurate description may prove evasive unless you are familiar with the broader context. For example, imagine that you are writing on the disparate penalties among the States for financial frauds against senior citizens. The following statutory provision, defining "economic crime" within Ohio's elder protection law, thus serves a key function in your Note's "Background" section:

> *Economic crime* is hereby defined as those illegal acts which are characterized by deceit, concealment or violation of trust and which are not dependent upon the application or threat of physical force or violence.

At first read, the definition appears to be of great utility. It evidences both a concise definition and also the legislature's concerted attention to the issue.

But upon a closer read, the definition—by itself—tells the reader very little. How do we define "deceit"? Which relationships may serve as a basis for a "violation of trust"? And can a crafty villain simply incorporate violence into the equation to remove himself from the definition? Finally, since the predicate acts must be illegal to begin with, the provision is actually reliant upon another statute (e.g., the Penal Code of Ohio). Thus, a thorough understanding of this provision by a Note author warrants a full read of the subject statute as well as a review of the implied/referenced companion statutes. Only after such diligence can the Legal Writer ensure an accurate analysis.

Stated otherwise, even when you feel comfortable with a statute, do not stop your reading. Explore commentary; read the statute it replaced. Review the examples below for illustration of the more comprehensive approach:

WEAK:

> In Ohio, a concise passage within the Elder Protection Law defines "economic crimes" against seniors as illegal acts "characterized by deceit, concealment or violation of trust" in the absence of physical violence.

BETTER:

> In Ohio, a definition within the Elder Protection Law of 2011 informs that covered "economic crime" is "characterized by deceit, concealment or violation of trust." Pre-existing case law defines the key terms within that definition. Contemporaneously, the Ohio Revised Code covers financial crimes resulting in physical manifestations of harm, while the traditional Penal Code covers threats or application of violence.

The second Chapter IV point worthy of reiteration concerns case summaries. Such tools, even if consistently progressing from to "accident/crime to checkbook/jail time," may bury the Reader with details. To ease the reading, only offer a case for one of two clearly stated reasons: in explaining the status quo, or in support of an alternative to the status quo. Such clarification may require the addition of a second topic sentence in each relevant paragraph.

Witness the relative ease of use of the following two passages:

WEAK:

> The case law on piercing the veil of sole proprietorships is quite varied. A 2001 Georgia case concerned obligations under an insurance policy where the covered party was a sole proprietor. *Miller v. Harco Nat. Insur. Co.*, 274 Ga. 387 (S. Ct. Ga. 2001). The Georgia high court trivialized a trade name as nothing but an "alter ego" for the policy holder, thus finding coverage. However, a 1994 Montana case shielded the sole proprietor debtor because the statute did not expressly indicate that owners of unregistered businesses could be potentially liable on a personal level. *Jerry Martin & Assoc., Inc. v. Don's Westland Bulk*, 884 P.2d 795 (S. Ct. Mt. 1994). Thus, change is needed.

BETTER:

> The case law on piercing the veil of sole proprietorships is quite varied. State benches have exhibited a variety of means at reach-

ing a just end. These means often center on a stated or unstated reliance upon a finding of an "alter ego."

An example of the stated approach comes from a 2001 Georgia case which concerned obligations under an insurance policy where the covered party was a sole proprietor. *Miller v. Harco Nat. Insur. Co.*, 274 Ga. 387 (S. Ct. Ga. 2001). The Georgia high court trivialized a trade name as nothing but an "alter ego" for the policy holder, thus finding coverage.

An example of the unstated reliance on a finding of an alter ego is the *Martin* case. *Jerry Martin & Assoc., Inc. v. Don's Westland Bulk*, 884 P.2d 795 (S. Ct. Mt. 1994). In that 1994 Montana case, the sole proprietor debtor was shielded from the creditor because the statute did not expressly indicate that owners of unregistered businesses could be potentially liable on a personal level. Both approaches belie the certainty that businesses and business law consistently seek. Thus, change is needed.

The first example relies heavily on transitional words (e.g., "however") to keep the Reader engaged. Such words, while very helpful when initially learning coherence, may not be up to the task when Writing gets more complicated (as in a Note).

The second example requires more time—both in analysis and its presentation. But its benefits are many. First, the diligent Reader feels educated in learning two judicial approaches. Second, supporters of both approaches remain engaged, as the purpose of the passages is repeatedly made clear. Finally, the longer case summaries allow for the interruptive cite—a frequent occurrence in Notes—to be harmlessly placed at the end of the first sentence.

Recognize that even if a series of case summaries succeeds as consistently engaging the Legal Reader, an effective Note would nonetheless add a transitional paragraph after the summaries (e.g., "Thus, clearly existing law is not providing for consistency of approach ..."). Indeed, such transitions smooth out many of the disparate missions and sections of a Note, the individualized preparation of which is detailed below.

V. A Step-by-Step Example of the Note Process

This example recites the steps in this Chapter thus far while providing more concrete details.

Imagine that you are curious about the previously described 1981 decision by President Ronald Regan to fire over 11,000 air traffic controllers. You have read varying opinions on the event, ranging from accolades for strong, central action to doubts over the legality of the move. A quick check on the Internet yields many examples of relevant secondary authority; your piercing scan of one such item directs you to Executive Order 11491. That White House pronouncement, decades before the firings, ostensibly outlawed the strike that the controllers threatened in 1981, thus paving the way for Reagan's drastic action. Alternatively, Order 11491 was outdated and/or taken out of context, rendering the 40th President's bold move beyond Constitutional authority.

Such a tangible determination is still weeks away. At this point, you now (happily) have some primary authority—albeit a bit generic and a good deal less dramatic than the actual 1981 firing (the footage of which appears on the Internet[3]). The first step is to attempt a title—perhaps something playing with an aviation theme, such as "THE DOOMED AIR TRAFFIC CONTROLLER STRIKE OF 1981 AND THE LIFT IT PROVIDED EXECUTIVE ORDERS." Do not be shy here. The campier titles tend to please editors and Readers alike.

After you have a working title, create a rough outline. This structure would inform you of the research that awaits you, namely, the pinpointing of Constitutional provisions, the most famous examples of Executive Orders, and the commentary on both (e.g., your answer to Exercise One of this Chapter).

After familiarizing yourself with the empirical data, only then may you begin to investigate the limitations on executive orders, a political reality loosely grounded in our Constitution at Article II, section 1. With little effort you will learn of other bold moves by Presidents under the auspice of Executive Order authority—to wit, President Lincoln's suspension of habeas corpus in 1861 provides an interesting tale with which to evaluate the frequency and scope of this curious power of the Chief Executive. Now conversant with the relevant events, you are well on your way to outlining the "Background" section of your Note.

The next section, "Issue," carves out a category from the "Background." To wit, you will focus on when Presidents *not* faced with a war or a national labor problem perhaps exceed the Constitutional

---

3. *See, e.g., Reagan fires 11,359 air-traffic controllers, available at* http://www.history.com/this-day-in-history/reagan-fires-11359-air-traffic-controllers.

power bestowed upon them. Generally, your inspiration here harkens back to your reason for selecting the Note topic. More specifically, your research will seek a list of factors the Supreme Court has used in evaluating the necessity for the Executive Order action. The *Youngstown* case exhibited a direct judicial analysis of the President's bold actions— did other benches subsequently adhere to that approach? It is doubtful that all courts evaluating inherent Executive authority follow the exact same approach; such distinctions create your Issue.

Here is a good point to engage in a preemption check. If another student has published a Note examining this specific genre of executive power, examine the conclusion. Can you state the counter-analysis? Perhaps you can salvage the originality of your idea by focusing on one of the tangential approaches to evaluating Executive Orders (e.g., by centering on one of the numerous concurring decisions within the Supreme Court's *Youngstown* decision).

Next, you will offer a tentative answer to the Issue in your "Resolution" section. Students falter at this point when they stick too closely to their initial themes; remember, you ultimately will either approve of Executive Order 11491 (and call for further use of this form of action) or disapprove of it (and call for limitations, likely set by Congress, the courts, or the citizens themselves). Either way, the Reader will need to be able to picture your solution. Draft actual text; be a legislator here.

Overall, while working on sections 2–4 (i.e., Background-Issue-Resolution), you will revise your title, adjust your premise, and perhaps even delay drafting the exact language of the Issue (or Resolution). Such delay is fine, as is a change of heart. Perhaps you will start to opine that President Reagan was well within his authority in firing the air traffic controllers. Perhaps you will not. The ultimate opinion matters less than the depth of analysis and coherence of your Note.

Finally, you will sum up your Note in your "Conclusion" section. The Conclusion section amply provides room for closing thoughts and periodic updates (e.g., whether President Obama's immigration Executive Orders will ultimately be undercut by the federal courts). As a last step, you will adjust the roadmap within your "Introduction" section to accurately reflect what you have written.

As you can see, no section works in isolation, and your exact theme is subject to constant change (so save all drafts). The Note process should feel new and a bit uncomfortable, but the process gets exponentially easier each time it is subsequently attempted. Most importantly, the methodology described herein will ensure that such work at perfecting your brand of scholarship is consistently productive.

To begin the process of subsequent attempts, below is an Exercise asking simply for the "Introduction" section of a Note:

Exercise Two: Writing an Introduction Section

To tie the Chapter's lessons together, write out a full first section of a Note based upon the Executive Order debate described above. At this point, your position and depth of familiarity are secondary. Strive to create two meaningful paragraphs (of six–ten sentences) both clarifying your topic and the Note's structure. Include a title, each section's purpose, and a roadmap of the Note.

VI. Conclusion: Follow Your Heart

To be sure, completion of a law school Note is a long, arduous, frustrating process. Deadlines will seem impossible; insights will appear and then vanish unpredictably. But possibly no law school thrill compares with receiving word that your Note has been selected for publication by your Journal. Likewise, few job interview props shine more than a bound copy of your Note or Comment in response to a request for a Writing sample.

I have been fortunate enough to both advise a great many law student Notes during my years in teaching and witness a large number of these authors "get published." One particular story stands out.

A few years ago, a student who had been in my year-long Legal Writing class shared with me her good fortune in being selected for publication. Her Note examined the effects of and solutions to an online company's gathering of an incalculable number of books for digital reproduction. When I asked her how she had arrived at this topic, she said simply that, upon her learning of this unique commercial event, she had uncovered a law story that had to be told.

The student's success continued to grow. Months later, a federal judge cited her work repeatedly in his decision in a case involving the very same dispute on which she had opined. Thus, before she had even graduated law school, the student's research had helped shape the debate on a dynamic, crucial area of intellectual property. In short, the student was inspired by having a story to tell, instead of feeling overwhelmed at her Journal's instruction to tell a story.

Students who recognize this distinction ultimately find the writing of a law school Note a most rewarding adventure. Half the battle is committing to telling of a Legal confrontation without ready remedy, and never questioning your revelation's worth. For if you believe that you are making a valid contribution to the storied world of "scholarship," the hard work shall always seem justified.

Find your spark. Diligently learn the subject area. Write—and rewrite—until a solution comes to you. And consistently follow your outline (and your heart).

Chapter XI

A New Deal: The Agency Comment Letter

Chapter Objectives:
- Recognizing the Import of Practice at Professional Writing
- Learning the Proper Tone and Structure of Commentary on Agency Rulemaking
- Organizing Technical Commentary Through Varied Legal Writing Tools
- Drafting an Effective Comment Letter

Substantive Takeaways:
- "Section 553 Rulemaking"
- The "Volcker Rule" (Post-2010 Regulatory Limitation on Bank Trading Accounts)
- Local E-Cigarette Regulation

I. Background

While teaching in Germany, I learned of the perceived novelty of the American administrative process. "I've read your Constitution," a German student with a Ph.D. told me. "Agencies are listed nowhere in it."

The student was absolutely right, although it is quite often and effectively asserted that the "Necessary and Proper" Clause (Art. I, section 8) and "Faithful Execution" Clause (Art. II, section 3) justify the creation of agencies by, respectively, the legislative and executive branches. Nonetheless, from these humble authorizations have grown enormous bureaucratic entities with billion-dollar budgets. These agencies sometime flex their muscles in enacting disciple against foreign nationals whose business practices affect American citizens (as was the case that inspired the curt Constitutional critique by the German Ph.D.).

More importantly for our purposes, the enormity of this agency structure and attendant rulemaking protocol provide a fertile ground for Legal Writers, as is described below.

II. Section 553 Rulemaking

Federal Agencies are authorized by the constitutional provisions reminding that the Congress and the Executive must have the authority to get things done. In the nation's darkest hours (i.e., 1929–1945), new and existing agencies alike took on the role of effecting expedient reforms. This "fourth branch" of government proved to be much more effective in meeting needs than, for example, the national legislature. Thus, the "New Deal" of the 1930s saw tremendous growth in rulemaking by agencies.

Concerned with the power of this largely unscripted branch of government, Congress passed the Administrative Procedures Act in 1946 ("APA"). The APA was once called "a bill of rights" for those regulated by agencies. APA Section 554 (as interpreted by federal case law) thus grants specific, enumerated rights to those affected by agency decisions. For example, parties brought before agency hearings, which are like trials, are afforded statutory rights (e.g., to counsel).

APA Section 553 governs agency rulemaking, which provides ample opportunity for public input into pending rule proposals. On a routine basis, agencies include on their web sites (under headings such as "Regulation" or "Proposed Rulemaking") formal proposals as they appear within the daily Federal Register.[1] Comments are normally accepted (and finalization of the proposed rule halted) for a period of 30 days. Such proposals create voluminous opportunities for lawyers, law firms, and members of the public to champion the rights of those who are or would be affected by agency rulemaking.

It is a tribute to the democratic process that responsive public "Comment Letters" are collected, read, categorized, and displayed by the agency. Indeed, America may be unique in the amount of resources allocated each year to providing an avenue for administrative insights offered by the layman. Such a pro-

---

1. The Federal Register is the medium by which the public learns of agency notices, proposed rules and final rules. It can be accessed at https://www.federalregister.gov/.

tocol ensures that agencies issue informed regulations, and that relevant business models have time to prepare for new oversight. Such Comment Letters are also a priceless tool for the aspiring Legal Writer, who can simultaneously prove to be part of the democratic process, practice drafting a piece to be read by professionals, and earn a line on his/her resume.

III. A Concrete Sample

In 2012, several of my students and I prepared a Comment Letter to the Commodity Futures Trading Commission on a proposed measure to limit investments made by federally chartered banks (who were thought to have speculated too much prior to the 2008 Recession). The Letter appears in large and relevant part below, with its internal footnotes in italics:

April 19, 2012

Mr. David A. Stawick

Secretary of the U.S. Commodity Futures Trading Commission
Three Lafayette Centre
1155 21st Street, NW
Washington, D.C. 20581

Re: RIN #3038-AD05, Prohibitions and Restrictions on Proprietary
Trading and Certain Interests in, and Relationships With,
Hedge Funds and Covered Funds

Dear Mr. Stawick:

The undersigned are a group comprised by an associate professor and five upper class students at the Hofstra University Maurice A. Deane School of Law ("The Group"). Collectively, the Group has long followed and researched the remedies debated since the onset of the Financial Crisis in 2008.[1] We thus appreciate the opportunity to Comment on this issue of great moment for both regulators and the regulated alike.

1 The Group includes a Professor who served as a regulator for over 10 years and who has taught Securities Regulation every year since 2000, and law students who have since 2009 studied, litigated, and authored articles on the law governing financial services. Three of the students in the Group are pursuing joint JD/MBA degrees. Nearly all of the students have interned/externed with a securities arbitration clinic, or securities regulators at the State/SRO level. All views expressed herein are purely personal to the authors.

This Comment Letter represents our collective efforts at evaluating the CFTC proposal referenced above. The Comment Letter is divided into two parts: 1) comments on the proposed final proprietary trading limitations, and 2) comments on the proposed limitations of investment in private equity enterprises.

As a preamble, the Group wishes to express two global thoughts:

i. The nation's economic challenges occasioned by Wall Street practices are not over.

Remarkably, some newspaper commentary from the spring of last year triumphantly declared the nation's recession to be over; concurrently, publicly available data on the repayment of "TARP" (*i.e.*, initial Bailout) monies continue to suggest that a "reset button" has been successfully pushed. The Group feels strongly that such forgetfulness of the lingering damages occasioned by market excesses in recent years augurs only more collective setback. On a national level, the depressed housing market, the continued trading in exotic derivatives, the unfaltering downward trends in employment, and even the shockingly low interest rates paid on retail bank account deposits all speak to a crisis that has yet to abate. Stated more directly, the efforts by forces both governmental and private alike—while perhaps necessary—did not completely succeed, as the bank failures and mortgage defaults have simply hot halted, and the taxpayer monies extended via TARP simply did not come back at par.[2]

2 *See* "A.I.G. Shares Fall Amid Treasury Sale," **The New York Times** (March 8, 2012).

ii. Stronger (and more pointed medicine) may still be required.

Concomitantly, the Group is somewhat concerned that stronger action did not result from the shattering disclosures of 2008. More meaningful net capital requirements at the banking level, stronger circuit breakers at the nation's stock exchanges, and vastly increased staffing levels at the SEC and CFTC all might have succeeded in both improving financial regulation and investor morale. While [Dodd Frank Act] Section 619's isolation and limitation of distinct business lines hints at a return to the cautious days preceding Gramm-Leach-Bliley, the fact remains that a completed and implemented Volcker Rule arguably remains a relatively small victory for those favoring more regulation of American markets.

Nonetheless, the Group feels that the Volcker Rule should proceed toward implementation. Concurrently, the Group would hope that alarms sounded in recent months by both government entities (confessing missed deadlines) and Wall Street lobbyists (sounding practiced refrains of "complexity") do not work to forestall implementation of final rules at or near the July 2012 deadline. To assist with the weighty efforts being undertaken by various government agencies charged with implementing the Volcker Rule, the Group hereby offers its Comments on five of the more salient points raised by the Proposal.

I. Definitional Challenges

With the implementation of the Dodd-Frank come a few new terms that require clarification. The most prominent term that we held worthy of notable attention was the definition of a "trading account." A trading account is defined by the Proposal "as any account used for acquiring or taking positions in securities." It is further noted that a firm takes positions in a trading account when there is intent to sell so as to profit from price fluctuations in the near term.

We agree that CFTC determination of a trading account is difficult to implement since a governing body cannot readily determine the intent of a party entering into a position. However, the presently proposed definition perhaps creates some difficulties in both its interpretation and its proper execution. To wit, the three prongs noted above successfully define what is classified as a trading account; nevertheless a rebuttable presumption is afforded to rebuff institutional arrangements from being classified as such.... [further reasoning omitted]

To that end, it may be both more just and expedient for the present rulemaking to simply adopt existing definitions of "proprietary account" as defined by the stock exchanges in the context of audit trail rules.[3] ...

3 See, e.g., New York Stock Exchange Rule 7410(p) ("... The funds used by a Proprietary Trading firm must be exclusively firm funds and all trading must be the firm's accounts ..."). See also NYSE Rule 95.10 (permitting Floor members to exercise discretion when liquidating positions as part of "bona fide arbitrage").

Separately, the Group respectfully suggests that the CFTC must determine the appropriate authority to perform the independent testing of the financial institutions' trading activities ...

II. The Registration Matrix

The Group is also concerned with the piecemeal nature of the presently proposed "provisional registration." One benefit of provisional registration is that it will allow Swap Dealers ("SD") and Major Swap Participants ("MSP") to slowly integrate under the new legislation. Secondly, this form of registration will allow the National Futures Association ("NFA") to sort through the registration materials much more closely to ensure compliance instead of reviewing all documents in one submission date ...

Notwithstanding these positive benefits, the Group is concerned that the negative implications of this approach may outweigh the advantages.... [*further reasoning omitted*]

It is respectfully urged that the presently proposed deadlines be consolidated into fewer submission dates. This will ensure adequate compliance as well as alleviate the burden on the NFA when reviewing the registration materials.

III. Proprietary Trading v. Market Making

The Group is also concerned with the Proposal's possible inspiring of market confusion over what constitutes "proprietary trading," which is prohibited, and what constitutes "market making," which is exempted. The proposed regulation does provide six key principles for distinguishing these activities ... While the Group recognizes that these standards may lack the certainty of bright line rules, we believe that even broader standards are necessary to effectuate the intent of the Rule and accommodate the dynamic demands of an evolving marketplace....

Without providing concrete guidance for banks by both adopting broad-based standards and, where appropriate, narrowly defining rules, the Volcker Rule could inhibit legitimate activities. Alternatively, completely novel standards could hinder the prohibition on proprietary trading through a bank's willingness to continue the practice under the guise of market making. A mixture of new, bright line rules and established standards would provide the best solution, thus emboldening the Volker Rule to effect its intended (and salutary) purpose.

IV. Prohibitions on Private Equity Sponsorship and Funding

The Group feels troubled by the Volcker Rule's prohibitions on private equity sponsorship and funding by banking entities. The dual 3% limits that will be imposed on banking entities by the Volcker Rule will significantly decrease liquidity in the private equity market, thus limiting the ability of firms to raise funds and pursue the purchase of companies that are troubled or have unrealized potential. Such purchases often result in a net positive for the U.S. economy....

The ultimate goal of the Volcker Rule is to stem the imposition of risk on depositors and taxpayers by banking entities. By attempting to treat one excess (*i.e.,* a concentration of assets at regulated entities), the proposed Volcker Rule will unsettle revenue streams in the United States financial system by imposing an unqualified limitation that would be equally, if not more, detrimental to their stability and growth. It is respectfully submitted that a preferable alternative to the presently proposed restrictions on Private Equity would be the imposition of more flexible limits on private equity investment and sponsorship by banks ...

V. International Implications of the Volcker Rule

The Group is also concerned by the possible international ramifications of the Volcker Rule as currently drafted. We recognize that modern trading centers are inherently interconnected and global in scale. Accordingly, any effort to regulate American markets must be conscious of the effect of domestic regulations on international markets and entities. To that end, U.S. regulators should ensure that rules and regulations promote fair and open markets and avoid protectionism. Concurrently, it is imperative that U.S. regulators maintain their role as leaders in financial regulation in order to ensure the stable and efficient operation of U.S. markets. Therefore, we believe that the international implications of the Volcker Rule, while requiring redress, do not preclude implementation of the rule.

Some have voiced concern that the Volcker Rule will significantly damage U.S. companies' ability to remain competitive because it applies differently to U.S. and foreign banking institutions. This is because the ban on proprietary trading restricts U.S. banking entities' global operations, whereas the ban only restricts foreign banking entities' U.S. operations. We recognize the importance of maintaining the competitiveness of American markets. We do not believe that prudent market regulation should embrace a regulatory "race to the bottom" that would weaken U.S. markets and expose them to the same frailties that contributed to the financial crisis of 2008....

Accordingly, to best serve the dual goals that 1) American regulation stand at the forefront of global responses to the crisis, while 2) giving credence to the concern that the Volcker Rule potentially threatens the liquidity of foreign sovereign debt markets, the Group believes that the proposal's exception for trading in U.S. sovereign debt should be extended to include any nation of similar strength and stability to the U.S....

Conclusion

The Group reiterates its hope that the Volcker Rule be finalized in conformance with the deadline set by the Dodd-Frank Act, passed nearly two years ago. In sum, vagaries attending the adoption of pivotal terms (and their implementation) can be assuaged through the efforts of regulators who have been charged with updating and enforcing regulations for decades. The matrix governing effective dates for registration should be simplified and its requirements made more uniform. Separately, the 3% limits to be implemented on private equity investments may be too singular in effect to warrant inclusion. Finally, the Group is confident that crafters of the final rules called for by Section 619 can concurrently advance the nation's model body of regulation in a way that does not signal political isolation to nations whose aid may still be enlisted in fashioning responses to the persisting worldwide economic crisis.

We thank the Commodity Futures Trading Commission for the opportunity to share the thoughts included herein.

Sincerely,

[signatories]

The published Letter excerpted above[2] (obviously penned by experienced Business Law students) was the result of a good deal of discussing, planning, and revising. For **Exercise One** of this Chapter, see if you can reverse engineer the Letter by creating an outline of its five positions. You need not be familiar with the subject matter, as the Letter abounds in topic sentences and clearly conveyed sentiments.

Meanwhile, I have had numerous other students who prefer drafting and submitting individual Letters on their own time. Regardless of its scope of content and participation, a Letter can be said to adhere to two equally important forms of guidance: Formatting, and Content.

---

2. The original version of this Comment Letter can be found at http://comments.cftc.gov/PublicComments/ViewComment.aspx?id=57424.

IV. Formatting Guidance

A. Subject Line

The challenge of earning reputation commences immediately when preparing a Comment Letter.

Specifically, the proper identification of the topic is articulated by express reference to the label chosen by the proposing agency. In the example above, the technical-laden "EIN" data has been created by the CFTC; the Commenter's job is to simply parrot this language. The reason for the specificity is practical: The agency shall receive countless Comments during the course of a year. Ensuring that the correct subject line has been utilized will guarantee that the Comment finds its way to the appropriate reviewer.

B. Choice of Persona

For better or worse, ersatz Comment Letters are sometimes written in bits resembling passionate scribbling on cocktail napkins. The goal of a law student is to distinguish his/her submission from those of the maddened (but excessively informal) crowd. Accordingly, use of the first and second person is discouraged. "I feel ..." connotes the proverbial lone voice in the wilderness. "You should change" needlessly personalizes the criticism, and possibly offends some of the hardest working government employees involved in the rulemaking process.

Simply address your comment to ideas, rules and proposals, which—at worst—are "misguided," "unfounded" or "overbroad." The people who penned them were doing their job. The product of that job is fair game for polite but impassioned debate.

C. Choice of Language

Contrary to a primal lesson of this book, sophisticated language should be considered; the audience has expertise, and a new goal is the impression upon the Reader that the Commenter has similar expertise (see footnote 1 of the Letter).

Further, the clarity of presentation may depend upon repetitive use of a term introduced by the proposal. For example, the CFTC coined the phrase "registration matrix." While the Commenter is free to recast that technical phrase as "schedule," such artful re-phrasing actually works to cloud the communication. Students here would do best to abide by the guidance offered for terms of art created in a statute: Sometimes a standard has to be repeated verbatim, or, as suggested in Chapter VI, sometimes we all need to walk like ducks.

D. Aides to Coherence

As can be seen in the example above, the Comment Letter strives to explain itself—the opening paragraph clarifies that the Comments shall be presented in two parts. Further, the Letter relies heavily on reading aides, to wit, sub-headings, a numbered outline, and varying fonts. There is rarely a dictated style in this art form. Instead, utilize any arrow in your Writing quiver that shall keep the Reader engaged.

Footnotes are also fair game, as long as they serve a vital purpose and are limited in number. In the example above, footnote 3 displays the Commenters' knowledge of the technical subject matter and field. Footnote 2 generates credibility by providing support for a strong assertion.

E. Routing/Distribution Requirements

The agency's proposing release normally includes routing instructions, which may seem cumbersome (e.g., "If submitting in hard copy format, five copies of the Letter must be sent to the Secretary and ..."). Commenters must adhere to these instructions, or else face the likelihood that the Letter will be disregarded.

It should be noted that agencies will often accommodate a reasonable request to submit a Comment Letter slightly beyond the Comment Period. Such a request for an extension should be made well in advance of the deadline.

F. Preamble and Conclusion

A respectful Preamble is suggested (but not required). While agencies are required by the APA to open a Comment period, specific dates and formats are left to agency discretion. It thus behooves the Commenter—who might find himself facing an obstacle to timely submission on the present proposal or a future one—to express gratitude for the overall professionalism of the agency.

In such a pointed critique, the Conclusion is effectively required. In those parting words, it is, again, customary to express a certain amount of gratitude to be able to weigh in on a proposed measure at a meaningful stage of its preparation. This gratitude takes the form of both a statement of appreciation on page one of the Letter, and a more concrete "Thank You" in the document's last paragraph. Such inclusions, for many reasons, are simply good business.

More importantly, as discussed below, it may become difficult for the reviewer to comprehend or classify your Letter unless its myriad working parts are summed up.

V. Substantive Guidance

A. Edit the Targets

The recent Recession has seen a surge in agency rule proposals, and these proposals were more often than not complicated. The above-referenced Dodd Frank Act alone called for over 300 governmental studies/rules.

A successful Comment Letter is thus the result effectively limiting the scope. Congressmen send sole-paragraph exhortations that a measure be adopted or abandoned; such a model would not aid the Writer's goal of practice. Conversely, industry lobbyists pen impassioned works sometimes numbering over 20 pages. A goal of 5 pages and 3–5 specific topics therein would work for the first-time Commenter.

For example, the Comment Letter excerpted above concerned a lingering and highly controversial proposal spurred by the White House and steadfastly opposed by market interests. The proposal was subject to repeat Comment periods (by several federal agencies) and drew over 15,000 Comments. Nonetheless, in an attempt to present meaningful insight, the Commenters behind the Letter above narrowed down the proposal's scores of questions to a handful of topics; correspondingly, references to opposition are few. Streamlining a Letter to address a subset of topics/questions posed is not only permitted but quite often applauded. Again, the term "inter alia" may be the most brilliant contribution to Legal Writing ever offered.

B. Proceed within a Disciplined Approach

Within each of the five subdivided sections in the above Letter, there is presented, sequentially, 1) the specific concern, 2) a summary of the relevant language within the proposing release, 3) the particular problem(s) occasioned by the language in its present state, and 4) a suggested, detailed alternative. The Reader/reviewer thus becomes accustomed to the disciplined approach.

Perhaps this is the reason why the Letter above, among literally thousands, is expressly listed on a companion agency's web page.[3]

Note also the inclusion of a counter-analysis ("Some have voiced concern ..."; three paragraphs from the end). Such a weapon permeates persuasive documents, as does the accompanying guidance that the counter-analysis should not be the last thing a Reader sees on the topic.

C. Make Individual Positions Clear

The Preamble and Conclusion communicate the Commenter's overall feelings about the proposed measure. But savvy Letters combine positions of support, opposition, and hope for modification. Such even-handedness serves many goals, including objectivity, respect for the proposal, and familiarity with the subject matter.

For example, in the excerpted Letter above, the group of Commenters urged the adoption of the proposed rule, but opposed its definition of "trading account" and its implementation schedule. The Letter simultaneously suggested modifications to the proposed regulation's exceptions. Thus, there are five individually stylized positions expressed in the Letter. These varying positions are briefly stated within the first and/or last paragraph of each section headed by a Roman numeral (and repeated within the Letter's "Conclusion" section).

VI. Conclusion

Understand that, on a large scale basis, the greatest thrill offered by the Comment Letter is often the mere possibility of express recognition of your viewpoint prior to minor changes to the final regulation.[4] As has been often noted, agencies are not legally obligated to substantively consider each Comment submitted.

---

3. *See* https://www.sec.gov/comments/s7-41-11/s74111.shtml (providing a list of certain Comment Letters dually submitted to the CFTC and SEC). The Letter above is approximately number 40 on the list.

4. For an example, see Self-Regulatory Organizations; Order Approving and Notice of Filing and Order Granting Accelerated Approval to Amendment Nos. 2 and 3 to the Proposed Rule Change by the National Association of Securities Dealers, Inc. Relating to the Delivery Requirement of a Margin Disclosure Statement to Non-Institutional Customers, *available at* http://www.federalregister.com/Browse/Document/usa/na/fr/2001/5/3/01-11049 (noting, at footnote 5, the submission of the Comment Letter of J. Scott Colesanti prior to final changes to NASD Rule 2341).

But on a much smaller basis, the Comment Letter process is a tremendous opportunity for fans of both the democratic process and the need for practice at Legal Writing. The New Deal gave Americans many safety nets we now take for granted, including federally insured bank deposits and a social security retirement system. Concurrently, how fortunate that it also inspired agency rulemaking that allows lawyers and law students to serve civic duties while becoming a bit better at their craft. To start such practice, try your hand at Exercise Two below, which concerns the E-Cigarette debate introduced in Chapter VIII.

Exercise Two: Drafting a Comment Letter

Using the tools described in this Chapter, as well as the considerations detailed below, draft a brief Comment Letter (i.e., 2–3 pages) opposing or supporting the following measure. The proposed State regulation from a State agency reflects an effort to limit the sale and use of E-Cigarettes:

Notice of Rulemaking:

Concerned that federal regulation is late in coming, the State Respiratory Health Agency ("SRHA") has opened for Comment the proposed measure.

> **Rule 15-1598.** *No establishment employing more than 15 individuals shall permit the use of E-Cigarettes on or near the premises. Also, no establishment selling food, beverages, or personal sundries shall sell E-Cigarettes to anyone under 18 years of age.*
>
> *The penalty for each occurrence of violation is a fine in the amount of $1,000.*

All comments should be addressed to Miles Standish, Secretary, SRHA, and should reference Rule Proposal 15-1598—Electronic Cigarette Limitations. Only hard copy Comments shall be accepted by the SRHA.

Noteworthy Authorities/Considerations:

• In June 2014, New York's highest appellate court struck down a 2012 New York City Board of Health measure attempting to limit the sale of sugary drinks of 16 ounces or more. The court ruled that the Board had exceeded its authority. The court also reasoned that the measure was arbitrary and capricious because, inter alia, customers could lawfully purchase two 8-ounce drinks at a time.

The dissent noted that the Board had previously banned lead paint in homes.

• The Department of Sanitation of the City of New York later adopted a measure limiting the use of Styrofoam packing peanuts. That measure was also struck down by the court as arbitrary and capricious; among other reasons cited in the September 2015 lower court decision was the fact that alternative means of recycling the discarded Styrofoam containers had not been effectively weighed.

• It has been estimated that E-Cigarettes are being used by over 10 million "vaping" consumers across America, and that over 1,000 business enterprises presently manufacture related paraphernalia. Although E-Cigarette "juices" contain no nicotine, they can contain other undesirable elements (e.g., tar). It has been argued that the product helps to wean cigarette smokers from tobacco products.

• Nothing in the proposed vaping ban prevents an individual over 18 years of age from purchasing E-Cigarettes or vaping products and then immediately handing them to a minor.

• The Federal Drug Administration has not to date finalized regulations defining E-Cigarettes as a food or tobacco product that comes under its jurisdiction, although such a broad response is pending.

———————

Chapter XII

Drafting the Accusatory Instrument (That Dream Job)

Chapter Objectives:
- Understanding the Purpose of the Varied Forms of Accusatory Instruments
- Properly Implementing the Four Basic Requirements of Such Documents
- Recognizing the Two Major Formatting Additions of Instruments
- Avoiding the Pitfalls of Poor Drafting of Initial Pleadings
- Drafting a Basic Criminal Complaint

Substantive Takeaways:
- Requirements of a Federal Securities Fraud Violation
- Right of Publicity Allegations
- Lanham Act Violations for Infringements of Sports Apparel Trademarks

---

I. Background

For years I have been meeting 1L students who desire foremost to have more "job-like" responsibilities. While immersed in case law books, they wish to design trial strategies and argue for/against charges. Such impatience is endearing until the wish is granted, and suddenly the law student must actually point the finger of blame at someone.

That finger of blame is enabled by the accusatory instrument ("Instrument"), which is characterized by four, basic sections: 1) the statements of jurisdiction/venue, 2) the provable facts, 3) the claim for relief, and 4) the remedy sought.

These substantive sections are bookended by two formalities: the captioned cover page, and the submitting attorney's signature (also known as an "Indorsement"). The six requirements are collectively elaborated on below. They are also displayed concretely within example documents within the Chapter.

A. Cover Page

Even the most basic of instruments contains a cover page. Such formality helps not only the parties but others who may be tasked with having to file or store such documents. A standard Cover Page conveys, at least, four bits of information:

- The specific court hearing the dispute (including circuit/district)
- The official caption of the case (e.g., "Roe v. Wade")
- The document's title (e.g., "Complaint")
- The name and contact information for the submitting attorney

B. Statements of Jurisdiction/Venue

The Statement of Jurisdiction ensures both that the court has the authority to hear the case and that the parties are at the right level thereof. It normally also includes a statement of venue, which ensures that, within a level of court, the physical locale of the adjudicating bench is proper.

C. Provable Facts

This section comprises the bulk of the work. Simply put, number each paragraph, list one fact at a time, and only include a fact for which evidence already exists.

WEAK:

> 12. The defendant then telephoned Jones, who was uninterested in his scheme, or in being part of any conspiracy. Jones then slammed the phone down and contacted his lawyer.

BETTER:

> 12. The defendant then telephoned the defendant, who was uninterested.

> 13. After the phone call, Jones contacted his lawyer.

The first example includes four facts, two of which (at best) are provable by a sole witness/affidavit. The second example separates the allegations into two distinctly provable paragraphs (while eliminating commentary that, even if provable, adds little to the violation, or is ultimately a decision for the judge/jury).

D. The Cause of Action (a.k.a. "Claim for Relief")

This section serves as both point of entry to the courthouse and safeguard against spurious claims: If a cause of action cannot be alleged in good faith, the accusing attorney must either find more facts or advise the client of the bad news.

Ordinarily, each violation of a law, regulation or case law standard is listed separately.

E. The Remedy Sought (a.k.a. "Prayer for Relief")

This section often represents a combination of the remedies permitted by the cause of action (e.g., treble damages in antitrust price gauging) and the particular needs of the client (e.g., an equitable injunction). Pleading accurately here is significant; courts are known to exclude relief not requested.

F. The Indorsement

An attorney (or attorneys) sign the Instrument, thus at once affirming its preparation upon best accurate belief and providing a point of contact for questions.

II. Samples

Overall, the Accusatory Instrument is strikingly similar in all of its civil, administrative, and criminal incarnations. Below is an example of the administrative variety; as is the practice of this book, the parties and facts are hypothetical, but the law is real.

A. The Administrative Agency Action

In this hypothetical example of a government action alleging securities fraud due to misleading press releases issued by a public corporation, note the interdependence of the factual paragraphs and the legal claims:

UNITED STATES DISTRICT COURT
WESTERN DISTRICT OF LUXURY

————————————————————————————————————X

SECURITIES ENFORCEMENT AGENCY,   :

        Plaintiff,   :

                                                                  :   **15 Civ. 7073**

        -against-   :

                                                                  :

DANIEL CHRISTOPHER CRESTIN,   :

        Defendant.   :

                                                                  :

————————————————————————————————————X

COMPLAINT AND REQUEST FOR SANCTIONS

Of Counsel:

Thayman Walshoe

S.E. Agency, Luxury Office

————

JURISDICTION AND VENUE

1. This Court has jurisdiction over this action pursuant to Section 27 of the Securities Exchange Act of 1934. 15 U.S.C. §§ 78aa (West 2012).

2. Venue is proper pursuant to Section 1391 of the United States Code. 28 U.S.C. § 1391. The Defendant, directly and indirectly, has made use of the means of interstate commerce, or the mails and wires, in connection with the transactions, acts, practices and courses of business alleged herein.

FACTS

3. Defendant Daniel Christopher Crestin ("Defendant" or "Crestin") resides in Ridge Falls, Luxury. Crestin began working in the marketing department of Landess, Corp. in August 1999. By August 2005, he had risen to the company's Chief Executive Officer.

4. Landess, Corp. is a public company located in the state of Luxury. The common stock of Landess, Corp. is presently listed and traded on the New York Stock Exchange.

5. In the month of March 2008, Landess, Corp. was preparing to go public. At a special Board Meeting that month, the Landess, Corp. Board quite vocally expressed concern that the offering price of $30 was not sustainable after the offering concluded.

6. Also at the March 2008 Board meeting, several members of the Landess, Corp. Board made it clear to Crestin and other members of upper management that their employment contracts would be terminated if the stock price did not stay in the $30 range until at least December 2008.

7. In or around April 2008 (the month of the Landess, Corp. initial public offering), Crestin and several other Landess, Corp. officials developed a plan to keep the

company stock price near the offering price through the distribution of false earnings results via highly publicized press releases.

8. Commencing in May 2008 and continuing through the end of the year, the company issued press releases that painted a glowing picture of Landess, Corp sales.

9. For example, a press release from May 15, 2008 stated the following in relevant part:

> ... our accounting department further believes that domestic growth will exceed all analyst expectations for at least the next three quarters....

10. Further, a press release from August 2008 stated the following in relevant part:

> ... It seems that the public simply cannot get enough of our new product line. Additionally, contracts are nearly completed that will result in the listing of Landess, Corp. stock on no less than three European stock exchanges ...

11. In fact, there were no contracts with any European stock exchanges, and the sole contacts with any such markets at that time consisted of the mailing of press kits to the marketing departments of the London and Frankfurt stock exchanges.

12. As CEO, the Defendant saw all press releases before they were transmitted to, among other places, the New York Stock Exchange for public distribution.

13. Crestin, who was familiar with the company strengths and weaknesses from his long tenure there, either knew or was reckless in not knowing that the statements detailed above in paragraphs 9 and 10 contained material misrepresentations.

14. Due to his efforts at creating (or recklessness in not detecting) the misleading press releases described above in paragraphs 9 and 10, the Defendant earned in excess of $200,000 in profits from falsely inflated personal holdings of Landess, Corp. stock.

15. At his Agency testimony in March 2009, Crestin denied playing any part in the creation or distribution of press releases that misrepresented Landess, Corp. finances and/or prospects.

16. Also at that Agency testimony, Crestin was advised by the staff attorney that a parallel criminal investigation was underway, and that the criminal case might delay resolution of the Agency investigation for some time. Crestin protested that he did not understand the meaning of this delay, but he was nonetheless on notice of the possible time lag in bringing charges.

17. To date, criminal charges have been brought against five other members of Landess, Corp. management. The most recent charges were brought in this District in May 2012. No convictions have yet been obtained.

FIRST CLAIM FOR RELIEF

Violations of Section 10(b) of the Securities Exchange Act and Rule 10b-5

18. Paragraphs 1 through 17 are re-alleged and incorporated by reference as if set forth fully herein.

19. From at least April 2008 through December 2008, the Defendant, in connection with the purchase and sale of securities, directly and indirectly, by use of the means and instrumentalities of interstate commerce or of the mails and/or wires, has employed devices, schemes and artifices to defraud; has made untrue statements of

material fact and has omitted to state material facts necessary in order to make the statements made, in light of the circumstances under which they were made, not misleading; and has engaged in acts, practices and courses of business which operated as a fraud and deceit upon investors.

20. · By reason of the activities described herein, the Defendant violated Section 10(b) of the Exchange Act [15 U.S.C. § 78j(b)] and Rule 10b-5 [17 C.F.R. § 240.10b-5] promulgated thereunder.

SECOND CLAIM FOR RELIEF

Aiding and Abetting Violations of Section 10(b) of the Exchange Act and Rule 10b-5

21. Paragraphs 1 through 17 are re-alleged and incorporated by reference as if set forth fully herein.

22. From at least April 2008 through December 2008, Landess, Corp., in connection with the purchase and sale of securities, directly and indirectly, by use of the means and instrumentalities of interstate commerce or of the mails and/or wires, employed devices, schemes and artifices to defraud; made untrue statements of material fact and has omitted to state material facts necessary in order to make the statements made, in light of the circumstances under which they were made, not misleading; and engaged in acts, practices and courses of business which operated as a fraud and deceit upon investors.

23. By reason of the activities described herein, the Defendant aided and abetted violations of Section 10(b) of the Exchange Act [15 U.S.C. § 78j(b)] and Rule 10b-5 [17 C.F.R. § 240.10b-5] promulgated thereunder.

PRAYER FOR RELIEF

WHEREFORE, the Agency respectfully requests that the court enter a final judgment against the Defendant granting the following relief:

I.

Finding that the Defendant violated the securities laws and rules promulgated thereunder as alleged herein.

II.

Permanently enjoining the Defendant, his agents, servants, employees and attorneys and all persons in active concert or participation with them who receive actual notice of the injunction by personal service or otherwise, and each of them, from committing or aiding and abetting future violations of Section 10(b) of the Exchange Act [15 U.S.C. § 78j(b)] and Rule 10b-5 thereunder [17 C.F.R. § 240.10b-5].

III.

Permanently restraining and enjoining the defendant from ever again holding the office of Chief Executive at any public company.

IV.

Directing the Defendant to disgorge his ill-gotten gains, an amount of approximately $200,000, plus prejudgment interest thereon.

V.

Granting such other and further relief as this Court seems just and proper.

Dated: Luxury   SECURITIES ENFORCEMENT AGENCY
           July 30, 2013

                                         By: <u>Wallace Horvip</u>

                                         Wallace Horvip, Esq.

                                         Regional Director

                                         Securities Enforcement Agency

---

Note that the claim for relief is meaningless if not tied to the underlying facts. Thus, there is the need for the awkward "realleges herein" language of paragraphs 18 and 21.

Concerning the content in general, note that precision is paramount, and that basic Legal Writing guidance yields to the demands of trial strategy. For example, paragraph 8 deliberately includes "press releases" instead of "several releases" (which normally means at least three) or "numerous releases" (which connotes even more). There are but two provable violations, and to overstate the case in its initial paperwork can only make the charging attorney's job more difficult.

Note that the foremost goal of linking a paragraph to its proof leads to short, distinct allegations (e.g., paragraphs 9 and 10 above). Recognize also that the "strong-weak-strong" guidance for storytelling (from prior Chapters) must yield. Specifically, this "story" ends on a down note (i.e., the government has lost related criminal cases) in the interest of full disclosure—to leave that fact out risks it being first disclosed by the defendant, which can only hinder persuasion.

Finally, observe the terse but vital request offered by "V." above. Formally asking the court for "any and all" relief not articulated by the Writer can ultimately salvage a claim (e.g., where an action at law is transformed, sua sponte, into an equitable action). To neglect to include that option can be fatal to an Accusatory Instrument, as I learned while watching my very first administrative hearing (the charging attorney sought to add a form of relief, and the administrative law judge denied the request by yelling "That train done left!").

In sum, students are routinely surprised by the brevity of and lack of color within Instruments, which are most serious documents. The concise nature owes directly to the concomitant needs to state a violation while reserving flexibility and confidentiality in overall trial strategy. The next example—the civil complaint—perhaps speaks a bit more to the Legal Reader's curiosity.

B. The Civil Lawsuit

The private plaintiff perhaps expends more effort detailing a cause of action, if for no other reason than fear of a hasty dismissal for vagueness. In the hypothetical example below (concerning a dispute over lookalike sports jerseys), note the inclusion of specifics meeting the legal standard of Section 43a of the Lanham Act:

In the Northern District of California

MAJOR LEAGUE INDOOR SOCCER,

Plaintiff,

v.

MILIEU VENDORS, INC.,

Defendant

Case No. C-14-3290

COMPLAINT FOR
INJUNCTION AND
DAMAGES

L. Percival Neumonic
Neumonic & Associates, LLC
Telephone: (123) 887-6500
Attorney for Plaintiff

PARTIES

1. Plaintiff Major League Indoor Soccer (hereinafter "MLIS") is the holder of all trademark rights in the family of registered marks for the eight professional sports teams that compete in its league. These registered marks have been used (and continue to be used) in commerce for a sustained period of time since 1999. MLIS is a California corporation, headquartered in Santa Barbara, California.

2. Defendant Milieu Vendors, Inc. is a Delaware corporation located in Oakland, California. Defendant produces, markets and distributes sports jerseys and other clothing items. These items are sold outside of MLIS events and through various retail outlets. Upon information and belief, Defendant has never submitted an application for registration of the marks to which MLIS claims exclusive ownership.

JURISDICTION

3. This court has jurisdiction pursuant to 15 U.S.C. § 1121 and 28 U.S.C. § 1338(a) (2008) because this case arises under the trademark laws of the United States, 15 U.S.C. §§ 1051 et seq. (2008).

VENUE

4. Venue is proper in this District pursuant to 28 U.S.C. § 1391 because Defendant conducts business in this District and sells and offers to sell its products in this District via its retail stores and the Internet. Defendant sells its products to consumers within this District at its stores located in, among other cites, the cities of Lapp, Creepy Harbor, Palo Tenor and Lawson's Creek.

FACTUAL ALLEGATIONS

5. MLIS was founded in 1999 and has for the past 10 years provided entertainment through live soccer contests held in various cities throughout the United States. After a reorganizational respite during the years 2003–2005, the league extended the distribution of its product via a television contract with a national broadcasting network. Said network continues to nationally broadcast one game a week during the MLIS season (approximately February through May).

6. At the present time, MLIS consists of ten professional teams: The Boston Bullets; the Northern California Sharks; the Philadelphia Sound; the Trenton Dogs; the Chicago Chiefs; the Jacksonville Cats; the Portland Blazers; the San Francisco Bears; the Los Angeles Braves; and the Houston Rigs. The full names (including city names) of each of these ten teams were duly registered by MLIS with the United States Patent and Trademark Office during the years 1999–2003.

7. The jerseys, t-shirts, caps and other items of sports apparel bearing these team names in whole or in part have become quite popular all across America.

8. At least one consumer has evidenced confusion at the time of purchasing one of Defendant's jerseys.

9. Further, at least one user has evidenced confusion as to the ultimate source of the Defendant's jersey.

10. At no time did MLIS grant a license or its equivalent to the Defendant to sell jerseys bearing MLIS team marks.

11. By letter dated August 15, 2008, MLIS ordered Defendant to cease and desist in its practices of producing and distributing Jerseys.

12. The Defendant has ignored the MLIS cease and desist request and continues to sell its jerseys.

ALLEGATION OF IRREPARABLE HARM

13. By reason of Defendant's acts, Plaintiff has suffered and will continue to suffer damage to its business, reputation and goodwill, and the loss of sales and profits which Plaintiff would have realized but for Defendant's acts. Unless restrained and en-

joined, Defendant will continue to engage in the acts complained of herein and will irreparably damage Plaintiff. Plaintiff's remedy at law is not adequate to compensate Plaintiff for all the injuries resulting from Defendant's actions.

FIRST CLAIM FOR RELIEF

14. Plaintiff hereby repeats, re-alleges, and incorporates by reference each and every allegation previously made herein as if the same were more fully set forth at length herein.

15. The Defendant, by reason of the facts alleged herein, violated Section 43(a) of the Lanham Act, 15 U.S.C. § 1125, by falsely designating his sold sports apparel in a manner likely to cause confusion or mistake, leading to damage or likely damage to the Plaintiff.

SECOND CLAIM FOR RELIEF

16. Plaintiff hereby repeats, re-alleges, and incorporates by reference each and every allegation previously made herein as if the same were more fully set forth at length herein.

17. The Defendant, by reason of the facts alleged herein, violated Section 43(a) of the Lanham Act, 15 U.S.C. § 1125, by falsely designating the origin of its sold products by misrepresenting the nature or quality of its sports apparel, leading to damage or likely damage to the Plaintiff.

PRAYER FOR RELIEF

WHEREFORE, Plaintiff prays for judgment in favor of MLIS and against Defendant Milieu Vendors, Inc. as follows:

1. That the court issue a permanent injunction enjoining and restraining defendant and its employees, agents and servants, and any person acting in participation or concert with them, from selling items bearing the Plaintiff's trademarked names or otherwise using in commerce the names detailed below:

    (i)   "Boston Bullets" and/or "Bullets";

    (ii)   "New York Sharks" and/or "Sharks";

    (iii)   "Philadelphia Sound" and/or "Sound";

    (iv)   "Trenton Kings" and/or "Kings";

    (v)   "Chicago Chiefs" and/or "Chiefs";

    (vi)   "Jacksonville Cats" and/or "Cats";

    (vii)   "Portland Blazers" and/or "Blazers";

    (viii) "San Francisco Bears" and/or "Bears";

    (ix)   "Los Angeles Braves" and/or "Braves"; and

    (x)   "Houston Rigs" and/or "Rigs".

2. That Defendant be ordered to account to Plaintiff for any and all profits derived from Defendant's sale of unfairly competing or falsely designated goods;

3. For damages in the amount of Defendant's profits together with damages sustained by the Plaintiff, trebled;

4. For interest, costs, and reasonable attorney's fees; and

5. For such other relief as this court may deem proper.

DATED: January 23, 2009

Neumonic & Associates, LLC

By: _____

L. Percival Neumonic, Esq.

Attorney for Plaintiff,

MAJOR LEAGUE INDOOR SOCCER, INC.

In the above example, note the use of boilerplate in paragraph 13, often copied from authorities within the jurisdiction. Note also that the Writer has added some discretionary sections to aid with the document's comprehension (e.g., "PARTIES"); however, the numbering of the paragraphs continues uninterrupted. Finally, note that the claims for relief are drafted almost verbatim from the statute (to ensure that a violation has been properly alleged); further, note that a single statute can support more than one claim (here, for causing confusion, and for misrepresentation).

Thus, the drafting of an Instrument requires—at a minimum—the following preparatory tasks:

- Familiarizing yourself with the totality of the supporting evidence,
- Carefully reviewing the applicable standard giving rise to the claim, and
- Organizing of the document's paragraphs into "Facts," "Claims" and "Relief."

Before moving on, complete Exercise One, which asks you to identify and complete required parts of a complaint alleging a violation of a common law right of publicity (as introduced in Chapters V and VIII).

Exercise One: Identifying Complaint Parts

Practice the new vocabulary used in describing Complaints and other Instruments by titling or inserting required language into the 7 passages/sections labeled with letters in the sample below. The document should be titled "Civil Complaint," and the submitting attorney is you.

STATE OF LUXURY SUPREME COURT
LAPP COUNTY, THIRD JUDICIAL DISTRICT

DARLENE DRUDGINS   )

(a.k.a. "Dolly Dakota"),   )   Case No. C-2007-189

Plaintiff,   )

vs.   )   A. _____

CITY OF LAPP TOWN COUNCIL,   )

Defendant   )

                                                 B. _____

GENERAL ALLEGATIONS

1. Plaintiff Darlene Drudgins (a.k.a. "Dolly Dakota") is an individual and is now, and at all times mentioned in this complaint was, a resident of Lapp County, in the State of Luxury.

2. Plaintiff alleges, upon information and belief, that Defendant City of Lapp Town Council is, and at all relevant times was, a municipal entity organized under the laws of the State of Luxury.

3. All events complained of herein took place in Lapp County, in the State of Luxury.

SPECIFIC ALLEGATIONS

4. Plaintiff incorporates each allegation contained in paragraphs 1–3.

5. Plaintiff is a popular musical entertainer, earning substantially all of her income from activities related to the recording and live performance of popular music played on radio stations and web sites all around the world. Plaintiff also appears regularly on a hugely popular television program that airs four days a week on a national network aimed at teenagers and pre-teenagers.

6. In early April 2015, Plaintiff learned that, on or around March 31, 2015, the Defendant began displaying a large, holographic image clearly intended to represent the Plaintiff's appearance, mannerisms, characterizations, stylings, and/or performance gestures.

7. Specifically, a "Rock & Roll Pavilion" (hereinafter "Pavilion") erected at the entrance to Lapp City Park featured (and continues to feature) a human-sized, 3-dimensional holographic image of a young woman clearly intended to portray Ms. Drudgins.

8. Upon information and belief, there are no other images (or 3-dimensional portrayals) of any type in the fledgling museum. In the main, the museum displays magazine pictures and old musical instruments, showcased

on bare canvas walls amidst an "atmosphere" provided solely by free music from a radio receiver.

9. At no time did the Defendant request permission to use Plaintiff's image or in any manner communicate that said image was being prepared for public display. Upon learning of the unauthorized usage, Plaintiff's counsel immediately contacted the Defendant and demanded that the usage cease. Defendant refused.

10. Upon information and belief, Defendant charges $15 per individual admittance to the Pavilion.

11. Upon information and belief, the Pavilion, which is open to the public 9 hours a day, at least 6 days a week, has grossed over $200,000 in proceeds from the entrance fees to the Pavilion.

12. The Defendant's unauthorized use of the appearance, mannerisms, characterizations, stylings, and/or performance gestures of the plaintiff constitute a use of the plaintiff's identity.

13. The Defendant's unauthorized use of said identity was solely for the defendant's commercial benefit.

14. The Defendant's unauthorized use of said identity was without the consent of the Plaintiff or her agents.

15. The Defendant's unauthorized use of Plaintiff's identity caused the plaintiff immediate and irreparable financial and reputational injury.

SOLE CAUSE OF ACTION

16. (C) _____

17. Defendant City Council of Lapp, through its unauthorized use of the identity of Dolly Dakota for its own commercial profit, has violated (D) _____.

(E) _____

1. For an injunction to prevent further irreparable harm;

2. For compensatory damages;

3. For punitive damages;

4. For costs of suit and reasonable attorney fees; and

5. For _____ (F) _____.

(G) _____

_____

III. The Pitfalls

A. Including Unnecessary Color

Students and interns attempting Accusatory Instruments often mistake elaboration for precision. Witness the danger of the following numbered fact:

EXAMPLE:

> 27. Because he intentionally sold numerous jerseys bearing the Plaintiff's fully copyrighted trademarks for substantial profits, the Defendant is liable for treble damages under the Lanham Act.

The addition of the colorful language—perhaps beneficial in a trial summation—here sets unnecessary obstacles. Specifically, the Lanham Act provision does not require knowledge of a "full copyright," nor multiple offenses, nor "substantial" profits. Further, a close reading of the trademark fact pattern presented earlier in the Chapter discloses that the Plaintiff, while dutifully filing trademarks for the full team name, in fact did not seek to protect the "nickname" part of the team's title (e.g., "Sharks" or "Bullets"). Thus, to carelessly state that the marks at issue are "fully copyrighted" overreaches.

As a good rule of thumb, include only the words that 1) can be proven—by testimony, incontrovertible facts, or physical evidence, and 2) that are necessary to satisfy the relevant Legal standard. Any other descriptions or additions merely raise the hurdle of proof and ultimately set back the Writer's efforts.

B. Forgetting Formalities

A brilliant Instrument is of little use if not properly labeled on its cover page (or Indorsed on its final page). Skilled attorneys rarely leave these nagging requirements entirely to co-workers. Proofread for these items.

C. Including Facts Not Necessary to Prove the Offense

More facts do not prove an accusation; *appropriate* facts prove an accusation.

D. Misstating the Causes of Action

Legal Writers often neglect to proofread against the statute, thus jeopardizing a cause of action and/or the relief sought. I had a supervisor who suggested reading backwards, aloud, one word at a time. While such ritual may be superfluous, the point to be taken is that proper pleading of the law must be exact, and careless errors thereat are unforgiveable.

To practice the rules governing the inclusion of appropriate facts and causes of action, try Exercise Two below, which furthers the insurance fraud hypothetical of Chapter IV.

Exercise Two: Drafting a Complaint

Utilizing the information provided below, write a 3-page criminal Complaint (including a Cover Page) culminating with two alleged violations (one sounding in "Conspiracy"). Be sure to include allegations, charges, and relief requested, as described earlier in the Chapter.

• JURISDICTION: Subject matter jurisdiction is conferred by New York Criminal Procedure Law section 20.20.

• FACTS:

• Jacoby Levvan (the father) abandoned New York for Arkansas on May 27, 2015 as part of a plan to stage his own death and wrongfully collect his life insurance proceeds.

• Alicia Levvan (the daughter) was 16 years old at the time of his fictitious report of the drowning death of his father. The report was made on May 28, 2015.

• Alicia telephoned the missing persons report to the police and faxed a claim form to the insurance company.

• A news report stimulated public interest. The hoodwinked townspeople spent two days volunteering their time searching for the "victim," and

• The insurance policy, valued at $100,000, was submitted for redemption but the crime was discovered before the check was cashed by the father, who had been located en route to Arkansas.

• LAW:

ARTICLE 240.50 *Falsely reporting an incident in the third degree.*
A person is guilty of falsely reporting an incident in the third degree when, knowing the information reported, conveyed or circulated to be false or baseless, he:

1. Initiates or circulates a false report or warning of an alleged occurrence or impending occurrence of a crime, catastrophe or emergency under circumstances in which it is not unlikely that public alarm or inconvenience will result; or ...

2. Reports, by word or action, to an official or quasi-official agency or organization having the function of dealing with emergencies involving danger to life or property, an alleged occurrence or impending occurrence of a catastrophe or emergency which did not in fact occur or does not in fact exist; ...

Falsely reporting an incident in the third degree is a class A misdemeanor.

ARTICLE 176

A fraudulent insurance act is committed by any person who, knowingly and with intent to defraud presents, causes to be presented, or prepares with knowledge or belief that it will be presented to or by an insurer, self insurer, or purported insurer, or purported self insurer, or any agent thereof:

1. any written statement as part of ... a claim for payment or other benefit pursuant to an insurance policy or self insurance program for commercial or personal insurance that he or she knows to:

(a) contain materially false information concerning any fact material thereto; or

(b) conceal, for the purpose of misleading, information concerning any fact material thereto;....

176.10 Insurance fraud in the fifth degree.

A person is guilty of insurance fraud in the fifth degree when he commits a fraudulent insurance act.

Insurance fraud in the fifth degree is a class A misdemeanor.

105.00 Conspiracy in the sixth degree.

A person is guilty of conspiracy in the sixth degree when, with intent that conduct constituting a crime be performed, he agrees with one or more persons to engage in or cause the performance of such conduct.

Conspiracy in the sixth degree is a class B misdemeanor.

IV. Conclusion

The dream legal job can rapidly become a nightmare if a student attempts to exercise professional judgment through imprecise or unfocused Writing. Some professionals feel that an Instrument is an ideal blend of industry boilerplate and provable fact; perhaps, but the document still requires the highest attainable levels of relevant substance, consistent formatting, and flawless punctuation, spelling, and grammar.

These daunting, concurrent goals can be met by a law student attempting an initial Instrument through careful adherence to a short list of guidance, as reiterated below:

- Always include a cover page that details the court, the case caption, the title of the accusatory instrument, and the submitting attorney;
- Include only the Facts that can be proven and that establish the violation;
- Add subheadings, sections, and titles that ease the burden for the Reader;
- Prepare causes or action/charges that precisely mirror the statute or standard;
- Preserve all appropriate forms of relief; and
- Indorse the document.

Chapter XIII

When Battles Go Well: Drafting a Settlement

Chapter Objectives:
- Acknowledging the Purpose of the Settlement Document
- Identifying Four Key Parts of Settlement Documents
- Recognizing the Goals Behind the Operative Parts
- Preparing a Settlement Contract

Specific Takeaways:
- Registrable Trademarks Under Federal Law
- Actual (vs. Apparent) Authority of Corporate Presidents
- State Consumer Protection Claims and Organic Food Labels

I. Background

Authorities and layman alike concur that at least 90% of all litigated matters settle. Every dispute, from a multi-million dollar award to a small claims court tussle, is, statistically, much more likely to be resolved by way of a written agreement than decided by a champion's oratory. Indeed, the unheralded compromise is the lynchpin of the American civil and criminal dockets. Contrary to the books and movies, it is the Settlement—or the refusal to fight on—that marks the wisdom of our system.

And yet, so little attention is given in law school to drafting the document that actually codifies the agreement to cease fire. Hopefully, this Chapter meets that need.

The Settlement is a form of contract. It reflects a "meeting of the minds," and it is only conscionable when evaluated for consideration (no matter how small). But the Settlement goes far beyond a contract in duration and scope. The document needs to concurrently bear a specific date and to apply forever; it needs to formally bind the parties and still apply to their future, unnamed agents. Overall, the Settlement must be broad enough to have effect outside of the specific contest it terminates while contemporaneously concrete enough to clarify the precise nature of that contest. It comes in many forms and names (e.g., "stipulation"; "consent order"; "release") but, at its core, it contains a short list of universal attributes.

II. The Operative Parts

A. Recitals

This section summarizes the postures and events to date while identifying the parties. In truly dispassionate (some might say bland) language, it tells the reader who is settling and why. Despite the occasional presence of some uncomfortable legalese (e.g., "Whereas"), its chief requirements are twofold: Identifying the specific case that has come to end, and to ensure that a similar action does not arise in the future.

In the example below, evaluate which Settlement opening would give you more comfort as a party to the dispute:

WEAK:

> WHEREAS the parties wish to cease all hostilities between them, they have jointly decided to end the dual litigations pending in Civil Court.

BETTER:

> WHEREAS the parties wish to settle the matter captioned "American Can Distributors, Inc. v. Mulvoy," No. CIV 15-14553, as well as the related counterclaim, No. CIV 15-14977, and all related matters, they have freely entered into this Settlement and Release, each without admitting or denying guilt.

The first example, while saluting the cooperative spirit, is open to future interpretation (e.g., whether a pending motion for attorney fees qualifies as part of the "dual litigations" that, by signature of the document, have disappeared). The second example clearly terminates the dual lawsuits as well as "all related matters." Note that the "freely entered" clause is an express attempt to prevent later allegations of duress.

Note also that the drafting of the Recitals section is more than just an example of legal precision. In administrative Settlements, the Legal Writer may need to ensure that the settled matter shall not become evidence in a subsequent civil/class action. While such occurrence can never truly be eradicated in the first action, it is made far less likely via the inclusion of language denying wrongdoing. Charges against Wall Street firms are notorious for language expressly stating that the accused settles "without admitting or denying guilt" and/or "for the sole purpose of settling this proceeding." Indeed, attention to this detail up front may alleviate some of the Legal Writer's concern over the substantive facts included in the Settlement, the drafting of which is discussed below.

B. Terms and Conditions

This section contains the agreed upon actions and awards. It represents the heart of the agreement. The terms and conditions, sometimes summarized as "Rights and Obligations," normally fall into three wide categories:

- Actions to be taken
- Actions to be halted
- Money damages to be accorded, or penalties to be imposed

All that has been agreed to should be codified; further, the Legal Writer should anticipate that the Parol Evidence Rule applies (i.e., contracts shall be presumed to be whole, a lesson to be learned from your Contracts class). To firm up the totality of the deal, a clause attesting to the "complete agreement of the parties" is often utilized.

Nonetheless, the temptation to the Legal Writer to presume items to be universally understood is strong. For example, review the examples below:

WEAK:

The Parties agree to cease all unlicensed sales efforts and to respect each other's territories as they existed as of year-end 2014.

BETTER:

The Parties agree to cease all unlicensed sales efforts as described in paragraph "II" above and to respect each other's territories as they existed as of year-end 2014, as reiterated in the map attached as "Appendix 1."

Note that any vagary over the definition of "unlicensed sales efforts" or the expanse of the relevant territories is cleared up by two, clear references to other parts of the Settlement. Both additions answer the Reader's likely questions on scope while reinforcing the supremacy of the document's "complete understanding" clause.

C. Representations and Warranties

This section of the Settlement can speak to the authority of the signatories to conclude the agreement, as well as to any documents incorporated by reference in the Settlement. In a specific sense, the "reps & warranties" can be used to reflect the situation of the businesses at the time of the Settlement. In a more generalized sense, the section can add to (or subtract from) significant responsibilities in the Terms and Conditions section.

Note that there are historical differences between the terms "warranty" (signifying a substantial, material part of the contract) and "representation" (signifying a collateral, secondary part of the contract). Moreover, some attorneys like to include the term "covenant," signifying an action to be avoided (e.g., "covenant not to compete" within a salesman's employment contract). The tension between traditional names and modern usage is, again, best remedied through clear language (e.g., a definitional section of the Settlement distinguishing material terms, promises premised upon presently known facts, and actions to be undertaken via good faith efforts).

D. Signatory Section

A Settlement is void unless signed by the properly authorized party. Normally, such authority becomes evident during negotiations; further, the "Representations and Warranties" section can be amended to clarify that the proper people have concluded the litigation.

Nonetheless, on occasion, an issue will arise as to the legal authority for a party representing an entity to settle a matter on behalf of that entity. Note that this triggers an agency law analysis, and that a precise answer for the specific corporate form within a specific jurisdiction may be difficult to locate.[1] Thus, a

---

1. *See, e.g.*, Stephen Bainbridge, *Agency Authority at the Corporate Apex, available at* http://www.professorbainbridge.com/professorbainbridgecom/2012/12/agency-authority-at-the-corporate-apex.html (Dec. 24, 2012) ("Corporate presidents are regarded as general agents of the corporation vested with considerable managerial powers. Accordingly, contracts that are executed by the president on the corporation's behalf and arise out of the ordinary course of business matters are binding on the corporation."). Professor Bainbridge also notes that the law is unclear concerning subordinate officers.

Of course, partnerships and LLCs present their own "apparent authority" issues.

skilled Writer independently ensures that—by operation of written delegation or by operation of law—the Settlement has been signed by the right person.

III. The Unspoken Goals

I once attended a day-long corporate seminar where all 30 lawyer attendees were at once advised to settle a contested disciplinary matter, but to not speak first in the process. Many of us simply stared across the table at each other for minutes on end.

Such pointless posturing can easily overwhelm the preparation of the Settlement (particularly between parties similarly schooled in negotiations and drafting). To keep the process productive, never forget the needs of your client, phrased within the context of the document. In other words, focus on the omnipresent obligation to prepare a durable document that ends all hostilities. With a "hard copy" solution as the goal, the mind numbing competition recedes.

To verbalize that goal, recognize the four overriding aims of the Legal Writer within the Settlement drafting process, as discussed below:

A. Clarity

Err on the side of overstating—or understating—the obvious. Each statement within the document should clearly reference the party governed in the most user friendly of terms.

WEAK:

> The Plaintiff, Sunset Life Advantage Control Industries, Inc. ("SLACII"), hereby agrees ...

BETTER:

> The Plaintiff, Sunset Life Advantage Control Industries, Inc. ("Sunset Life"), hereby agrees ...

In the first example above, the awkward acronym poses difficulties (as well as the case for the contract attorney's traditional use of "Party of the First Part" and "Party of the Second Part"). In the second example, a much easier term for the Reader to remember has been phrased, and it was crafted in a manner that is not insulting to either party (i.e., the identifier did not label one party as "Advantage").

B. Finality

Clarify that subsequent parties in interest will be bound by the agreement, and that other documents do not address the resolution of the dispute. Settlements are of little value if a successor company can revive a claim, or an election creates a new agency management intent on revisiting prior discipline.

The standard "Successors and Assigns" clause usually suffices here. Trust boilerplate versions of this clause, and be wary of short variations thereof. At least one law firm counsels its clients to err on the side of verbosity and anticipation, as detailed by the second example below:

TRADITIONAL:

> This agreement is binding upon, and inures to the benefit of, the parties and their respective successors and assigns.

PROGRESSIVE:

> This agreement is for the benefit of and is binding upon the parties, their respective successors in interest by way of merger, acquisition, or otherwise, and their permitted assigns. This section does not address, directly or indirectly, whether a party may assign its rights or delegate its performance under this agreement.[2]

On a related note, many a practitioner has been foiled by an unforeseen debate over the effective date of the Settlement. Stated in simplest terms, pick one effective date, repeat it throughout the document, and have both of the parties sign the Settlement on that date. Clarify that an e-copy is as good as the original.[3]

C. Comprehensiveness

Cover all things agreed upon in negotiations. Vagaries will be filled by the governing law on contracts and shall be construed against the document's drafter (as he/she was better situated to prevent them). Since experienced attorneys recognize that no document is infallible, provision is normally made for the forum or choice of law that governs a future dispute over the scope of the Settlement.

---

2. *See* Sheila J. Baran, *Don't underestimate the boilerplate*, SMART BUSINESS ATLANTA (Feb. 2004), *available at* http://www.kslaw.com/library/pdf/baron_article.pdf.

3. In June 200, Congress made effective the Electronic Signatures in Global and National Commerce Act, Pub. L. 106-229. This law upholds the validity of e-signatures in matters of interstate commerce.

WEAK:

> The Parties agree that this Settlement reflects all intentions at the present time.

BETTER:

> The Parties mutually warrant that there are no known disputes outside the scope of this document as of the date of its signing, and that any and all disputes arising from the Settlement will be resolved in accordance with the Uniform Commercial Code and its most recent interpretations within this jurisdiction.

Equally important to one or both parties is the guaranty that there shall be no lingering disagreement over—or unseen parties to—the dispute. It is thus customary to strike the compromise that a signatory knows of no further issues with the counterparty, or others claiming the disputed rights that are subject of the Settlement.

D. Miscellaneous Considerations

Apart from the components and goals inherent to most Settlements, there are additional stylistic considerations to be relied upon. Three such factors are described below.

- Use the "block format" of relaying information (i.e., discuss Party A first, then Party B).
- Make sure that, wherever possible, all actions and references are governed by a time period.
- Avoid an excess of formalistic language, which signals a possible over-reliance on textbook forms.

Now conversant with the goals and operative parts of a Settlement, try your hand at matching the sample language at the left with its category on the right:

Exercise One: Matching Settlement Language with Its Name

Each phrase on the left fits within one or more categories on the right. List the name of the category/categories by including its letter on the line next to the phrase. Note that some categories may be used more than once, or not at all.

<table>
<tr><td>1. "… the parties knowing of no other litigation at this present time …" _____</td><td>a. covenant</td></tr>
<tr><td>2. "Party Number One shall cease all collection efforts …" _____</td><td>b. warranty/ representation</td></tr>
<tr><td>3. "Party Number Two promises not to Advertise its services …" _____</td><td>c. signatory</td></tr>
<tr><td>4. "… and agrees not to mortgage said property during the period of refinancing …" _____</td><td>d. recital</td></tr>
<tr><td>5. "Whereas the Parties have agreed to Settle their respective lawsuits …" _____</td><td>e. term/condition</td></tr>
<tr><td>6. "XYZ, Inc. shall pay ABC Corp. $100,000 in U.S. currency …" _____</td><td></td></tr>
</table>

Witness the full example of a Settlement below, which continues the introduction to the Lanham Act in Chapters V and XII. The hypothetical below concerns the dual use of a popular cartoon character by two companies selling children's breakfast cups and plates.

SETTLEMENT AND RELEASE

This settlement and release ("Settlement") is freely entered into between Child's Play Industries ("CPI") and Breakfast Bonanza, Inc. ("BBI") (collectively, "the Parties") on this 30th day of November, 2015.

I. RECITALS

WHEREAS, CPI is the plaintiff in Civil Action No. 08-CV-3535 in the United States District Court for the Northern District of Georgia, in which CPI asserts claims under common law against BBI; and BBI is the plaintiff in a related counterclaim titled Civil Action 08-CV-3591 in the same District Court (collectively, "the Litigation"); and

WHEREAS, the Parties wish to settle all claims and counterclaims stemming from the sale of logo products ("Products") asserted in the Litigation and wish to resolve any and all disputes between or among them, without any admission of fault or liability by any of the Parties, on the terms and conditions set forth herein;

NOW, THEREFORE, in consideration of the premises and the mutual representations, warranties, and agreements contained herein and for other good and valuable consideration, the receipt and sufficiency of which is hereby acknowledged, and intending to be legally bound hereby, CPI and BBI agree as follows:

II. TERMS AND CONDITIONS

(a) DISMISSAL OF ALL CLAIMS AND COUNTERCLAIMS. The effective date of the Settlement ("Effective Date") is the date on which it evidences signature by both of the Parties. Within three (3) business days of the Effective Date, the Parties will commence fulfilling their respective obligations under paragraphs (b) and (c) of this Settlement. Also, within two business days of the Effective Date, the Parties will each file a Stipulation in the Litigation dismissing all claims and counterclaims with prejudice, each party to bear its own costs.

(b) ROYALTY PAYMENTS TO CPI. If BBI sells any Products during the period beginning on the Effective Date and ending on the three (3) year anniversary of the Effective Date (the "Royalty Period"), then BBI shall pay an annual royalty on any sales made during the Royalty Period in accordance with the following terms and conditions: 25 American cents per plate, 15 American cents per tumbler.

(c) FINISHED GOODS INVENTORIES. Within one month of the Effective Date, CPI shall transfer to BBI all of its remaining Products and the attendant rights, title and interests therein to BBI at no cost to BBI.

III. REPRESENTATIONS AND WARRANTIES OF BBI.

BBI hereby represents and warrants to CPI as follows:

(a) BBI and the signatory executing this Settlement on its behalf are legally authorized to execute this Settlement, and the terms of this Settlement are binding upon, and, enforceable against, BBI, its principal, officers, employees, heirs and assigns.

(b) BBI is the lawful sole owner of all rights, title and interest in all BBI and "Comet Hamster" marks, said marks—either by nature "suggestive" or "descriptive" under applicable law—having been duly registered under § 1127(a) of the Lanham Act. BBI is unaware of any other person or entity who is currently claiming ownership of any BBI mark for any Product or service.

(c) As of the Effective Date, there is no legal action pending or threatened against BBI, other than the Litigation, relating to BBI's rights or obligations concerning the Products, or to any related products.

IV. REPRESENTATIONS AND WARRANTIES OF CPI.

CPI hereby represents and warrants to BBI as follows:

(a) CPI and the signatory executing this Agreement on its behalf are legally authorized to execute this Settlement, and the terms of this Settlement are binding upon, and, enforceable against CPI, its principal, officer, employees, heirs and assigns.

(b) CPI is the lawful sole owner of all rights, title and interest in all of its marks, exclusive of the "Comet Hamster" mark.

(c) As of the Effective Date, there is no legal action pending or threatened against CPI, other than the Litigation, relating to CPI's rights or obligations concerning the Products, or to any related products.

V. **SIGNATORIES**

THE PARTIES do hereby agree that the Settlement represents the sole and entire agreement concerning the resolution of their respective claims, and that disputes arising from the Settlement, if any, will be resolved in accordance with Georgia statutory and common law.

Lorne Hesser   Date
President, Child's Play Industries ("CPI")

Alphonse De La Croix   Date
CEO, Breakfast Bonanza, Inc. ("BBI")

Note that the example contains many separate paragraphs, but each paragraph expresses a sole conclusion. Note also that the Settlement is not bound to a universal form; it serves the parties. In paragraph III(b), the parties have agreed that the "Comet Hamster" logo has been duly registered with the government. Remember one of the key lessons of Chapter III on Facts: Parties may stipulate that the sea is shallow and the sky green. Settlements are not displays of model fact-finding (or style). More than any other document explained in this book, they are examples of purely functional Legal Writing.

IV. Conclusion

To be sure, there exists a healthy debate over which clauses in a Contract are most vital. Two other clauses not discussed by this Chapter concern confidentiality and severability of provisions. Further, the nature of the Settlement could trigger duties specific to a variety of fields.[4]

---

4. *See, e.g.,* Steven L. Harris & Charles W. Mooney Jr., *How Successful Was the Revision of UCC Article 9?: Reflections of the Reporters,* 74 Chi.-Kent L. Rev. 1357 (June 1999) (discussing the new applicability of U.C.C. Article 9 ["Secured Transactions"] to rights of payment under tort claim settlements); Jeffrey M. Stein et al., *SEC Requirements for Disclosure/ Accrual of Litigation, Governmental Proceedings and Other Loss Contingencies,* Client

Untold qualifications and authorities aside, this Chapter focuses on developing a starting grid for drafting meaningful Settlements. Such grid would adhere to some very discernible advice. Clarify parties and dates. State the fundamental terms. Be specific in citing terms and conditions. Memorialize all concessions. Include only one effective date. Reference the effect of future disputes and parties. And use legalese and boilerplate where it works, but not to excess.

To be sure, Settlements take an untold variety of forms and sometimes seemingly evidence no structure at all. Still, familiarity with the elementary notions introduced in this Chapter should place a young Writer in a solid position to commence drafting. To start practicing these drafting skills, try your hand at creating a Settlement of the dispute described below. The Settlement ends a hypothetical claim against a farm labeling foods "organic," a dispute that has heated up since the California high court's December 2015 ruling that suits may be commenced under the State's "Consumers Legal Remedies Act" even where FDA labeling standards have been met.

Exercise Two: Drafting a Settlement

In January 2015, a class of consumer plaintiffs headed by Wilshire Rights International sued Pettbrock Farms over the labeling of its produce products. The action alleged that seven different food items were labeled "organic" when, in fact, these products were grown with the assistance of genetic engineering. The seven subject products sold by Pettbrock Farms are detailed below:

- "Grown Green Olives"
- "Harbored Right Lettuce"
- "Water Purified Onions"
- "Short Shaded Beets"
- "Air Taught Cucumbers"

NEWSLETTER OF KING & SPALDING LLP (March 2013), *available at* http://www.kslaw.com/imageserver/KSPublic/library/publication/presentation/2013/SECTreatmentofLitigation GovernmentalProceedings-Mar2013.pdf (discussing disclosure provisions within S.E.C. Regulation S-K applicable to public companies); John B. Isbister et al., *Seven Steps to a Successful Class Action Settlement*, ABA ONLINE, *available at* https://apps.americanbar.org/litigation/committees/classactions/settlement-class-action.html (last visited December 22, 2015) (discussing the Class Action Fairness Act of 2005, which imposed "transparency" upon settling parties in order to protect class members wishing to "opt out").

- "Mighty Millenial Beans"
- "Rose Pure Cabbage"

In turn, Pettbrock Farms (which owns several subsidiaries, inside and outside of the State), countersued for slander of title, asserting that FDA standards on organic labeling had been clearly met in all instances.

The two sides now wish to settle the competing matters, which constitute the only litigation either side has ever faced. The plaintiff consumer group, represented by President E. Shensington, shall receive coupons valued at $50,000 (but only valid after January 1, 2017). The defendant food producer/distributor, represented by CEO Dolph Landacks, agrees to conduct a substantial study of the effects of irradiation and genetic engineering on farm products. The results of the study shall be made public, although details on the breadth of that disclosure were not delineated at the time of Settlement.

In a contract no longer than three pages, utilize the parts described in this Chapter to draft a Settlement that the plaintiff consumer group would be pleased to sign. Remember to lock in dates (but also account for future responsibilities), to specify the actions being settled (but best preclude subsequent legal actions by third parties), and to establish the authority of the signatories.

———————

Chapter XIV

Conclusion:
Meaning Business

Chapter Objectives:
- Exploring the Professional Challenge of Legal Writing
- Revisiting the Specific Lessons of Each Chapter
- Recognizing the Theme Common to All Forms of Legal Writing
- Charting a Plan for Future Growth as a Legal Writer

Substantive Takeaways:
- Statutory Authority for Federal Reserve Board Regulation T
- The UIGEA and Online Daily Fantasy Sports

I. Background

A law student once informed me, "I hate writing, but I like having written." Another student commented that, "The only way to learn this skill is 'on the job.'" Most recently, a particularly sincere student once asked me how I learned "to like to write." I informed him that I always liked to write; I just never knew it.

There is less facetiousness in my revelation than first appears. The feeling I always enjoyed was the satisfaction at having effectively conveyed a point. I first felt that sentiment as a competitive speaker at Saturday morning tournaments in high school. I later occasionally experienced the triumph of communion with the audience as a fledgling songwriter. But, as a practicing attorney, progress was so intertwined with the client's success as to obscure whether or not I was getting any better at the craft.

Finally, as a law professor, I was simultaneously obligated to write and to train others. The latter responsibility by far provides the greatest reward. Watching the new law student effectively register and then repeat notions that are but days old is a rare joy for an educator of any ilk.

Thus, wholly apart from the law review articles and panel presentations, the greatest success I have earned in the past decade has been in propelling the approximately 500 students I have helped to prepare and complete a Note, a Brief, a Memo, or a Research Paper. I could never have foreseen the sense of achievement that has attended watching law students shed their rookie year concerns of inadequacy to become confident, accomplished authors. Many of them later explained that all they had needed was direct guidance and an ability to read the audience, a message and a skill I truly enjoy imparting.

In short, I always liked to write—I just did not know it.

II. Book Summary

This coursebook had three aims: 1) To provide a robust introduction to the dictates of "Legal Writing," 2) To provide more specific instruction for seven different examples of common legal documents, and 3) To provide a substantial set of business law standards as takeaways.

Chapter I ("Choosing Collars ...") distinguished Legal Writing from the collegiate experience. Organization and brevity were valued over vocabulary. The Legal Writing "Formula" was introduced, while outlining and preparation were emphatically urged.

Chapter II ("The Magna Carta ...") expanded upon the notion of a Rule. Both thoroughness and a greater appreciation for the Legal Reader were encouraged.

Chapter III ("Locating Facts ...") tackled the goal of all Legal Writing: Formal application of the identified law to new facts. The Chapter revealed one of the profession's dirty little secrets: that few lawyers can adequately define a "Fact." Five tenets of Rule Application were offered.

Chapter IV ("... Statute and Case Summaries") was the first of two Chapters designed to help deepen analysis. The effective summary of statutes was tied to scrutiny of both the statute itself and outside sources. The effective summary of cases was explained as a multi-step process.

Chapter V ("... Rules and Rule Applications") strove to take insights further. It was explained that a Rule can be made weightier by adding an inferred or "translated" principle. Moreover, the organization of a Rule Application can usually be varied. And it was noted that analysis can always be made more substantive (e.g., via a counter-analysis or a Policy argument).

Chapter VI ("Walking Like A Duck ...") sought to fill the hole created by the abandonment of flowery language. The notion of writing for the "Legal Audience" was stressed. Yet, a modicum of legalese was encouraged. Fifteen style conventions were offered, with formatting and word choice suggestions added in Appendices.

The second half of the Book dwelled on concrete examples. Chapter VII ("That Old Frame") focused on the staple of nearly all first year Legal Writing courses, the Office Memorandum. Six components—as well as the predictive vocabulary—were explained and exemplified.

Chapter VIII ("... The E-Memo") provided guidance on the E-Memo, a variation in many ways comprising the modern law firm's expectations of Legal Writing. That art form perhaps speaks more to preservation of privilege and ease of use than to traditional tools of analysis.

Chapter IX ("Into the Fray ...") served up entry into the world of contested litigation and professional persuasion. The Office Memo was adapted for a public audience. Universal structures such as Point Headings and the Formal Outline were applauded and learned. A Motion "shell" was referenced as Appendix E.

Chapter X ("... Having a Story to Tell") outlined the approach to a Law School Note, a distinct form of Legal Writing that at least 50% of all second year law students shall undertake. Towards the end of even deeper legal analysis, case summaries and statutory interpretation were studied in detail.

Chapter XI ("A New Deal ...") elaborated on the context for and utility of the industry Comment Letter. The student learned that the preparation of a formal Comment could simultaneously afford an opportunity for valuable practice and input into agency legislation.

Chapter XII ("... That Dream Job") edified on the terse, unforgiving requirements of drafting documents that commence formal proceedings.

And Chapter XIII ("When Battles Go Well ...") heralded the Settlement, the omnipresent document that can be hazardously taken for granted. Four segments of the document were explained and practiced, each with the goal of ensuring that the real thing would never leave out necessary codifications.

The keen eye will recognize that a proper Rule would fit neatly in nearly all of the document examples described above. Witness the universality of this passage:

> On the federal level, the initial extension of margin credit to purchasers of securities is governed by section 7 of the Securities Exchange Act of 1934, 15 U.S.C. § 78a et seq. (West 2012). This statutory pro-

vision authorizes Regulation T of the Federal Reserve Board. 12 C.F.R. §220 (2012). While there is no requirement that investors be accorded credit, since 1975, Regulation T has capped the discretionary credit amount at 50% of the purchase price of the security. The private sector serves to reinforce the seriousness of a violation of this cap. *See, e.g.,* "Regulation T FAQ," https://research.scottrade.com/ ("Reg T violations can have serious consequences, so it's important to understand the rules before you trade.").

The above passage could accurately state the governing Rule of a Memo, E-Memo, Trial Motion, Appellate Brief, Student Note, and Accusatory Instrument (and possibly find its way into a Settlement). Hence, the reader should appreciate the promise of the first Chapter: That Legal Writing consists of, to one extent or another, simply identifying and applying the law. While that modest aim can be amplified or condensed depending upon the audience found and the relief sought, it is almost shamefully tied to a short list of discernible basics.

Those basics were hopefully explained, supplied, practiced, and cross-referenced within this book. As another student once commented to me, "Legal Writing is what it is. I guess I just have to do it." Fair enough. If you have diagnosed yourself as a "never fan" of Legal Writing, at least allow for the possibility that if you practice it enough you will meet the demands of the profession. The next section provides a template for such practice.

III. Practice All You Can

In nine years of lecturing on Legal Writing, I have foremost learned one thing: You cannot *lecture* on Legal Writing. It is a skill that requires some structured introduction, followed by a large amount of practice.

When I meet 1L students, I immediately advise them to never waste an opportunity to write. Send text messages in full sentences; compose e-mails that provide a context. For those students desiring more guidance on how best to rehearse, I offer a series of my own dedicated proofreads.

Imagine that I were requested to sum up the state of the law regarding daily fantasy sports (the legality of which remains disputed as this book goes to press). Proper preparation of the passage would start with an exploratory outline that looks something like this:

- Constitutional silence on gambling (any sort)
- Any recent Congressional act?

- Proliferation within the private sector; varying forms
- Traditional State stances—legal in Nevada?
- Any New York State law?
- N.Y. attorney general action, Fall 2015
- Handful of States oppose
- Current status/changes in the immediate future

From that humble outline—glued together only by its adherence to the Hierarchy of Authority—comes a disjointed but slowly crystallizing first draft:

> In the past decade, Congress passed a law outlawing online gambling. That federal law contained an exception for "games of skill." The ensuing case law was scattered and relatively uninformative. Perhaps seizing upon a loophole, entities began facilitating online "daily fantasy leagues" around 2010. Those enterprises—existing in most States—rapidly reached unforeseen proportions and profits. In or around 2014, State regulators began examining the legality of these businesses.

That first draft was based upon my recollection of some milestone events. The draft was foremost designed to remind myself of what I do and do not specifically recall of the legal debate. The passage lacks introduction and conclusion, making it a bit frustrating to read. Further it lacks citation and specifics, generating little credibility. Hence, a second (improved) draft might look like this:

> In 2006, Congress passed the Unlawful Internet Gambling Enforcement Act ("UIGEA"). 31 U.S.C. §§ 5361–66 (West 2012). The sponsors of that measure proclaimed that it would target underage and addictive gambling (comments of Calif. Rep. Pelosi). Nonetheless, the definitional section of UIGEA contained exemptions for "fantasy sports games" not "predominated" by chance. *See generally* § 101. This exception paved the way for the daily sports fantasy leagues that have since proliferated, claiming millions a day in participant contributions. *See generally* Max Miceli, *Betting on the Fantasy World*, U.S. NEWS (Oct. 30, 2015) (estimating total 2015 entry fees at $3.7 billion).

> In 2014, a number of State regulators commenced inquiry into the operations of daily sports fantasy leagues, but the leading enterprises openly advertise that their offers are invalid in a only a handful of states. *See* https://www.draftkings.com/help/why-is-it-legal.

> In November 2015, the New York State Attorney General sent cease-and-desist letters to the two largest daily sports fantasy concerns op-

erating in New York State. The next month, a New York court sided with the Attorney General in halting all "wagers," but a contemporaneous stay from an appellate court allowed the business to continue.

The passage now generates credibility, but to an uncertain end. The third draft—with even greater specificity—provides a beginning, middle and end. It also adds paragraphing (while concurrently shortening sentences) to convey thoughts in resolute but digestible chunks:

> In 2006, Congress passed the Unlawful Internet Gambling Enforcement Act ("UIGEA"). 31 U.S.C. §§ 5361–66 (West 2012). The sponsors of that measure proclaimed that it would target underage and addictive gambling. § 5361 (preamble). Nonetheless, the definitional section of UIGEA exempted "fantasy" sports from the definition of "bet" or "wager." § 5362(1)(E)(ix).
>
> This federal, "game of skill" exception paved the way for the creation of daily sports fantasy leagues between 2006 and 2010. These leagues have since proliferated, claiming millions a day in participant contributions. *See generally* Max Miceli, *Betting on the Fantasy World*, U.S. NEWS (Oct. 30, 2015) (estimating total 2015 entry fees at $3.7 billion).
>
> In 2014, some State regulators commenced inquiries into various Site business practices; Nevada made headlines when, in October 2015, it banned the practice as unlicensed gambling. *DraftKings, FanDuel banned in Nevada*, NEW YORK DAILY NEWS (Oct. 15, 2015).
>
> Further, in November 2015, the New York State Attorney General sent cease-and-desist letters to the two largest daily sports fantasy concerns operating in the State. The next month, a New York court sided with the Attorney General in halting all "wagers." However, the enterprises obtained a contemporaneous stay from an appellate court, thus allowing their businesses to continue to solicit State participants. *See Stay Lets DraftKings, FanDuel Keep Operating in New York*, NBC NEWS ONLINE (Dec. 11, 2015). Finally, facing potential fines, the two companies halted litigation and ceased operating in New York in March 2016.
>
> Nonetheless, these enterprises continue to advertise that their offers are invalid in a only a handful of states. *See* https://www.draftkings.com/help/why-is-it-legal.

Note the implementation of many lessons of the book. The passage proceeds from highest authority to most local, and from then known to the unknown. It avoids commentary and flowery language. Citation is rational (rather than repetitive). The passage tells a story with a beginning, middle, and (unknown) end.

To follow this guidance, the final product required an outline and three drafts. So too should all your writing proceed: 1) Create slowly, and with planning. 2) Progress with the intention of routinely acquiring precision and ultimately displaying a chronology. 3) Revise repeatedly, mindful that no one is as familiar with the topic as you are.

The last advice—repeat revisions—may be the most important. For if writing from the hip is a priceless method of assuring that you will have enough pages to turn in, then writing multiple drafts is the best possible means of efficiently answering the question(s) posed to you.

To those who would resist so many edits, the strongest advice I can offer is to learn to appreciate the journey. Looking back, there was much to be applauded in the candid comments of the students I have taught. To wit, both the students who solely enjoy having written and those who rationalize that command of Legal Writing takes years were both correct. Then again, Legal Writing class does not accord high grades for perpetually wearing a smile, or for instantly exhibiting a practitioner's skill set.

Accordingly, the goal would seem to be a recognition that no one is born a Legal Writer. Practice being a necessity, it should feel as little as a burden as possible. Once you enjoy tackling that next draft, the craft takes on a whole new reward. Show that you are willing to engage in routine re-writes (i.e., that you "mean business"), and your Reader will always appreciate the effort. And once you are applauded at having successfully communicated what you intended, you shall realize that you were actually a fan of Legal Writing all along.

—*J. Scott Colesanti, June, 2016*

Appendices

Appendix A:
Two Bluebook Exercises

Exercise One

1. The Supreme Court recently held in *Obergefell v. Hodges* that marriage is a fundamental right protected under the Due Process Clause of the Fourteenth Amendment. The decision is not yet available in the Supreme Court reporters. We thus call such an opinion a(n)

    a) Temporary Opinion

    b) Slip Opinion

    c) Parallel Cite Decision

    d) Interim Holding

2. Which of the following cases, based off its name alone, is unlikely to indicate an appeal in which the defendant lost at the trial level:

    a) *United States v. Newman and Chiasson*

    b) *Pennoyer v. Commonwealth of Massachusetts*

    c) *Gabelli v. Securities and Exchange Commission*

    d) *Thomas v. Linklater*

3. You would like to cite to a New York Times article by James Jaffrey in your memo to support your argument that elected officials should be required to share their computer records with the public. The headline is "Justice Department and Thumb Drives," appearing in the August 12, 2015 issue on page A13. Which of the following is the correct cite?

a) James Jaffrey, *Justice Department and Thumb Drives*, N.Y. TIMES (Aug. 12, 2015), at A13.

b) *Justice Department and Thumb Drives*, N.Y. TIMES (Aug. 12, 2015), at A13.

c) N.Y. TIMES (Aug. 12, 2015), at A13 ("Justice Department and Thumb Drives").

d) Jaffrey, *Justice Department and Thumb Drives*, N.Y. TIMES (Aug. 12, 2015), A13.

4. *Burwell v. Hobby Lobby*, the controversial 2014 Supreme Court case on the Religious Freedom Restoration Act of 1993, includes a heavily discussed dissent by Justice Ginsburg on the issue of women's health care and contraception costs. After providing the formal case citation, which of the following is the best way to indicate that you are citing to that dissent?

a) (This is a dissent authored by Justice Ginsburg.)

b) (Ginsburg J., dissenting).

c) (Justice Ginsburg Dissenting)

5. In *Miranda v. Arizona*, the Supreme Court's opinion quoted *Malloy v. Hogan* in saying that a person should be guaranteed the right to silence, declaring that "to remain silent unless he chooses to speak is the unfettered exercise of man's own will."

According to the Bluebook, which of the following is not a permissible parenthetical explanation?

a) Miranda v. Arizona, 384 U.S. 436 (1966) (case found that a right to remain silent during arrest resided in the U.S. Constitution).

b) Miranda v. Arizona, 384 U.S. 436 (1966) ("[T]o remain silent unless he chooses to speak is the unfettered exercise of man's free will.").

c) Miranda v. Arizona, 384 U.S. 436 (1966) (finding that a right to remain silent during arrest resided in the U.S. Constitution).

6. As you know, section 10 of The Federal Arbitration Act provides 4 bases of relief for parties unhappy with their arbitration decision. Which of the following is a proper long cite to that section?

a) Federal Arbitration Act, 9 U.S.C. § 10 (1946).

b) Federal Arbitration Act, 9 U.S.C. § 10 (West 2014).

c) Federal Arbitration Act, 9 U.S.C. § 10 (2014).

d) None is proper.

7. True or False: This block quote is in correct format:

> Yet, the court found the defendant guilty, stating
> There is—and never has been—an unqualified right to withhold
> facts from the police. Such disobedience mocks the foundation
> of authority.

New York v. Carson, 433 N.Y.2d at 289.

8. Please read this passage:

> A great many courts have held that recklessness does not satisfy
> the "conscious disregard" standard. _____ *New York v. Wilk-*
> *ers*, 141 Misc. 2d 266 (N.Y. 1989). _____ *New York v. Joneston*,
> 142 Misc. 2d 754 (N.Y. 1991) (finding recklessness to satisfy the
> standard).

Which pair of signals works best in the spaces above?

a) *See generally ... Accord ...*

b) *[no signal].... See also ...*

c) *See, e.g., ... But see*

d) *See ... See, e.g., ...*

9. Which of the following citations is correct?

a) *SEC v. Quinlan*, 231 F.Supp. 2d 144 (E.D. Mich. 2008).

b) *S.E.C. v. Quinlan*, 231 F.Supp. 2d 144 (E.D. Mich. Nov. 7, 2008).

c) *S.E.C. v. Quinlan*, 231 F. Supp. 2d (E.D. Mich. 2008).

10. Which of the following is not a permissible short cite for the *Miranda* cite
provided above in question number 5?

a) *Miranda*, at 439.

b) *Miranda*, 384 U.S. at 439.

c) 384 U.S. at 439.

d) All are not permissible.

Exercise Two

Use your Bluebook to answer each question. You may also have to use the In-
ternet to answer certain questions.

1. The most important case for a discussion of legalized abortion is the 1973
Supreme Court decision in *Jane Roe, et al., v. Henry Wade*. The case can be
found at page 113 in the 410th volume of the United State Reporter. Please

type the official cite, paying close attention to such details as spacing and punctuation.

2. Which of the following cites is least likely to indicate a criminal case, and (in one sentence) why?

    a) *U.S. v. Chiarella*

    b) *Gad v. Longfellow*

    c) *Commonwealth of Massachusetts v. Merrill Lynch*

    d) *N.Y. v. Delan*

3. On August 13, 2011, *The New York Times* published on page C1 an article entitled "That Student Loan, So Hard to Shake." The article was written by Jonathan D. Glater. How would you cite to the article in a court petition to freeze a graduate student's loan payments?

4. An interesting book about the Supreme Court of the 1960s is titled, "Super Chief, Earl Warren and His Supreme Court—A Judicial Biography." The book was published in 1983 by New York University Press. It had only one edition, and the author was Bernard Schwartz. How would you write a cite to pages 166–168 therein? (NOTE: Assume that you have not previously cited the book.)

5. The following is a cite to a law journal article written by a law professor: Norman S. Poser, <u>Liability of Broker-Dealers for Unsuitable Recommendations to Institutional Investors</u>, 2001 B.Y.U. L. Rev. 1493 (2001). In one sentence, explain how the citation would differ if a law student authored the piece.

6. The duty of police officers to advise suspects of their right to counsel can largely be traced to the 1966 Supreme Court decision in *Ernesto A. Miranda v. State of Arizona*, which can be found at page 436 within the 384th volume of the United States Reporter. The dissent to that decision authored by Justice Clark on pages 499–502 argued against a "doctrinaire" holding that such rights must always be given to the accused. Please write the complete cite to that portion of the dissent.

7. The courts of the Southern District of New York adhere to a procedural rule governing the filing of a bankruptcy petition (formerly Local Bankruptcy Rule 9(a)). First, what is the number of that rule? Next, what's the web address you used to locate it?

8. Which of the following citations to the two relevant reporters is correct:

   a) <u>Wellman v. Dickinson</u>, 475 F.Supp. 783 (S.D.N.Y. 1979), <u>aff'd</u>, 682 F.2d 355 (2d Cir. 1982).

   b) <u>Wellman v. Dickinson</u>, 475 F. Supp. 783 (S.D.N.Y. 1979), <u>aff'd</u>, 682 F.2d 355 (2d Cir. 1982).

   c) <u>Wellman v. Dickinson</u>, 475 F. Supp. 783 (S.D.N.Y. 1979), <u>aff'd</u>, 682 F. 2d 355 (2d Cir. 1982).

9. Write a citation for that part of the United States Constitution requiring two witnesses for any conviction premised upon an allegation of treason.

Appendix B:
20 Common Legal Terms

These terms appear enough in Legal Writing to safely escape the label of "legalese."

1. dicta

2. gravamen

3. demurrer

4. with/without prejudice

5. sub nom

6. concurrence/dissent

7. res ipsa loquitur

8. red herring (as a distraction in a criminal investigation; as a preliminary prospectus in securities law)

9. certiorari

10. en banc

11. per curiam

12. pro hac vice

13. pro bono

14. inter alia

15. remand

16. de facto (vs. de jure)

17. enjoin/injunction

18. disgorgement

19. arguendo

20. equity

And a Dozen Legal Euphemisms
(To Replace Slang/Harsh Language)

- misguided (instead of "ignorant")
- ill-advised (instead of "foolish")
- ill-fated (instead of "losing")
- unfortunate (instead of "weak")
- curious (instead of "bizarre")
- opportunistic (instead of "greedy")
- misrepresented (instead of "lied")
- similar (instead of "like")
- untimely (instead of "late")
- novel (instead of "dangerous")
- unprecedented (instead of "weird")
- approximately (instead of "about")

Appendix C:
Distinguishing Vocabulary

These word pairs are often confused. Note the "non-words" therein.

1. Affect (as a verb: to change an outcome) and effect (as a noun: the change)

2. Alternate (a substitute, one of two choices) and alternative (one of many choices)

3. Birth (start of life) and berth (space for a boat or a playoff team)

4. Climatic (relating to climate) and climactic (deciding or ultimate)

5. Complimentary (praising) and complementary (completing)

6. Consequently and consequentially (same thing, latter is preferred)

7. Dessert (a treat) and desert (to abandon)

8. Differing (disagreeing) and different (separate or unusual)

9. Dual (two of something) and duel (a fight)

10. Disoriented (confused) and disorientated (not a word)

11. Discreet (using good judgment) and discrete (distinct)

12. Discriminating (perceptive) and discriminatory (marked by prejudice)

13. Disinterested (impartial) and uninterested (bored)

14. Ensure (to confirm a result) and insure (to guarantee financially)

15. Fewer (before a plural noun, like "shelves") and less (before a mass noun, like "sugar")

16. Flammable and inflammable (mean the same thing)

17. Forego (to go before) and forgo (to abstain or do without)

18. Foundering (for inanimate objects, such as buildings) and floundering (for live things, such as a fish)

19. Further (as in depth of subject) and farther (as in distances)

20. Incent and incentivize (both used as verbs by corporate America, although "motivate" might be the more conventional choice)

21. Ironic (unexpected, satirical) and ironical (not a word)

22. Loath (reluctant, unwilling) and loathe (to detest, abhor)

23. Mischievous (inclined to pranks) and mischievious (not a word)

24. Nauseous (ability to make one feel sick) and nauseated (feeling sick)

25. Oral (spoken) and verbal (relating to words)

26. Principal (the person) and principle (the standard)

27. Regard (to look at) and regards (best wishes)

28. Precede (to come before) and proceed (to continue)

29. Pled and pleaded (both are the past tense of "plead")

30. Preventive and preventative (same meaning; latter is perhaps more prevalent)

31. Skewed (altered, such as facts) and skewered (cooked food, such as meat)

32. Titled (a book that has been named) and entitled (right to an inheritance)

33. Unwieldly (not a word) and unwieldy (difficult to master or control)

Appendix D:
A Starter Set of 15 Helpful Legal
Writing Conventions

Use these rules in the absence of a clear formatting or style pronouncement from an instructor, supervisor, or court. These Conventions are offered in addition to those appearing in Chapter VI of this book.

1. Use 1-inch margins.

2. Use only 12-point, Times New Roman font.

3. Insert two spaces between each period and new sentence.

4. Double space all text (with exceptions for headings and block quotes, which should be limited to 1 per page).

5. Number all pages (at the bottom of the page, in the center of the page).

6. Staple once, in the top left corner (no industrial staples).

7. Consistently use either words or numbers to represent numbers. Modify the convention for the start of a sentence (e.g., "Eleven jurors voted for acquittal.") or for hyphenated terms (e.g., 12-point font).

8. Use a comma after each item in a series.

Example: The trunk contained tools, drug paraphernalia, and a spare tire.

9. Use the third person instead of the second person.

10. Place commas and periods within quotation marks. Place semicolons outside quotation marks. Place question marks outside quotation marks unless they are a part of the quotation.

Example: The court found that argument "patently absurd," and the bench added that "[s]anctions are always within reach."

11. Do not use bold, italics, or underlining for emphasis. Such tools have distinct meanings in Legal Writing.

12. Use ellipses correctly: 3 dots to replace part of a sentence, 4 dots to replace a complete sentence or multiple sentences.

13. When organizing sequentially, use the following terms:

> First,
> Second,
> Third,
> Finally,
>
> (i.e., do not use "Lastly")

14. Do not start a new Component on the last line of a page.

15. One semi-colon per page.

Appendix E:
Trial Motion Shell

UNITED STATES DISTRICT COURT
IN THE SOUTHERN DISTRICT OF NEW YORK

DANIEL CHRISTOPHER CRESTIN,

Petitioner,

    against

U.S. SECURITIES ENFORCEMENT AGENCY,

Respondent.

MOTION FOR EXCLUSION OF SETTLEMENT DATED

NOVEMBER 12, 2014

Miles Nifteck

Attorney for Petitioner

New York, N.Y. 10023

*For educational purposes only. All names and events are fictitious.

TABLE OF CONTENTS

TABLE OF AUTHORITIES

STATUTES

None.

CASES

State v. Simms, 539 A.2d 601 (Conn. App. Ct. 1988)

Weisman v. First UNUM Life Ins. Co., 44 F. Supp. 2d 512 (S.D.N.Y. 1999)

....

MISC.

§ 10-48: The Answer—Express Admissions and Denials to Be Direct and Specific, CT R SUPER CT CIV § 10-48, Conn. Gen. Stat. Ann. (West 2012).

....

PRELIMINARY STATEMENT

In January 2013, Daniel Christopher Crestin, the Petitioner in this matter, received notice that he was being investigated by the governmental body known as the Securities Enforcement Agency ("Agency"). This investigation centered on his prior employment at a registered broker-dealer. In May 2013, Mr. Crestin received a similar notice of investigation from the private party known as the Universal Stock Exchange ("Exchange"); the two investigations specifically related to a foreign broker-dealer client later convicted of money laundering.

In November 2014, Mr. Crestin concluded the Exchange investigation by means of a settlement ("Settlement"). The Agency now seeks admission into evidence of the Settlement into its own disciplinary hearing process....

ISSUE PRESENTED

Whether a signed stipulation ending a private disciplinary inquiry may be introduced into a governmental hearing commenced by an agency when the stipulated settlement contains the words "solely for the purpose of settling this private disciplinary hearing"?

STATEMENT OF FACTS

Mr. Crestin served as an entry level bookkeeper for a public company. His days entailed checking trading desk entries against the prior day's "blotter." He had little customer contact …

ARGUMENT

BECAUSE THE SETTLEMENT DATED NOVEMBER 12, 2014, BY ITS OWN TERMS, IS INADMISSIBLE IN PARALLEL PROCEEDINGS, IT MUST BE EXCLUDED.

A. *In contractual matters, the law on subsequent admissibility is clear.*

In the Second Circuit, disciplinary settlements are governed by contract law.…

B. *In numerous cases, this Circuit follows the "textbook" guidance on this topic.*

In the *Weisman* case, a District Court made clear that.…

C. *In the instant case, the Settlement unequivocally falls within the Circuit law.*

Mr. Crestin and the Agency concluded an agreement dated November 14, 2014.…

CONCLUSION

In these troubled times.…

For all of the above reasons, the Settlement should be deemed inadmissible.

NOTES

1. There is no universal Cover Page template. Strive to communicate the jurisdiction, the case caption, the title of the Motion, and the name/address of the submitting attorney.

2. Within the Table of Contents, use lower case Roman Numerals (or other font means of distinguishing Table pages from text pages).

3. Within the Table of Authorities, follow alphabetical order (first name of case or statute, last name of author of secondary material).

4. Within the Preliminary Statement, avoid argument. Simply sum up the procedural history of the case.

5. Within the Issues Presented, use upper case Roman Numerals when listing more than one Issue.

6. Within the Argument, the Headings should appear exactly as they appear in the Table of Contents, thus making the latter a substantive index for the Motion.

7. The Conclusion should always stay within page limitations.

Index